SHAWANGUNK ROCK CLIMBS

The Trapps

This we know:

The earth does not belong to man—
　man belongs to the earth.
All things are connected, like blood
　which connects one family.
Whatever befalls the earth befalls
　the children of the earth.
Man did not weave the web of life—
　he is merely a strand in it.
　Whatever he does to the
　web, he does to himself.

CHIEF SEATTLE, 1854

THE AMERICAN ALPINE CLUB
CLIMBER'S GUIDE

SHAWANGUNK ROCK CLIMBS
The Trapps

Dick Williams

THE AAC PRESS
NEW YORK

© 1991 Dick Williams

All rights reserved

First Edition 1972
Second Edition 1980
Third Edition 1991

ISBN: 0-930410-36-X

LIBRARY OF CONGRESS CATALOG NUMBER 91-061758

Cover and Book Design: Carol Malcolm-Russo

Editorial Coordination: Jeanne Marie Gilbert

Frontispiece: The Shawangunks as seen from the Sky Top Memorial Tower.
Overleaf: Fritz Wiessner in the Trapps.
Photographs by Dick Williams.

Published by
The AAC PRESS
113 East 90th Street
New York, New York 10128-1589
USA

The AAC PRESS is an Imprint of The American Alpine Club, Inc.

The American Alpine Club, Inc. was founded in 1902 and began publishing in 1907. It is dedicated to the promotion and dissemination of knowledge pertaining to mountains and the art of mountaineering in all of its forms.

To my Father and Son,

with gratitude beyond words as we continue
to guide each other through
the years and the adventures of life.

In Memoriam

FRITZ WIESSNER
My dear friend and climbing partner.
His pure style and ethic demonstrated
his love and respect for
the rock; he will always serve as a
model for climbers worldwide.

D.W.

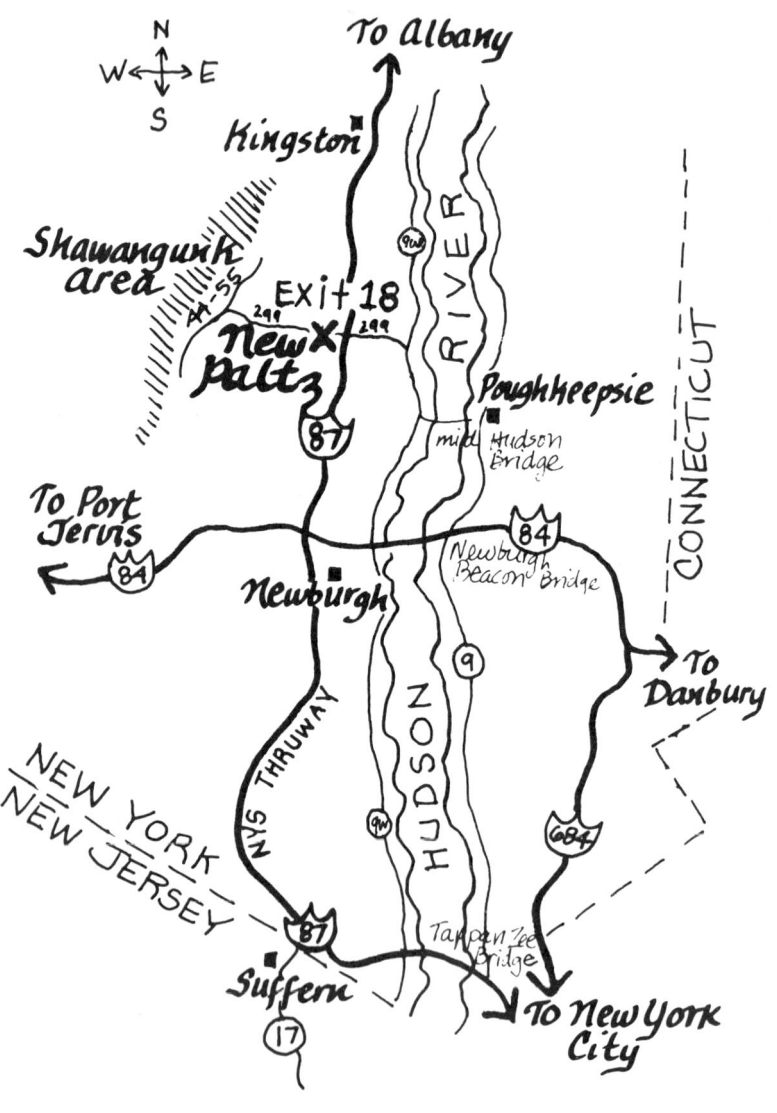

Acknowledgments

I COULD NOT HAVE DONE this guidebook without the help of many individuals who gave freely their time, suggestions, opinions, and honest recollections about routes and the style in which they were climbed. I would like to thank the following people in particular for their understanding and patience in helping me make this guide as complete and accurate as possible: Henry Barber, Kevin Bein, John Bragg, Joe Bridges, Russ Clune, Dave Craft, Jim Damon, Al Diamond, Steven Faludi, Scott Franklin, Mike Freeman, Rich Goldstone, Rich Gottlieb, Jeff Gruenberg, Lynn Hill, Darrow Kirkpatrick, Jim McCarthy, Jack Mileski, Frank Minunni, Felix Modugno, Jeff Morris, Russ Raffa, Bill Ravitch, Mark Robinson, Rich Romano, Jon Ross, Rich Ross, Mike Sawicky, Thom Scheuer, Mike Steele, Todd Swain, Brett Wolf, Steve Wunsch, my son Richard for letting me take away from playtime so I could work on this book, and last but not least my dogs Lea and Cruz, who many times on my trips to the cliffs in the heat or cold or rain would stare at me wondering, "What in the world is he doing?"

Sincere appreciation is expressed to
Fritz Wiessner and Hans Kraus

In the June 1960 issue of *Appalachia,* Fritz Wiessner wrote:

It is rare in our days of over-exploitation of the land to find, near a large city, country which is still unspoiled by man and as beautiful as when it was created. Greatest gratitude is due to the Smiley families at Lake Mohonk and Lake Minnewaska who, by great sacrifices, have protected and kept this beautiful land as their grandfathers found it one hundred years ago. . . . and so it is today.

Special and most grateful thanks to the Smiley family, the Mohonk Preserve, and the Mohonk Mountain House for their patience with climbers and for allowing us to climb.

Contents

Introduction	13
History	29
The Trapps	57
Route Photographs	257
Indexes	329

Introduction

WELCOME TO THE SHAWAN-
gunks, an internationally known climbing area that is one of the most popular and extensive in the United States.

Located in Gardiner, New York, a few miles west of New Paltz and about 90 miles north of New York City, the "Gunks" consists of a series of gleaming white quartz conglomerate cliffs up to 260 feet high that extends for 8 miles along several ridges. It is renowned for its horizontal holds, spectacular overhangs, and high-quality routes at every level of difficulty. In fact, it is one of the few places in the world where it is common to find classic beginner's routes side by side with desperate test pieces.

This is the 3rd edition of Shawangunk Rock Climbs, and it is by far the largest and most comprehensive. Over 1000 routes and dozens of variations are included on the four most popular cliffs in the area: Millbrook, The Near Trapps, The Trapps, and Sky Top. Because of the large number of routes, the guidebook has been divided into three volumes so that each will be small enough to carry conveniently on multipitch climbs. Other new features include the increasingly popular G-PG-R-X protection rating system and a star system to indicate the quality of the routes. In addition, much time and effort has been put into revising and updating the route descriptions and photographs to ensure their accuracy. Climbing has undergone significant changes in the years since publication of the last edition of this book, and many of these changes are reflected in this edition. For the first time, toprope climbs and the style in which many of the first ascents were done are included.

The weather in the Shawangunks is normally moderate, even during the winter, but spring and fall usually offer the best climbing conditions. Most of the cliffs face east and receive morning sunshine and afternoon shade.

The map in the front of each volume shows the main parking locations and how to reach the area from the surrounding highways.

You will find the local climbers to be friendly and helpful, so enjoy your visit, climb safely, and be considerate of others. And please remember that the cliffs and most of the surrounding land are on private property, and it is therefore **especially important to respect the environment,** the local climbing traditions, and the regulations so that the privilege of climbing here will continue to be granted to all for many years to come.

Of course, in any work of this size, errors and omissions are bound to occur, despite the best intentions of the author. So please send any corrections, constructive criticism, and new route information to Dick Williams, Route 1, Box 444, High Falls NY 12440.

ARRANGEMENT AND USE OF THE GUIDE

The guidebook is divided into three volumes because of the large number of routes. Volume 1 contains all the introductory material and the Trapps, Volume 2 contains the Near Trapps and Millbrook, and Volume 3 contains Sky Top. Each volume has an index that lists the routes and named variations in that volume both alphabetically and by grade.

Each cliff is introduced with a brief description of its characteristics and prominent features. This is followed by detailed direc-

INTRODUCTION

tions on how to reach the area and information about descent routes and trails along the top and bottom of the cliff. Restrictions, if any, are also noted.

The route descriptions are numbered so they can be easily cross-referenced with the photographs. However, because of lack of space, not all the routes are shown on the photos. This should not be a problem because the route descriptions are hopefully detailed enough to stand by themselves.

MOHONK PRESERVE AND MOHONK MOUNTAIN HOUSE

The Mohonk Preserve and the Mohonk Mountain House resort are separate entities that share a common heritage but are not legally associated with one another. The Mountain House resort was founded in 1869 by the Smiley family, who spent many years acquiring hundreds of acres of land in the northern Shawangunks. In 1963 the Mohonk Preserve (then called the Mohonk Trust) was established, and through the generosity of the Smileys, it was opened to the public for recreational activities compatible with preservation of the area. The Preserve is a nonprofit corporation dependent for support on memberships; charitable contributions from individuals, outdoor and conservation groups, and businesses; government grants; and an endowment fund. Today the Preserve contains over 5600 acres of rugged wilderness, which includes 22 miles of carriage roads and 26 miles of hiking trails that give access to one of the most beautiful mountain ridges in the Northeast. Each year between 75,000 and 100,000 people visit the area to rock climb, hike, bicycle, cross-country ski, and enjoy the natural surroundings.

Of the four major cliffs in the guidebook, however, only the Trapps and the Near Trapps are completely within the Preserve boundaries. Sky Top is owned by the Mohonk Mountain House resort, and Millbrook is divided between the Preserve and several private landowners, whose property begins in the valley below.

A day-use pass or a semiannual or annual membership is required to use the Mohonk Preserve. These may be obtained for a fee from the Preserve rangers (who are usually stationed at the Uberfall in the Trapps on weekends or are on patrol at other

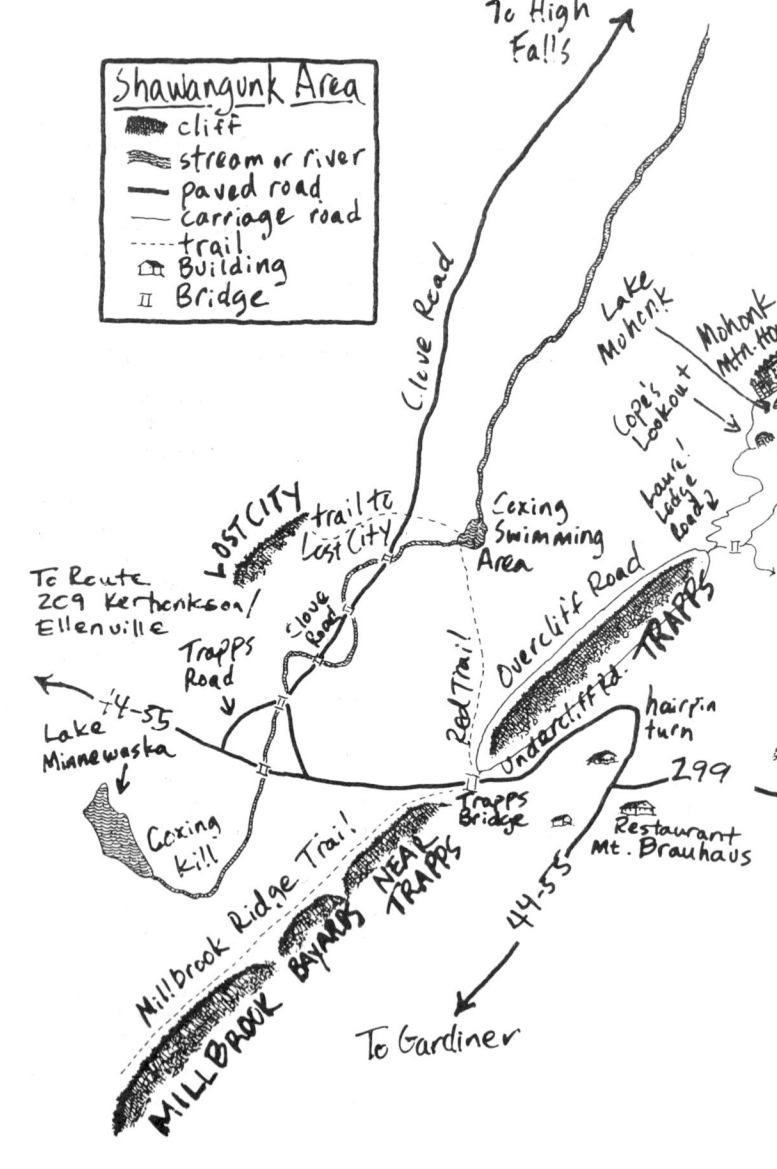

THIS MAP IS NOT ACCURATE IN SCALE

times) or at the Visitor Center on Mountain Rest Road (see map). Memberships may also be obtained by contacting the Mohonk Preserve, Inc., Mohonk Lake, New Paltz, NY 12561, telephone (914) 255-0919. The fees are used to defray the costs of maintaining the land through the provision of outhouses, ranger patrol, litter cleanup, trail maintenance, and other activities necessary to ensure safe and sanitary conditions. A reciprocal agreement with the Mohonk Mountain House allows Preserve members to visit the resort grounds (excluding the hotel and its facilities, and the beach). Visitors entering the resort via the gatehouse are required to pay the normal Mountain House charge unless they have an annual membership in the Preserve, in which case they are required to pay a parking fee of $1 per person. They also must keep all climbing equipment inside packs out of sight of the general public. Questions regarding the Preserve can be directed to the above address. A flyer with a trail map is available at the Visitor Center, or it can be requested through the mail by sending a stamped, self-addressed envelope.

Signs are posted throughout the cliffs stating that rock climbing is inherently dangerous, and those who climb do so at their own risk. Skill and training are essential. Neither the Mohonk Preserve nor the Mohonk Mountain House provide any supervision, inspection, or maintenance of the cliffs or any climbing gear found thereon, and the rangers are not authorized to instruct or advise climbers, nor are they responsible for warning of dangerous conditions or practices.

REGULATIONS AND RESTRICTIONS

The Shawangunks is a popular area close to a number of large cities and is subject to ever-increasing population pressures. Beginners, hotshots, and every other kind of climber use the cliffs and the surrounding environment, and each has an obligation to maintain the area in a state that all can enjoy. Climbing is only one facet of the land and its use, and it cannot take place in isolation. Climbers are part of a larger community that must be respected, and this includes nonclimbers as well as the flora and fauna.

The restraint that climbers should exercise in preserving the rock and the standards of the sport should also be applied to the environment. Please keep the area clean and try to avoid trampling new growth and damaging larger vegetation whenever possible by using talus blocks and established trails. Many of the cliffs and talus fields harbor birds, snakes, and other wildlife, so care should be taken to avoid frightening them away from their homes and nesting sites. Quiet behavior is always desirable.

Camping and Fires: Indiscriminate camping and fires are not permitted because of their adverse impact on the environment and the danger of forest fires.

Motor Vehicles and Bicycles: Motor vehicles of all types, including automobiles, motorcycles, snowmobiles, and all-terrain vehicles (ATVs), are prohibited. Bicycles, including mountain bikes, are permitted on most of the carriage roads but are restricted from all of the hiking trails. The core area of the Mohonk Mountain House resort is posted with No Biking signs, and bicycles are not allowed in the area around the hotel. Those using bicycles are requested to ride safely and be considerate of other people on the roads who often do not hear them approaching.

Access Trails: Climbers are urged to stay on the designated access trails (see line drawings) that connect the carriage road with the base of the Trapps. This will help prevent erosion.

Littering: Littering mars the beauty of the landscape and is prohibited, and glass bottles are not allowed on the property. Climbers are urged to leave the area cleaner than when they arrived by disposing of cigarette butts, cans and bottles, wads of tape, plastic wrappers, toilet paper and related matter, and any other trash found at the cliffs or alongside the trails. Also, slings left fixed on the cliffs for protection or rappel anchors should closely match the color of the rock so they are not an eyesore.

Noise: Climbers should refrain from loud and abusive language. Radios are NOT permitted without the use of earphones.

New Routes: No new routes are allowed in the Sleepy Hollow area of the Trapps, from the route Wegetables to the right (north) end of the cliff. This restriction has been imposed to protect wildlife and the delicate environment as much as possible so that it can be compared to some of the more heavily used areas to access climber impact.

Tree Cutting, Rock Trundling, and Hold Chopping: Prohibited.

Bolts and Pitons: Prohibited because they alter the rock and are inconsistent with the preservation ethic of the area. The only exception is that bolts and pitons placed prior to November 1986 may be replaced as necessary, provided that every effort is made to use the same hole.

Professional Guiding and Climbing Instruction: Neither climbing instruction nor guided or group activity of any kind is allowed at Sky Top or elsewhere on Mohonk Mountain House property.

Guides and instructors planning to use Mohonk Preserve must register with the Preserve in advance. The Preserve has requirements for professional guiding and climbing instruction which must be strictly observed. All instructors and guides must carry liability insurance, be certified in first aid, be accredited by the American Mountain Guides Association, and hold a guiding license from the New York State Department of Environment Conservation. For details, contact the Mohonk Preserve directly.

Sky Top: As mentioned earlier, Sky Top is owned by the Mohonk Mountain House resort, whose principal interest is the safety and well-being of the hotel guests. Climbing is not officially sanctioned on the property, and guiding is thus specifically prohibited. Any such action may lead to further restrictions on the use of the land. Climbing is a very special privilege that could be rescinded if climbers do not abide by the rules and show courteous respect for the hotel guests and the environment. This includes refraining from behavior that could interfere with the activities and pleasure of the resort's paying guests.

In addition, the following rules also apply:

- Dogs are not permitted in or around the hotel or at Sky Top.
- Climbers should not be seen without shirts on, and all climbing equipment should be kept inside packs out of sight of the general public when traveling to or from the cliff.
- Climbing left (west) of the Crevice is prohibited on Fridays, Saturdays, Sundays, and holidays from the beginning of Memorial Day weekend in the spring to the end of Columbus Day weekend in the fall.

INTRODUCTION

- Climbers should not use the Crevice as a descent route when the above restriction is in effect.

SAFETY

The primary virtues of a climber are self-control and restraint, and a realistic sense of one's abilities. Nothing said in this guidebook should ever preclude a concern for safety. If you cannot maintain the standard of a climb without endangering yourself or others, perhaps you should return to it another day when you are a better climber or not do it at all. Avoiding accidents is every climber's responsibility, so pay attention to the cardinal rule: Never assume anything.

EQUIPMENT

Virtually all the climbs in the Gunks require technical climbing equipment and knowledge of its use. It is not the purpose of this book to explain climbing techniques and the use of climbing gear. People interested in climbing are encouraged to seek instruction from a reputable guide service or a competent climber.

Most climbers wear flexible, smooth-soled climbing shoes made of sticky rubber. Because most of the holds in the Gunks are horizontal, shoes that edge well are sometimes preferred.

Ropes that are 150 and 165 feet long and 10.5 and 11mm thick are commonly used, but the longer ones are preferred for long pitches, toproping, and rappelling. Many climbers use double 9mm ropes because of their greater safety and versatility. Double ropes are well suited for the many wandering lines that zigzag through the overhangs that are so common in the Gunks, especially for reducing rope drag and making use of widely scattered protection.

Artificial chockstones ("nuts") provide adequate protection on most of the routes, and everyone should have a general selection of wedge-shaped nuts, camming devices, slings, and carabiners. Stoppers, rocks, RPs, steel nuts, HB offsets, Hexentrics, Tri-cams, Friends, Camalots, and TCUs (three-cam units) all work very well in the horizontal cracks. Many fixed pitons and a few nuts, bolts, and slings will be found on the routes. These tend to loosen and weaken with age because of the freeze-thaw cycle, rust (especially inside the rock out of sight), and sunlight (in the case of slings). What looks good at first glance might actually be dangerously unsafe, so it is very important to back them up whenever possible.

Loose rock in the Gunks is rarely a problem, so hard hats are seldom worn. However, they provide good protection from head injuries during a fall and should be considered.

Chalk is almost universally used but quite often becomes an eyesore. Studies have shown that it works best when applied sparingly. The Mohonk Preserve strongly encourages the use of gray chalk that closely matches the color of the rock and also recommends that brightly colored slings not be used for permanent rappel and toprope anchors.

ROUTE DESCRIPTIONS

Standard terminology is used to describe the routes, although a few terms have special meaning in the Gunks. A "crack" is a verticle crack, while a "horizontal crack" is described as such. An "open book" is an inside corner that faces straight out, as opposed to being left-facing or right-facing. An overhang is described as an "overhang" when it is 3 feet or less in size, a "ceiling" if it is between 3 and 6 feet in size, and a "roof" if it is greater than 6 feet in size. If an overhang varies in size along its length, different parts of it may be referred to as an overhang, a ceiling, or a roof. These sizes are only approximate, as not every overhang has been measured. Ceilings and roofs may be tiered and composed of a series of smaller overhangs. "Mungy" and "grungy" mean bushy, mossy, grassy, or lichen-covered and/or wet. Trees are often used as reference points even though they don't last forever; however, most will probably last as long as this edition of the guidebook is in print.

The first feature of the route description is the name line, which includes the name of the route, the difficulty grade (5.0–5.14 with A1–A5 as necessary), the protection grade (G, PG, R, X, or combinations thereof), the quality rating (0–3 stars), and the word "toprope" if the route is a toprope climb. The difficulty and protection grades refer to the crux pitch on the route.

The "start" identifies the exact feature that marks the beginning of the route and relates it to one or more nearby climbs.

Each pitch description is followed by the length, difficulty, and protection for the pitch, if these are known. If certain parts of a pitch are more poorly protected than others, this is usually mentioned. Variations are indicated by V1, V2, etc. where they start in the pitch.

Variations are described after the pitch descriptions and are named and graded when this information is known.

A comment section sometimes follows the pitch and variation descriptions. In this section additional information about the route may be included.

The last feature of the route description is the credit line, which may include comments about the ethics and style used on the first ascent. FA means first ascent and FFA means first free ascent. The latter indicates that the route was originally climbed with aid. A single name on the credit line does not necessarily imply a solo; it usually means that the leader was belayed and no one followed.

GRADING OF CLIMBS

The Decimal System (5.0–5.14) is used to describe the relative difficulty of the free climbs in the guide. In this system the easiest grade is 5.0, and the ascending numbers represent increasing levels of difficulty, with 5.14 being the hardest at the time of this writing. Within each grade there are often noticeable differences, so minus (−) or plus (+) signs sometimes have been added to indicate "easy" or "hard" for the grade. (Some climbing areas use a-b-c-d subgrades instead of minus and plus. In this system "a" is equivalent to minus, "d" is equivalent to plus, and "b" and "c" fall in between.)

A few routes have been rated 3rd or 4th Class. A 3rd-Class route generally involves scrambling up broken, low-angle rock where a rope is seldom necessary. A 4th-Class route is steeper and often requires a rope between belay stances but seldom needs protection (nuts and slings) between the stances, as on 5th-Class routes.

The grades have been assigned by consensus whenever possible,

INTRODUCTION

but keep in mind three things: 1) Many of the newer routes have not been repeated, and thus their grades have not been confirmed; 2) Broken holds and rockfall may cause some grades to change over time; and 3) All grades are very subjective in nature. Climbers with different strengths, body sizes, and climbing abilities often will have different impressions about the difficulty of any given climb, and in a certain sense all will be correct. When height seems to be a significant factor, a comment in the route description has usually been made.

The chart below compares some of the more well-known rating systems.

Decimal	UIAA	British	Australian	French
5.0	III	2b	5	
5.1	III +	2c	6	
5.2	IV −	3a	7	
5.3	IV	3b	8	
5.4	IV +	3c	9–10	
5.5	V −	4a	10–12	
5.6	V	4b	12–14	4c
5.7	V +	4b–4c	14–16	5a
5.8	VI −	4c–5a	16–18	5b
5.9	VI	5a–5b	18–19	5c
5.10	VI +	5b–5c	20–22	6a–6b
5.11	VII −	6a–6b	22–25	6c–7a
5.12	VII	6b–6c	26–28	7b–7c
5.13	VII +	7a	29	8a
5.14		7b		8b

Aid climbs are graded A1–A5, with the higher number being the hardest. Only four are listed in the guide, and these may eventually go free.

The protection grades G, PG, R, and X are used to describe the quality and availability of the protection, which in turn defines the level of commitment required to free climb a particular route, assuming that the climber is competent at placing protection. If anything, they are probably more important than the difficulty grades and thus have been assigned conservatively. Grade G means good protection that is closely spaced so that only short falls are likely. Grade PG implies that the protection is more widely placed or not quite so good, and that moderately long falls are possible. Grade R suggests that the protection is widely spaced or relatively poor in quality, and that a long fall (over 20 feet) is possible with a fair chance of getting hurt. Grade X means there is little or no protection, and that a very long fall is possible with a good chance of being seriously injured or killed. As new advances in climbing hardware are made, the grades on certain climbs may change for the better.

The quality of the routes is indicated by a system of 0–3 stars. The stars have been assigned conservatively and, like difficulty ratings, are subjective in nature. A 3-star route is a classic that should not be missed; a no-star route is only average in quality, although most of these can still be expected to offer some worthwhile climbing, as there are very few really poor routes in the Gunks.

ETHICS AND STYLE

Climbing ethics in the Gunks is concerned with rules of conduct and principles of morality and the relationship of climbers' actions that alter or damage the rock and its environment—such as placing bolts, pitons, chipping or manufacturing holds, and trundling boulders. Although standards have been established, the area has become overwhelmed with recent controversy. Hence the land and cliff owners—the Mohonk Preserve, has firmly stated what the rules of conduct will be: They are absolutely no bolt or piton placing, hold chopping, rock trundling, or tree cutting.

Style on the other hand refers to the form, philosophy, and standards concerning the actual manner in which climbing is done, such as free climbing or aid climbing, and is left to the individual. So whether or not you hangdog, redpoint, toprope, pinkpoint, or free climb—it's your choice. Whether you take the adventure climbing road or the sport climbing road, thank God it's a free country. Good climbing to all!

FIRST ASCENTS AND FREE ASCENTS

A first ascent occurs when a route is climbed for the first time.

It can be done free on the lead or on a toprope, or it can be done with aid. A free ascent occurs when a route is climbed from start to finish without any form of aid, such as tension from the rope or physical support from climbing gear or other climbers. In other words, only the rock and natural vegetation can be used to make forward progress. The perfect free ascent is one in which the climber does the route "on sight." This means that the route is climbed on the first try (no falls) the first day it is attempted without having prior knowledge gained by talking to other climbers; receiving "beta" (move-by-move instructions) from other climbers while climbing; toproping (in the case of a lead); hangdogging; and placing protection, cleaning, and inspecting on rappel. A first free ascent occurs when a previously aided route is climbed free. From that point on, such a route is considered to be a free route.

SERVICES

Public bus transportation is available to New Paltz from the larger nearby cities, but climbers will have to hitchhike, take a taxi, or make other arrangements to get to the cliffs from town.

Information about guide services and climbing can be obtained from Rock and Snow (914-255-1311), the local climbing store in New Paltz.

In case of an accident, contact a Mohonk Preserve ranger or call either the Mohonk Preserve Visitor Center (255-0919) or the Mohonk Mountain House (255-1000). The police can be reached at 255-1323. Area hospitals include Vassar Brothers (454-8500) in Poughkeepsie and Kingston Hospital (331-8566) in Kingston.

GEOLOGY

The Shawangunk Mountains are the most northern ridge system of the Valley and Ridge Province of the extensive Appalachian Mountain chain which runs along the Eastern seaboard. The ridge system rises near Rosendale, New York, and runs southwestward through New Jersey (where it is called the Kittatiny Mountains), Pennsylvania (the Kittatiny or Blue Mountains), and West Virginia (North Fork Mountain and Seneca Rocks) to Alabama. Only near New Paltz, New York, and Seneca Rocks, West Virginia, are the cliffs high enough and the rock durable enough to form a major rock climbing area.

The cliffs are formed by an unusual sedimentary rock called quartz conglomerate, an orthoquartzite composed almost entirely of quartz. It is composed of consolidated coarse gravels that were deposited along the edge of an inland sea by ancient streams in the Silurian Period, about 400 million years ago. The individual pebbles, which can still be readily recognized in the rock, were rounded by stream and wave action, and were later cemented together with silica.

Underlying the conglomerate is an older sedimentary rock called Normanskill shale, which is composed of fine-grained clays, muds, and silts that were deposited at the bottom of the inland sea during the Ordovician Period, about 450 million years ago. Being much softer than the conglomerate, it tends to erode very easily and does not provide suitable exposures for rock climbing.

The sheer escarpment that faces the Wallkill River valley today exists because of the collision of the African and North American plates, which resulted in extensive folding and faulting. This in turn was followed by eons of erosion and weathering that created the multitude of cracks, ledges, overhangs, and corner systems. The beds in the vicinity of New Paltz are fairly gentle in slope and dip 10–22° to the west, leaving horizontally exposed strata that account for the friendly nature of the climbing. In contrast, the strata exposed at Seneca Rocks dip vertically because the rock there was more severely deformed.

The most recent major geological event in the area was the glaciation that occurred during the Pleistocene Epoch, which ended about 10,000 years ago. Evidence of this can still be seen on the western slopes of the range in the form of large areas of bare rock, polished and scratched bedrock, and glacial erratics of nonnative rock that were transported by the ice from the Catskills and other areas to the north.

History

*F*RITZ WIESSNER, WITH HIS awesome enthusiasm and appetite for climbing, looms large in the history of mountaineering in North America and was the dominant figure in the early years of its evolution. An aura of legend surrounds his achievements, including his discovery of the Shawangunks in 1935.

Born in Dresden, Germany, in 1900, Wiessner became a brilliant and technically advanced climber who helped pioneer "free-climbing style" in the Elbsteingebirge, his home playground in Saxony. He later went on to establish bold new routes in the Kaisergebirge and the Dolomites that confirmed his reputation as perhaps the best rock climber of the time.

In 1929 Wiessner emigrated to New York City and soon began seeking out new climbing opportunities. Traveling throughout North America, he explored such diverse areas as New England (Ragged Mountain, Cannon, Wallface), Devils Tower in Wyoming, and Mount Waddington in British Columbia, and pioneered an incredible list of first ascents. During the 1939 American expedition to K2 (28,741 feet), the second highest mountain in the world (only 287 feet shorter than Everest), Wiessner came within 700 feet of the summit (and a first ascent) and was only stopped by darkness and later misfortune.

Wiessner did most of his climbing closer to home, however. Even though the Northeast did not have the same atmosphere and scale as the Alps and the Himalaya, he eagerly sought out what was available and left his mark wherever he went. While climbing at Breakneck Ridge in the Hudson River Highlands one late spring day in 1935, after a thunderstorm had thoroughly cleared the air, Wiessner looked about 30 miles to the northwest and spotted the gleaming white, 8-mile-wide rock band of the Shawangunk escarpment. He had just discovered what was ultimately to become the center of rock climbing in the Eastern United States.

On the following weekend, Wiessner set off in search of these tantalizing cliffs and, characteristically, made his way to the highest in the area, Millbrook, for an adventurous day of exploring with John and Peggy Navas. In the process, he climbed the first route in the Shawangunks, now known as Old Route (5.5), with his two friends; they were impressed by the extent of the cliffs and the enormous possibilities ahead. Although Wiessner had done far more impressive routes elsewhere, this was still a significant achievement because of the complex route finding involved, the primitive climbing gear used (hemp rope, soft-iron pitons, and rope-soled shoes or hiking boots), and the fact that he was climbing with relatively inexperienced beginners (as he often did) who placed their complete trust in his abilities. In those days, the prevailing school of thought was that "the leader does not fall," because a fall could mean disaster for the whole party. Thus it took a certain amount of courage for Wiessner and his friends to attempt such a route, knowing the uncertainties involved. But things worked out well, they enjoyed the climb, and a week later Wiessner returned with a stronger party.

It may seem surprising that the Shawangunks had not been noticed sooner by climbers, but in the early 1930s there were very few climbers around. The range was dominated by the Mohonk Mountain House and Minnewaska, two prominent resort hotels that provided fashionable accommodations for three generations of well-heeled travelers. Just how small the climbing community was in those days is revealed by the fact that no climbers had ever heard of either resort.

Wiessner's second foray into the Gunks brought him to the Mohonk House and Sky Top via the resort's extensive and easily accessible network of carriage roads. There, with the Smiley's consent, he put up another impressive climb with John Navas and a newcomer to the scene, Percy Olton. The route was named Gargoyle (5.5), and in later years Wiessner often soloed it by the light of a full moon.

The remainder of the decade saw virtually no activity; Wiessner, in fact, only visited the area once in the next four years, making his way back to Millbrook in 1937 to establish The High Traverse (5.5) with Percy Olton.

The turning point for the Gunks was 1940. During that year, Wiessner returned with his good friend Maria Millar and established White Pillar in the Near Trapps, notable for being the first 5.7 in the area and the first route in the Near Trapps. The climb was a magnificent achievement, not only because of its difficulty, but also because it was poorly protected by the soft-iron pitons they were carrying. Another milestone that year was Wiessner's initiation of a lifelong friendship and partnership with Hans Kraus, which was to prove so vital to the development of the Gunks. Kraus, an orthopedic surgeon, who later became an internationally recognized specialist in physical rehabilitation, had recently emigrated from Austria. Kraus was already an accomplished climber when he accepted Wiessner's invitation to climb. Coming from different backgrounds, though, they had contrasting climbing styles: Wiessner was a free climber, while Kraus, having been trained in the Dolomites, excelled in the use of aid. By employing their respective styles, these two highly creative and energetic personalities were to produce a wealth of future classics. Their first climb together was Overhanging Overhang (5.6) at Sky Top, which challenged their skills and paved the way for much future activity, including the first route in the Trapps, Kraus' Easy Overhang (5.2).

The following year, 1941, stands out as the year that produced many of the moderate classics. Most of the new routes were in the Trapps, which Wiessner had always avoided because he considered it a "dirty cliff" with too many trees and grassy ledges. However, after Kraus put up Northern Pillar (5.2) and succeeded in talking Wiessner into trying it, Wiessner at long last recognized the merits of the cliff and went on to establish a number of fine lines, including Baby (5.6) and Frogshead (5.6−). While both men often climbed with women at the time, each developing his own circle of female partners, they frequently joined forces and, in so doing, created the outstandingly popular Horseman (5.5) and the ultra-classic High Exposure (5.6+), whose spectacular, overhanging final pitch represented their most significant climb together. This was also the year that Betty Woolsey, a fine climber and skier in her own right, did the first lead of a new route in the Gunks by a woman, Betty (5.3−), and set the stage for the active participation of women on the sharp end of the rope, a trend that has continued to the present day. Yet another milestone was Emilio, the first aid climb in the area, on which Kraus and Wiessner employed a shoulder stand.

During World War II, climbing activity slowed down considerably, and only a handful of new routes were produced. Perhaps the most important of these were Kraus' Madame Grunnebaum's Wulst (5.6) and Wiessner's Gelsa (5.4), High Corner (5.5) and Yellow Ridge (5.7), the latter involving an initial off-width crack that was Wiessner's "piece of cake" or forte, followed by interesting route-finding problems. During this period, Mary Cecil, a protégée of Wiessner's, led Mary (5.2), the second new route to be established by a woman.

Shortly after the war, standards began to rise perceptibly, new approaches to climbing were tried, and new people began to appear on the scene. Perhaps the most impressive accomplishment in the immediate postwar era was Wiessner's 1946 ascent of Minnie Belle, the first 5.8 in the Gunks and one that was minimally protected at the time. For many years thereafter, this route retained its reputation as the hardest in the area. Meanwhile, Kraus, who had been concentrating mostly on free climbing during the preceding years as a result of Wiessner's influence, began experimenting with aid techniques to tackle some of the more formidable-looking lines, starting a trend that was to continue well into the 1960s. His first major achievement in this new direction was

Hardware Route, which required the extensive use of pitons and double ropes (no stirrups) for tension. This was a notable departure from some of his earlier climbs, where aid had only been used on the occasional move. Kraus' statement very much reflected the mountaineering philosophy of the time, in which the primary goal was to reach the summit (or the top of the cliff as the case may be). Style was not yet an issue. Also, because hemp ropes had a nasty habit of breaking easily, most climbers adopted a conservative approach and chose not to "run it out" on hard free moves when there was a chance of a long, potentially fatal fall.

During the late 1940s and early 1950s, most of the climbers frequenting the Gunks were associated with the Appalachian Mountain Club, whose power and influence was on the rise. Wiessner eventually moved away to Stowe, Vermont, and left Kraus as the dominant figure. The number of climbers was greater than ever, and on some weekends, as many as 50 or 60 could be found at the cliffs. Among these were several women who were easily the equal of any of the men in climbing ability. Outstanding among them was Bonnie Prudden, a physical fitness expert who is credited with over 30 new routes. Many of these she climbed with Kraus and Wiessner, and several of them she led, including such remarkable aid lines as Grand Central and Bonnie's Roof, and the free routes Wrist (5.6) and The Brat (5.6).

The growing reputation of the Shawangunks started to draw many new climbers to the area in the early 1950s, and most contributed in one fashion or another. In late 1951, a young Princeton undergraduate, in the person of Jim McCarthy, appeared on the scene. McCarthy, later to become a lawyer and president of The American Alpine Club, was destined to play a major role in the development of the Gunks. In the beginning, he showed considerable promise as he climbed many of the standard routes and rapidly worked his way up the scale of difficulty. Soon he attracted the attention of Hans Kraus; the two became fast friends and did their first route together at Millbrook, an aid variation to Wiessner's High Traverse called Recollection. Another newcomer to the area was Ken Prestrud, who added the ever popular Ken's Crack (5.7) in 1951 and established the second 5.8

in the Gunks with his 1952 ascent of Gaston, six years after Fritz Wiessner had done the first. These two climbs were considered the hardest in the Gunks through the mid-1950's. Though not as difficult as Gaston, the undoubted highlight of the period was Nobel Prize-winning physicist Bill Shockley's breathtaking 1953 ascent of Shockley's Ceiling (5.6), a spectacular overhang that still inspires awe in beginners today. Amazingly enough, all of these routes were being protected by the same thin soft-iron pitons that had been used before the war, and the very thinness of the pitons often made them inadequate for the wide horizontal cracks. To help alleviate this problem, Dick Hirschland, and later Norton Smythe, began making special pitons to fit the wider cracks, which opened up many new protection possibilities.

Over the next few years, McCarthy adopted Kraus' techniques and improved his skills to the point where he became the leading climber in the area. With considerable energy and enthusiasm, he actively joined in the search for new routes and was responsible for nearly half of the first ascents between 1954 and 1957, including a new 5.8 called Fat Stick, an awkward and technical climb with a long runout above the crux (no wired nuts or cams in those days) Fat Stick surpassed Ken's Crack and Gaston as the hardest route in the Gunks, and has remained popular to this day. Most of his new lines were climbed with aid, however, and such routes as Co-Op, No Glow, Le Teton, Try Again, and Foops were done during this period. On one aid climb, Double Crack, he actually used over 50 pitons! Years later, in the mid 1960s, these would all become well-respected free climbs. Hans Kraus continued to be active as well and concentrated more on free climbing, putting up V3 (5.7), Dry Martini (5.7)—the first route in the Gunks to receive a bolt, and the poorly protected Bitchy Virgin (5.6), the first route in the Gunks to receive a modern-day R rating. Considering the footwear then in use (stiff-soled boots), this was a bold accomplishment for its time. Art Gran and John Turner first visited the area at this time and soon began to challenge McCarthy's dominance. Gran, who a few years later was to publish the first Shawangunk guidebook, quietly established Thin Slabs (5.7); Turner, an expatriate Englishman who hailed from Canada, freed Gran's spectacular variation Thin Slabs Direct (5.7). While he was at it, Turner also free climbed Emilio (5.7+) and Yellow Belly (5.8), and led a new route of his own, Broken Sling, with a few points of aid.

The so-called Vulgarian era began in 1958. With the surge in climbing activity had come an influx of new climbers not associated with any club. Dave Craft, Claude Suhl, Al DeMaria, Roman Sadowy, Phil Jacobus, Steve Larsen, Dick Williams, and others became the nucleus of a rebellious group that was heavily involved with rock music, alcohol and the drug culture. Their vigor, sex-appeal, outrageous style and wild parties soon earned them the title "Vulgarians." The contrast between the new arrivals and the Appalachian Mountain Club or "Appies" is illuminated by the fact that both groups found the title "Vulgarians" appropriate. Depending upon who said it, the name was either an epithet, or a badge of independence. The clash in styles was evident and set the stage for confrontation.

Up until this point, most of the regular climbers (McCarthy and a few others being exceptions) were members of the AMC, which had been playing an active role in the training and development of new climbers since the 1940s. In 1945 a Safety Committee had been formed and was responsible for a training program that was considered by many to be stiflingly long and intolerably restricting, although it was able to boast a good track record. However, in 1959 the first fatality occurred at the cliffs, and fears were aroused that the owners of the property, the Smiley family, would restrict climbing because their insurance rates might be raised. To forestall this event, and perhaps gain control over the unruly Vulgarians, the AMC appointed itself the representative of the climbing community and presented the Smileys with a set of regulatory proposals. Tragedies could be averted, the AMC asserted, by allowing only "qualified" climbers on the cliff, and the Club would cheerfully undertake the role of training, certifying, and policing them. A climber would not be eligible to lead until satisfying the Safety Committee's requirements for reaching a certain level of proficiency.

As it turned out, the AMC soon discovered that it was not the uncontested voice of the climbing community, as the Vulgarians wanted no part of the Safety Committee's proposals. Not only were the Vulgarians not consulted about the proposals, but the whole underlying philosophy of control was the very antithesis of the freedom of expression and behavior that characterized their style of climbing.

Certain "Appies," fairly bursting with self-importance, used the issue as an excuse to further their confrontation with the Vulgarians and, in an attempt to enforce the new order, they patrolled the cliffs and ordered "unqualified" (i.e., unapproved) parties down. Ordering them down was one thing, though, but getting them down was quite another. The Vulgarians were simply not about to comply. Whether the AMC liked it or not, a new era had begun, and the Vulgarians made it a point to loudly proclaim their independence and remind the AMC that the Vulgarian Mountain Club was now the dominant force in the area. Not long afterwards, the whole regulatory system was dropped when Gerow Smiley bypassed the AMC and gave Dave Craft climbing applications for his fellow VMC climbers. The Vulgarians thus ushered in an exuberent period of hard climbing and hell raising that was to last for the next 10 years. Gone at last was the stolid old atmosphere of gentleman climbers and conservative attitudes.

The remainder of the decade saw a dramatic increase in climbing activity and further consolidation of the existing standards. The drive for new routes was spearheaded by Jim McCarthy and his Vulgarian friends, especially Dave Craft, and new ground was broken on several fronts. Also, for the first time, controversies over style began to appear, as past traditions about leading from the ground up were challenged. Important routes dating from this period were McCarthy's Birdland (5.8) and Pas de Deux (5.8), and aided ascents of Roseland, Birdie Party, and Turdland; Jim Andress' aptly named Drunkard's Delight (5.8−), and Krist Raubenheimer's Raubenheimer Special (5.7−), the first new 5.7 to be led by a woman. McCarthy, always experimenting with new approaches, aroused a storm of disapproval when he unethically rappelled down Pas de Deux and placed pitons for protection before leading it. Even though this wasn't as clearcut as standing in a sling, it was still considered aid by most everyone, and he quickly discontinued the practice. Another new tactic he tried was toproping a route before leading it, which is what he did on Madame Grunnebaum's Sorrow (5.8−), an obscure and rather unpopular climb today. This was just as radical a departure from past traditions as his actions on Pas de Deux had been, and the traditionalists once again were less than enthusiastic. Although the idea never really caught on until about 25 years later, in the 1980s, McCarthy had nevertheless opened the door.

The late 1950s saw several other significant developments as well. The 5.9 barrier was finally broken, on separate occasions, by Dave Craft and John Turner. In 1959 Craft free climbed the 5.9 crux of his new route, Inverted Layback, but then used two points of aid on the easier climbing above. Although his use of aid above the crux may seem hard to understand today, it should be remembered that in those days the major goal was to reach the "summit," not to deliberately climb in any particular style, as is now the case. Turner's 5.9 breakthrough was on the variation Maria Direct, which possibly may have predated Craft's ascent. Another development that pointed the way to the future was Art Gran's Never Never Land, which was the first major attempt to tackle a steep, blank-looking wall. Progress, in fact, was only made possible by the use of expansion bolts for aid.

THE 1960's

Climbing activity in the early 1960s took off like a rocket, as Phil Jacobus ushered in the decade with a very bold on-sight lead of Jacob's Ladder, the first 5.10 in the Gunks. Not only was this a grade harder than anything previously attempted, but it had virtually no protection and is now given a modern-day X rating. McCarthy, meanwhile, added three 5.9s in 1960 alone, the best among them being the classic M.F. At the time, this was considered to be 5.10 and the hardest route in the area. Another superb route was Arrow (5.8), by MIT undergraduate Willie Crowther, who wire-brushed the glistening white face clean of lichen and bolted it on rappel before leading it. Strangely enough, this ethical transgression failed to excite much of a response, as most climbers seemed only too glad to have clean rock and good protection.

The legendary Yvon Chouinard visited the Shawangunks for the first time in 1961 and brought with him an aura of the Yosemite hardman along with a selection of his new hand-forged chromolly pitons, which were to revolutionize climbing protection. Needless to say, the locals were eager to impress their visitor and began showing him around, ending up on Never Never Land. McCarthy volunteered to lead the climb and soon reached the belay safely. But before he could tie into the anchor, he inexplicably slipped and fell nearly 50 feet before Pete Geiser could arrest his fall. Trying to maintain his composure in front of the Western celebrity, McCarthy sheepishly grinned, "Welcome to the Gunks!" This welcome would return several years later when McCarthy took a long fall on the Nose route on Yosemite's El Capitan. Chouinard, the leader of the rescue party, greeted him with the words "welcome to Yosemite." After Never Never Land, Chouinard then proceeded to establish Matinee by free climbing the first pitch (5.10) and aiding the second. Since no one could follow the first pitch free, the route became an overnight sensation and an instant test piece, whose reputation for difficulty actually increased with time.

The following weekend, Dick Williams astonished his fellow Vulgarians by repeating Matinee's troublesome first pitch. And once again no one else could follow. Williams had begun climbing in 1958, when he was still on active duty with the U.S. Navy Submarine Service, but he wasn't able to devote full time to climbing until he was discharged in 1961. Coming from a gymnastic background, he brought a dynamic element to climbing that contrasted sharply with the static "three-points-of-contact" school of thought. When holds were out of reach, Williams used a controlled swing or "lunge" to reach them. This new style was well suited to the horizontal nature of the rock and was to have far-reaching effects on the history of climbing in the area.

As the decade advanced, the focus of climbing in the Gunks gradually began to change. The elimination of aid on existing routes started to gain almost equal status with the establishment of new routes. There were probably several reasons for this: Chouinard's new pitons finally offered safe and reliable protection, the footwear had markedly improved (*kletterschuhes* had just been introduced to the area by Dave Craft), and the standards had greatly increased. But perhaps the biggest reason was that aid-elimination projects were often less intimidating than new routes because they were usually on known ground that already had fixed protection in place. Reflecting this change in attitude, and with single-minded determination to retain his reputation as the leading climber, McCarthy made the first free ascents of Nosedive (5.10) and Retribution (5.10) in 1961, and led a bold new route called Tough Shift (5.10), which is still serious by today's standards, with an R. rating. In 1963 he also succeeded in making the first free ascent of the second pitch of Matinee, via a slight variation.

Aid climbing was by no means a lost art, however, as Williams nailed his way out of the huge Kansas City roof in 1962, and Art Gran, in a desire to practice his aid techniques for a trip to the Canadian Rockies, hammered his way up Twilight Zone, The Throne, and The Yellow Crack in 1963. Although Williams enjoyed aid, he also excelled in free climbing, and in 1963 managed to toprope the lichen-smeared Mental Block face and create the first 5.11 in the Northeast. At the time, it was only considered a boulder problem, but hindsight now recognizes it as a full-fledged route. Another Williams free climb of the period, Phoebe (5.10), had a more checkered history. After first toproping then leading it, he rappelled down, (mis)placed a bolt to make the route "safe," demonstrating that placing bolts on rappel then was just as misleading as it is today.

During 1964 there was a flurry of activity as Art Gran worked on the long-awaited first guidebook to the Gunks. Everyone rushed around trying to climb as many new routes as possible for inclusion in the book. Dick Williams climbed his test-pieces Double Clutch (5.9+) and Frustration Syndrome (5.10). However, a promising new talent, Steve Larsen, along with Williams, climbed Tweedle Dum, the area's first 5.11 lead. At the time, the route's significance was missed because it was considered little more than an expanded boulder problem, much like Mental Block. In those days, routes on the talus boulders were not taken very seriously; the longer multi-pitch routes on the main cliffs were thought of as the only "real climbs." Not until the 1980s was this way of thinking to be abandoned, as the leading climbers began to focus primarily on very short, extremely difficult problems, some scarcely 30 feet long.

Another important event in 1964 was Layton Kor's first visit to the Gunks. He introduced the locals to western tactics for big walls, and his awesome drive and talent expanded their concept of what was possible.

A Climber's Guide to the Shawangunks was finally published late in 1964, with 249 routes, and it was an instant success. The new guidebook covered the four major cliffs in the area: Millbrook, the Near Trapps, the Trapps, and "Mohonk," as Sky Top was then known. It also briefly mentioned a few of the rarely visited outlying cliffs, such as Lost City, Bonticou, and the Outback Slabs. The book's most outstanding feature was its use of aerial photographs to depict the cliffs and climbs. For the first time, climbers had a clear visual record of what had been climbed and what remained to be done, and this led to a surge in activity the following year.

An unprecedented total of 37 new routes were established in 1965, and seven former aid climbs were freed, the most important being Transcontinental Nailway (5.10) by Jim McCarthy. It was the most productive year since the Gunks were discovered 30 years earlier. The emphasis was overwhelmingly on free climbing, as only four of the new routes required aid. The pendulum was clearly swinging further away from aid climbing, and, in a few short years, aid would become virtually a lost art as the Iron Age of piton use was to draw to a close.

This was also the year that the leading "Gunkies" began to expand their horizons and travel to other areas around the country. Inspired by articles on Yosemite climbing in the 1963 and 1964 *American Alpine Journals,* Dick Williams and John Hudson visited the Valley and surprised the locals by successfully climbing the Steck-Salathé route on Sentinel Rock, the first Easterners to do so. Returning home with a wealth of experience, Williams then ventured north to Cannon Mountain in New Hampshire and teamed up with Yvon Chouinard and Art Gran to esablish the first big-wall aid climb in the East, the VMC Direct, complete with its own bivouac. This marked the beginning of a yearly exchange of visits between Eastern and Western climbers, and many partnerships were formed that broke regional boundaries and led to major accomplishments elsewhere in the world.

In the fall of 1966 Royal Robbins made his first visit to the

Gunks, leading the hardest climbs of the day, and leaving a lasting impression on the locals.

As interest in traveling to areas outside New York was kindled, activity in the Gunks declined in the late 1960s and early 1970s. There was a brief period of renewed interest in aid climbing, however, as many of the leading climbers worked on perfecting their big-wall techniques. Williams was especially active just before a planned 1966 trip to Yosemite and, among other climbs, put up The Yellow Wall, which included the first hanging bivouac in the Gunks. He then went on to do the fifth ascent of The Nose route on El Capitan with a VMC party, demonstrating that Eastern climbers, although trained on relatively small cliffs, were just as capable of climbing long, technically demanding, multiday routes as their Western counterparts.

Balancing the interest in aid climbing was a continuing and strengthening interest in free climbing, with the realization that styles would have to change if standards were to improve. During the preceding few years, climbing had not advanced much beyond the 5.10 level for essentially two reasons: Most climbers were still "weekend warriors," who did not train at home or in a gym during the week, and the "leader-never-falls" philosophy was still firmly entrenched, which meant that most climbers aspired to get up a route on their first try, even if aid was required. The idea of taking repeated falls was considered bad form that indicated a lack of ability. A few climbers, nevertheless, chose to ignore this tenet on climbs where they felt the end justified the means. McCarthy's M.F. (5.9) in 1960 and Williams' first free ascents of Jean (5.9) in 1964 and Turdland (5.10+) in 1966 are cases in point, but they were isolated incidents. In 1967, however, there was a concrete shift in attitude about sieging and yo-yoing that began with Richard Goldstone and Jim McCarthy's first free ascent of Coexistence (5.10+), which required five tries before success was achieved.

But it was another climber who was to carry this idea to its logical conclusion and point the way to the future. John Stannard, a relatively unknown climber who was a physicist by trade, had been quietly and methodically working out and improving his abilities for several years; later, in 1967, he took the Gunks by storm when he single-handedly free climbed the spectacular 8-

foot roof of Foops (5.11) in a monumental five-day effort. This magnificent achievement was the single most outstanding event of the decade, and it opened everyone's eyes to the promise of things to come. The route wasn't to be repeated until six years later, in 1973, when Henry Barber swept onto the scene during his meteoric rise in the climbing world.

Foops represented the concrete realization of a shift in attitude: it was indeed OK to siege a climb. The key to Stannard's ultimate success was not necessarily his talent, but his physical conditioning and persistence. It was now that the era of weekend climbs was at an end. Eventhough most climbing continued to take place only on the weekend, training in the gym and at home showed the commitment necessary to succeed on the hardest routes.

Spearheaded by Stannard, who was convinced that most of the existing aid climbs would eventually go free, a new wave of activity began in 1968 when, significantly, the number of first free ascents almost equalled the number of new routes. Stannard's crusade started at Millbrook, where one by one such routes as White Corner (5.9), Garden of Allah (5.10), Remembrance of Things Past (5.10), and Never Again (5.10) fell to his free-climbing tactics. Incredibly enough, he had very little competition at the time because few other climbers could follow him and most did not have the patience to spend days at a time working on a single route. So he had the field pretty much to himself for a while, and he continued on to free Fat City (5.10) in a four-day siege (with Gary Brown, who placed the crucial piton on this R-rated route), Comedy in Three Acts (5.11) after only one day, and Swing Time (5.11-) in a five-day *tour de force*. While many of these times may seem inordinately long by today's standards, it is important to remember that relatively stiff-soled climbing boots were then in use, and that pitons (which are heavier and harder to place than nuts) were still being used for protection.

The 1960s ended with a bang when John Gill, America's premier boulderer, visited in 1969 and soloed the left side of the Doug's Roof overhang, establishing the first 5.12 in the Gunks.

THE 1970's

The new decade began with the lowest level of climbing activity since the 1950's. The reason for the decline (and a similar one in

1967) are hard to pin down, but bad weather on weekends, trips to other areas and changing interests undoubtedly all had their effect. Only six new routes were established in 1970 and no first free ascents. The only really noteworthy climbs were Pete Carman's aid climb Half Assid and Rich Goldstone's Farewell to Fingers variation (5.11+). The most significant event actually occurred in New Paltz, where Dick Williams, Jim McCarthy, and several others started a successful retail climbing store named Rock and Snow, which Williams owns and still manages today.

In 1971 enthusiasm for new routes picked up once again, perhaps stimulated to some extent by the expected publication of a new guidebook the following year. A handful of new aid climbs appeared that represented very nearly the last of a dying breed. Dick Williams' Bird Cage, Dave Loeks' Open Cockpit, and Roy Kligfield's Kligfield's Follies, in fact, would all be free climbed within two years. Williams was also active on the free-climbing front, putting in Or Any Monday (5.11−) and reinforcing his reputation for boldness by leading Never Say Never (5.10), a poorly protected climb that ascended the blank-looking face immediately left of Never Never Land. Another serious route of the time was Walter Bauman's Something Boring (5.9), whose X-rated protection is unlikely to bore anyone.

Overshadowing all this activity, however, were several revolutionary changes that were to have a major impact on climbing in the Shawangunks and elsewhere around the country. Artificial chockstones or "nuts" had first appeared on a few climbers' racks in the late 1960s (the idea being imported from England), but they were crude in design and weren't taken very seriously in the Gunks because the cliffs already bristled with resident pitons, and the horizontal cracks were thought to be inhospitable to the newfangled gear. Since everyone already understood the capabilities of pitons, there seemed no reason to switch. However, in the early 1970s the ecology movement swept through the country, and man's impact on the environment came under close scrutiny. Climbers were just as affected by this as the rest of the population, and pitons increasingly became the focus of attention.

In the old days, soft-iron pitons had been used, and these generally bent to conform to the shape of the cracks, making them difficult to remove. As a result, most were left fixed in place. However, with the advent of hard-steel chromolly pitons, which didn't bend, the protection was easily removed. Unfortunately, the new pitons were much harder than the rock and left noticeable and growing scars (which can still be seen today) when they were repeatedly hammered in and out of the cracks by successive parties.

By late 1971, climbers were becoming increasingly concerned about all the damage caused by pitons and began searching for alternative forms of protection. At about the same time, new and sophisiticated nuts were becoming widely available, and more and more of the leading climbers began advocating their use. Foremost among them were John Stannard, who distributed a regional climbing newsletter called *The Eastern Trade,* and Yvon Chouinard, who published an article in his catalog by Doug Robinson entitled "The Whole Natural Art of Protection." Together, these and other climbers preached the new "clean-climbing" ethic with messianic fervor and, remarkably, in the next couple of years aid climbing in general and pitons in particular, especially in the Gunks, went almost completely out of fashion. To encourage the adoption of the new ethic, an "all-nut ascent" book was even maintained at Rock and Snow for a time.

Along with the clean-climbing revolution came a parallel advance in footwear, as flexible, smooth-soled climbing shoes with sticky rubber became available for the first time. In addition, there was a huge influx of new people into the sport, as the "back-to-nature" generation came into its own and demanded to be heard. As might be expected, the competition that inevitably arose between the newcomers and the old hands, combined with the advances in hardware and footwear, resulted in yet another major increase in the standards.

In 1972, *Shawangunk Rock Climbs* by Dick Williams was finally published, with 393 routes on the four major cliffs covered by Art Gran's earlier guide. This time there was no mention of any of the outlying crags because most of the locals felt that certain areas should be left undocumented so future climbers could experience the adventure of exploring on their own, a way of thinking that has prevailed ever since. Following Gran's example, Williams made extensive use of aerial photographs in the book, and its comprehensive format set a precedent for guidebooks nationwide. Among other things, the new guide included 38 aid climbs, which fanned the flames of Stannard's desire to completely eliminate aid from the Gunks.

Stannard was soon joined in this pursuit by several very talented new climbers with similar interests. Henry Barber, a rising young star who had begun climbing in 1968, first made his mark in 1972 by free climbing Bird Cage (5.10) with Bob Anderson. Barber quickly became known for his strict code of free-climbing ethics (including pulling the rope down after each try) and his bold and clean style of climbing. During the next few years he captured the imagination of the climbing world with his numerous difficult routes in the United States, Britain, and Australia, and his free solo of the 1600-foot Steck-Salathé route (5.9) in Yosemite, a feat that Royal Robbins hailed as "visionary."

John Bragg also made his debut at the cutting edge in 1972, when he joined Stannard in a successful four-day effort to free climb Help! (5.11+). Bragg, a Harvard graduate in physics, had started climbing only two years earlier, in 1970, but made rapid progress and eventually enjoyed a brilliant career that was to include ascents of Torre Egger and Cerro Torre in Patagonia.

Often teaming up together in 1973 and 1974, Stannard, Barber, Bragg, and Steve Wunsch, another free-climbing purist, systematically attempted to free climb every aid route in Williams' book and in the process firmly established 5.12 as a grade in the Gunks. Such routes as Crack of Bizarre Delights (5.11), Kligfield's Follies (5.11+), Open Cockpit (5.11+), Sling Time (5.11+), P.R. (5.11+), Kama Sutra (5.12−), The Throne (5.12−), To Have or Have Not (5.12), and Kansas City (5.12) testify to their dedication and great technical ability.

Since the majority of these ascents were done in 1973, the four climbers and their friends redirected most of their considerable energy to new routes in 1974. Stannard, although less active than he had been the previous year, nevertheless showed his determination to succeed by leading Persistence (5.11+) at Lost City from the bottom of the hole after 10 days of effort, setting a new record for endurance. Barber and Wunsch, on the other hand, remained much more active and picked up some of the slack left by Stannard. Barber's more significant contributions at this time were the sinister Crash and Burn (5.9), which required a frightening leap from the top of a pinnacle to the lip of an overhang on the main face, and True Grip (5.11−), which was X-rated at the time ("Friends" had not yet been invented) and still stands as a tribute to his mastery of the sport. In the meantime, Wunsch quietly put up the poorly protected Burning Bush (5.11+) and Cries and Whimpers (5.11) before turning his attention to an anonymous aid crack on a detached pinnacle at Sky Top.

After attempting the strenuous inch-wide crack with little success for two days, Wunsch began to realize the scope of the project and virtually set up camp at its base. A few days later he was still at it, and Kevin Bein half-humorously began to call the route "Wunsch Upon a Climb." Finally, after two weeks of unremitting work, the climb at long last yielded to Wunsch's exacting free-climbing style (which involved pulling the rope down after every try), and Supercrack, as it came to be called, became recognized as probably the hardest free climb in the world. As such, it was tentatively given the first 5.13 grade in America, a grade that seemed to be confirmed two years later, in 1976, when Californian Ron Kauk repeated the route after four grueling days and declared that it was two grades harder than anything in Yosemite. Today, of course, the grade has settled down to 5.12, but only because laybacking was eventually found to be easier than finger-stacking, as Wunsch and Kauk initially had done when they jammed up the relentlessly overhanging crack.

The remaining years of the 1970s constituted a period of consolidation and transition, characterized by an emphasis on traditional free-climbing values, and the rise of a new generation of climbers. Kevin Bein, Rick Cronk, Mike Freeman, Rich Perch, Ivan Rezucha, Russ Raffa, Mark Robinson, Rich Romano, Rich Ross, Mike Sawicky, Sandy Stewart, and others all became involved in doing what they humbly called "first human ascents" of the desperate test pieces pioneered by the reigning legends Stannard, Wunsch, and Bragg.

During this time, Wunsch retired from climbing to become a stockholder and Stannard made his last major contribution when he made the first free ascent of the formidable Wasp Stop (5.11+) in 1975, a route that had been intentionally aided in 1968 on the assumption that it could never be free climbed. Bragg, on the other hand, continued to be extremely active and dominated the scene for several years with his puritanical free-climbing standards. He tended to concentrate on very difficult routes, with less than perfect protection, and created a number of classics that included the first complete free ascent of The Yellow Wall (5.11) in 1977, with Russ Raffa, the ever-popular Shake Your Booty (5.11) in 1978, and the renowned Gravity's Rainbow (5.12) at Lost City in 1979.

Meanwhile, Rich Romano, who had been quietly leading 5.10 since 1973, suddenly made his first new-route appearance in 1975, when he powered his way up Void Where Prohibited (5.11+). Over the next few years, despite his determination to avoid publicity, he developed quite a reputation as a wildman by climbing such horrific X-rated climbs as Back to the Land Movement (5.11), in 1979. Other poorly protected, often loose routes convinced many climbers that Millbrook, where Romano did most of his climbing, was a dangerous place to climb, and few ventured out to the cliff. As a result, Romano had the place practically to himself and ended up doing most of the routes, all in traditional unrehearsed style. His long association with Millbrook has earned him the title of "Manager of the Bank" there, and he has done much to maintain its climbing traditions by setting a good example and declaring the cliff a "no-bolt" zone in the face of the mid-1980s Eurodog pro-bolting craze.

Also coming into his own was Kevin Bein, a Harvard graduate who was as skilled at playing the French horn as he was at climbing rock. Bein was a physical fitness fanatic, who often bicycled to the cliffs from New Paltz and who climbed at a very high standard for more than 20 years. He and his wife, Barbara Devine (a very talented climber in her own right, who counted Supercrack among her many successes), formed perhaps the best-known and most well-liked husband-and-wife climbing team in the United States for many years. Outgoing and friendly, Bein became known as the "Mayor of the Gunks, delighting in helping others out of difficulties and in giving visitors enthusiastic tours of the hardest routes in the area. Some of his best climbs during this period were Scene of the Climb (5.11−) and Creature Features (5.11). By far his best was No Comment (5.11+) in 1979, now considered a classic.

Creature Features was marred by questionable tactics when it was first climbed, and it generated quite a controversy for a time. Against their better judgment, Bein and Mark Robinson, with assistance from Sandy Stewart and Mike Sawicky, violated the high stylistic standards of the day by previewing the route and taking advantage of move-by-move instructions (known today as "beta") that Bein had memorized from his earlier toprope ascent of the route in 1975. When Henry Barber, whose free-climbing purism was well respected, heard of these developments, he unleashed a wrath of criticism in their direction that had a salutary effect. Robinson, for one, took Barber's criticism seriously and thereafter refused to be involved with any hangdogging, previewing, or preplacing of protection on any route.

Controversy again clouded the scene in 1978 when Dave Loeks and Dick Williams placed three bolts with aid on Beer and Loathing (5.11−). Although the bolts were placed on the lead, the two climbers and the route were heavily criticized because the bolts were seen as a violation of the sacrosanct clean-climbing ethic that was so well entrenched at the Gunks by then. Subsequently, the route has received more recognition, but only in the light of the ethical crisis that pervades climbing today.

Other than a few relatively minor transgressions like these, most of the new routes in the mid and late 1970s were climbed in traditional style and stand as examples of what dedicated climbers can achieve with patience, sound ethics, and good style. One of the most impressive accomplishments, other than Gravity's Rainbow (5.12), was Robinson and Sawicky's 1979 first free ascent of Happiness is a 110° Wall (5.12), after seven days of sieging that did not involve hangdogging or preplaced protection. Numerous other excellent climbs were created during this period as well, a few of the better ones being Freeman's Thunder and Frightening (5.11−) in 1979, Perch's Blind Ambition (5.11−) in 1978, Raffa's classic Graveyard Shift (5.10+) in 1978, Rezucha's Impenetrable

Ceilings (5.11) in 1978, and Robinson's Knockout Drops (5.11) in 1978 and Scary Area (5.12) in 1979.

THE 1980's

The 1980s opened with an explosion of new routes, largely stimulated by publication of the 2nd edition of Dick Williams' *Shawangunk Rock Climbs* in 1980, which described 530 routes. New equipment such as spring-loaded camming devices called "Friends," introduced in 1978 and the sticky-soled Fires in 1983, also contributed to the new route explosion. During that year, a record 49 climbs were established, but even that record was shattered in 1981 when a phenomenal 110 were climbed! In terms of sheer numbers of routes, the main activists were Ivan Rezucha (with 19 in 1980), Rich Romano (with 26 at Millbrook in 1981), and Todd Swain (with 37 in 1981).

At the upper end of the scale, so many fine lines were discovered or free climbed for the first time that only a few of the highlights can be listed: Rich Romano's Bank Shot (5.10), Birth of the Blues (5.11), Hang 'Em High (5.11) in 1980, Manifest Destiny (5.11), and X-rated Land Grab (5.11) in 1982; Russ Raffa's Project X (5.12+) in the Giant's Workshop, Point Blank (5.12) in 1981, Deep Chills (5.11+) in 1982, To Be or Not to Be (5.11+), and Tiers of Fiers (5.12) in 1984; Jack Mileski's Cookie Monster (5.12−) in 1981; John Myers' Lotus Flower (5.12) in 1981; Mike Freeman's Hocus Croakus (5.11+) in 1982; Russ Clune's first free ascent of Requiem for a Heavyweight (5.12) in 1982 and first ascents of The Sting (5.11+) and Flash Dance Arete (5.12−) in 1983; Jeff Gruenberg's Talus Food (5.11+) in 1983 and Nectar Victor (5.12+), Sudden Impact (5.12), and X-rated Skeletal Remains (5.11+) in 1984, the last being his best lead ever, by his own estimation; Jim Damon's Supper's Ready (5.12−) in 1984; Felix Modugno's Dark Side of the Moon (5.12) in 1984; and Jim Munson's Squeeze and Pump (5.11) in 1984. Many of these routes were poorly protected, so it can be seen that the average climbing ability of the area's top climbers was very high indeed.

One climber who served as an inspiration for all was Hugh Herr, who became legendary in circles far removed from the climbing world for his determination to succeed against all odds. Already an excellent climber by 1981, with such routes as Condemned Man (5.12−) and the first free ascent of Cilley Dickin' (5.12−) to his credit, Herr lost both legs below the knees to frostbite on New Hampshire's Mt. Washington in the winter of 1982. No one thought he would ever climb again, but everyone underestimated his iron will to recover. Incredibly enough, within a few months of his accident, Herr was back on the rocks with specially designed artificial legs, making an extraordinary comeback. So extraordinary, in fact, that in late 1982 he celebrated his return by making the first ascent of Mechanical Boy (5.11−). The following year he rejoined the ranks of the leading climbers by chalking up a number of very difficult new routes, including Footloose and Fancy Free (5.11), Cinnamon Girl (5.12), and Sticky Bun Power (5.12).

In 1983 another inspiration appeared on the scene in the person of Lynn Hill, a ray of California sunshine whose enormous talent was already apparent in the 1970s when she was climbing 5.11 at Joshua Tree and elsewhere. Acclaimed by many as the best female rock climber in the world, Hill was quickly welcomed by the locals and joined them on many of the hardest new routes. One of her most impressive leads during this period was the first free ascent of the scary and poorly protected Yellow Crack (5.12) in 1984. However, one of the first projects she actually became involved with was Vandals.

Ever since Supercrack was downrated to 5.12, the leading climbers in the Gunks had been searching hard for a genuine 5.13, and in 1983 they found it in the form of a roof at Sky Top. Jeff Gruenberg, Lynn Hill, Russ Clune, and Hugh Herr all set to work on it, and as luck would have it, Gruenberg finally succeeded in leading Vandals without using preplaced protection. Vandals was a significant achievement, not only because it was the area's first undisputed 5.13, but because it was done in fairly traditional style and was quickly repeated on the lead by all the other members of the party. At the time, the temptation to use the new Eurodog "aid" tactics, which were espoused by Clune (who had traveled more extensively to the world's major rock climbing areas than any other Gunks climber since Henry Barber) must have been great, but the four climbers showed remarkable and admirable restraint.

The 50th anniversary of climbing in the Shawangunks occurred in 1985, and it was celebrated in spectacular fashion by two of the leading climbers. Jeff Gruenberg free soloed the totally committing Foops (5.11), whose airy crux was 60 feet above the ground, and Russ Clune free soloed the relentlessly strenuous 80 foot Supercrack (5.12). The two outstanding new routes of the year were Lynn Hill's Artificial Intelligence (5.12+) at Bonticou, and Scott Franklin's Survival of the Fittest (5.13−) at Lost City, a very popular line that Scott Franklin led in traditional style, proving that extreme routes could be done from the ground up without resorting to preplaced protection. The rest of the activity that year was marked by harder lines being climbed using the increasingly accepted Eurodog techniques which involved hangdogging, toproping, rehearsing, and replacing of protection. Not all of the new routes were led, however, because toproping as an end in itself started to become more popular for a couple of reasons: Hard, well-protected lines were relatively scarce, and many climbers found it convenient to set up a toprope from an adjacent climb just to get a workout.

The year 1985 marked the culmination of a series of visits by top foreign climbers, who began parading into the area to test their skills in the late 1970s, as the reputation of the Gunks spread internationally. In 1980 Kim Carrigan arrived from Australia and basically climbed all the "hardest" routes on sight, including the first one-day ascent of Supercrack, the area's most prominent test piece. A year later Peter O'Donovan showed up from England and managed to lead Supercrack after only one fall, an achievement that none of the locals had ever been able to match. Then, in 1982, two more British climbers showed up and took the place by storm. Jerry Moffatt and Chris Gore climbed every difficult route they tried on sight, and Moffatt even managed to flash Supercrack with minimal protection, much to everyone's amazement. In 1984 Wolfgang Gullich appeared from West Germany, and he too quickly climbed everything the locals offered him, including Vandals. But it wasn't until 1985 that the single most impressive visit took place. In a fitting tribute to the 50th anniversary of Shawan-

SCOTT FRANKLIN on First Ascent of
CYBERNETIC WALL (Triple Right Cliff)
Cathy Bekeil

gunk climbing, French superstar Patrick Edlinger flashed every difficult route he was presented, on sight and with no falls, and gave his hosts a new perspective and perhaps a clearer vision of what was possible.

The foreigners trained on routes in Europe that had been bolted on rappel and, consequently, they all advocated the use of bolts. Many of the leading climbers in the Gunks and elsewhere around the country began to equate bolting with hard climbing. This led to a conflict between different climbing factions in the Gunks, and fueled an ethical crisis that continued to develop over the next few years.

Nineteen eighty-six was a watershed year for the Shawangunks. It began innocently enough with the publication of a pocket-sized guidebook, *The Gunks Guide*, by Todd Swain, who was a ranger for the Mohonk Preserve. The slender little volume was jam-packed with 881 routes and introduced to the area for the first time the popular G-PG-R-X protection rating system and a route quality system based on 0-3 stars. Significantly, the guide did not stimulate much new-route interest, as had all previous guidebooks, mainly because uncontrived, high-quality climbs were increasingly hard to find on the four major cliffs. Nevertheless, a number of excellent routes were discovered on both the major cliffs and the outlying crags, a few of the better ones being Russ Clune's Squat Thrust (5.12−), Al Diamond's Bone Hard (5.12), Scott Franklin's Diplomatic Strain (5.12+), Jeff Gruenberg's Clairvoyance (5.13) at Lost City, and Darrow Kirkpatrick's Future Shock (5.12−).

Most of these new routes were preprotected on rappel and some were climbed with dubious tactics (chiseled nut placements were used on Clairvoyance, for instance). On Twilight Zone, an aid route that Jeff Gruenberg and Jack Mileski had spent two years trying to free climb. Eventually they "succeeded," via a couple of variations called The Zone (5.13−) and The French Connection (5.12+), success came at the expense of the rock itself: holds were chipped and enlarged, forever preventing other climbers from attempting the route in its natural state. Another incident involved Pumping Pygmies (5.13), which was led after a bolt and other protection was placed on rappel and a tree was cut down. This

AL DIAMOND on MONKEY PUMP
Dick Williams

turned out to be the final straw: an outraged climber removed the protection to make an environmental statement.

The ethics controversy had a profound effect on Shawangunk climbing. Not only did it polarize the climbing community, but it led to an increase in toprope climbs and a new trend in naming routes to reflect the crisis; examples being Todd Swain's Trouble in Paradise (5.11 −) and Jim Munson's Explosive Bolts (5.11).

As the year wore on, the simmering ethics controversy came to a head. A climbers' meeting moderated by the Mohonk Preserve was called in November. The result, reflecting the sentiments of the participants, was an unofficial moratorium on placing new bolts or removing existing ones.

In the next year, 1987, the "bolting war" continued with a vengeance with some climbers placing and removing bolts with disregard for the bolting moratorium. This led to two more climbers' meetings moderated by the Mohonk Preserve, both of which reconfirmed the moratorium on placing or removing bolts.

New-route activity during 1987 was not very inspiring, due in part to the moratorium on bolts and the fact that several of the better climbers had moved away. Many of the new climbs were toprope problems, which were finally receiving more recognition, but a few notable leads such as Lynn Hill's Tweazle Roof (5.12+) were accomplished as well. Other notable leads first toproped and protected on rappel included Hill's Girls Just Want to Have Fun (5.12+), and Jason Stern's Death's Head Mask (5.12+). The award for most imaginative new route went to Ken Nichols and Dave Rosenstein for Great Wall of China (5.9), a 67-pitch, 9000-foot girdle traverse of the Trapps that may be the world's longest rock climb.

The most difficult new route and perhaps the hardest climb yet done in the Gunks was Scott Franklin's Cybernetic Wall (5.13+) at Bonticou, which he led after a marathon 21-day siege. Even more impressive though was his remarkable free solo of Survival of the Fittest, the first 5.13 to be soloed anywhere in the world.

In the Spring of 1988 the bolting issue was finally resolved. The Mohonk Preserve decided that enough was enough, and declared that there would be no bolting, chipping holds, or cutting trees on their lands, *period.*

In 1988, as in 1987, new route activity was minimal, with most of it siphoned off into little-known outlying areas. The hot, oppressive summer of 1988 began with the sad news of Fritz Wiessner's death. Then just as the climbing community began to recover, it was shocked again by the news of Kevin Bein's tragic death on the Matterhorn. The passing of these two dedicated climbers whose lives spanned the entire history of the Shawangunks marked the closing of an era.

Climbing activity for the remainder of the summer was hindered by an understandable lack of enthusiasm. But the fall began on a positive note with Lynn Hill's long-expected marriage to Gunks local Russ Raffa.

What does the future hold for the Gunks in the 1990's? If Minnewaska State Park is open to climbers, it would signal a new era, adding to what is already one of the world's greatest areas for "adventure" climbing.

The Trapps

The Trapps

THE TRAPPS (A NAME DErived from the Dutch word *treppen,* which means *steps*) is the most popular cliff in the Shawangunks. It is the longest and most accessible of the major cliffs and has a carriage road along its base. It also has the largest number of routes, including perhaps the greatest concentration of high-quality beginner and intermediate climbs to be found anywhere in the world. As a result, many of the climbs see considerable traffic.

The rock is generally clean and solid except on a few of the lessfrequented routes, and it ranges from 30 to 250 feet high. A prominent feature is the Grand Traverse Ledge (GT Ledge), which starts near the top of Pas de Deux and extends north (right) for most of the length of the cliff, with only a few minor breaks along the way.

The Trapps is only a short distance from Route 44–55, where parking is presently allowed on the south (downhill) side of the road above the hairpin turn. (Be sure to park inside the white line or the State Police will ticket your car.) Just uphill from a spring (pipe) beside the road is the main access trail, which follows a series of steps 100 feet uphill to the carriage road (Undercliff Road) in the vicinity of the Überfall. Two other marked access trails can also be found between the main trail and the steel bridge at the top of the hill. Climbers are urged to use these trails to prevent erosion elsewhere on the hillside.

The Überfall is the principal meeting spot for climbers in the Trapps and is where the Mohonk Preserve rangers can usually be found on weekends. It is also the site of the main descent route for the left end of the cliff.

The carriage road parallels the base of most of the cliff (except for a short section at the far right end), and most climbers follow this until they spot the climb they want to do and locate one of the established access trails (see line drawings) that connects the road with the cliff. A trail also follows the base of the cliff from just beyond the Überfall to the north end.

The four most popular descent routes are all connected by a trail that runs along the top of the cliff. For climbs on the far left (south) end, the easiest way down is via a trail that loops down around the left end of the cliff. For climbs between No Picnic and High Exposure, most climbers use the 4th-Class Überfall descent route. For climbs beyond High Exposure, Silly Chimney (5.1) is often downclimbed (or a rappel from a nearby tree is made) or Roger's Escape Hatch (3rd Class) is descended. Both of these are marked by cairns in the woods above the cliff.

Restrictions

No new routes are allowed in the Sleepy Hollow area, from the route Wegetables to the right (north) end of the cliff. This restriction has been imposed to protect wildlife and the delicate environment as much as possible so that it can be compared to some of the more heavily used areas to assess climber impact. Please cooperate.

COLORFULS BOULDER

Known by some as the Benign Behemoth, this huge boulder sits beside the carriage road near the steel bridge, just east of the junction of Undercliff and Overcliff Roads. The most prominent feature on it is an off-width crack that splits the boulder: Colorfuls

Crack 5.6 (FA 1960: Dick Williams). There are also several toprope climbs on either side of the crack, and there is an easy slab with a crevice on the backside.

BOULDERING AREA

About 65 feet left of Short and Simple is a trail that affords access to the top of The Brat and other nearby climbs. Follow the trail uphill for 2–3 minutes to an amphitheaterlike area that has a variety of short climbs and boulder problems. To the left is a slablike face and in the center is a zigzag crack called Reefer Madness. Just about everything here was climbed during the consciousness-expanding years of the 1960s.

1. SHORT AND SIMPLE 5.7 G
Start: At a blocky arête on the left end of the cliff, 100 feet left of Keyhole.
Pitch 1: Climb the left face of the arête and continue up the face and steep fault above to the top. (80 feet)
FA 1981: Todd Swain and Judy Paddon

2. BIRTHDAY BISCUIT BOY 5.9 G
Start: At a jumble of blocks on the left side of a rectangular orange block, 35 feet left of Keyhole.
Pitch 1: Climb past the blocks to a point just beneath three cracks or faults. Follow the right fault to the top. (70 feet)
FA 1979: Harvey Arnold and Kevin Bein

3. GREAT WALL OF CHINA 5.9 R
Start: Same as Birthday Biscuit Boy.
Pitches 1–67: Traverse the entire Trapps below the GT Ledge and finish on a dirt path that goes up the cliff about 100 feet beyond A Long Walk for Man.
This traverse extends for 9000 feet and is probably the world's longest rock climb. It took 5 days to complete and was quite an adventure in route finding. A detailed description is available

from the first ascent party. Beware of wasps, especially near Modern Times and The Yellow Wall.

FA 1987: Ken Nichols and Dave Rosenstein

4. KEYHOLE   5.7   G

Start: At a 4-inch-wide crack just left of a red maple with two trunks, 20 feet left of Katzenjammer.

Pitch 1: (V1, V2) Climb the crack and work up the back of the alcove to the overhang. Then traverse out right around the overhang and continue up to the top.   (40 feet)

Variation 1:   5.9+   PG   Climb the crack that arches left, 8 feet left of Keyhole.

Variation 2:   5.9   Climb the Y-shaped crack 8 feet left of Variation 1.

FA 1951: Doug Kerr

5. KATZENJAMMER   5.7   PG   ★

Start: At a vertical drill hole below a steep face, 8 feet left of The Brat and 20 feet right of Keyhole.

Pitch 1: (V1) Climb up the face until below a vertical fault, which is to the right of a ramp that goes up left. Then follow the fault to the top.   (60 feet)

Variation 1:   5.11+   R   Start at a crack system that arches up left, 9 feet left of the drill hole. Follow the crack until it bombays and then diagonal up right to the regular route.

FA 1958: Jim McCarthy and Jack Hansen
FA (Variation 1) 1969: John Gill

6. THE BRAT   5.6   PG   ★

Start: At a short crack in broken black rock, 28 feet right of Keyhole.

Pitch 1: Climb up 10 feet (V1) and traverse left for about 15 feet. Diagonal up right (V2) and traverse right 10 feet to a good stance. Continue up a left-facing flake or crack past a blast hole to a small ledge. Then go left a few feet and finish up a vertical fault. (70 feet)

Variation 1:   5.7   Continue straight up past a crack and some left-facing flakes to rejoin the regular route.

Variation 2: 5.9 PG–R Follow the left fault to the top. This route is rarely unoccupied on weekends.
FA 1946: Bonnie Prudden

7. HANDY ANDY 5.7 G–PG
Start: At a right-facing corner opposite a tree, 30 feet right and around the corner from The Brat.
Pitch 1: (V1, V2) Climb up to the first horizontal crack (V3), move up, and traverse left (V4) to the sharp outside corner. Then work up to a crack and continue to the top. (80 feet)
Variation 1: 5.10+ Start under the ceiling 10–15 feet left of the regular route. Clear the ceiling and move up to black rock. Then climb right around a small overhang and continue up to join the regular route.
Variation 2: 5.10+ Start just left of a thin crack between Variation 1 and the regular route. Climb up to the first horizontal crack and join the regular route.
Variation 3: 5.10 Continue up and a bit right, following a very thin crack or seam to horizontal holds. Then, either exit left (5.9) or continue straight up to the top.
Variation 4: 5.8 PG Climb straight up to the top from a point about midway along the traverse.
FA 1956: Jim and Louise Andress
FFA 1956: Gerry Bloch
FA (Variation 1) 1964: Dick Williams
FA (Variation 2) 1964: Steve Larsen

8. EASY KEYHOLE 5.2 G
Start: At the base of a broken, low-angle chimney, directly across the road from some large boulders and just right of Handy Andy.
Pitch 1: Climb to the top of the chimney and move up left to a ledge. (The route usually ends here.) (40 feet) 5.2 G
Pitch 2: Continue up the southeast side of the pinnacle above to its top. (30 feet) 5.0
Pitch 3: Step across to the ledge behind the pinnacle and go left about 15 feet to an open book, which is followed to the top. (50 feet)
FA 1950: Hans Kraus and Bonnie Prudden

9. BLACK FLY 5.5 G

Start: At a left-facing ramp which leads to a short left-facing corner capped by an overhang, 20 feet right of Easy Keyhole.

Pitch 1: (V1) Climb up to the overhang and exit right. Then move up, step back left, and continue up to a ledge. After an overhang, follow a crack up to a belay ledge. (45 feet) 5.0

Pitch 2: Scramble up right across a short face to a ledge with a tree. Continue up, following a crack to another ledge. (40 feet)

Pitch 3: Climb up past the right side of a tree to the top. (30 feet)

Variation 1: 5.6 G Start at a crack to the right of the ramp. Follow the crack to the ledge below the overhang on the regular route.

FA 1959: Gardiner Perry and John Bousman

10. ASTRO TRAVELER 5.10+ PG

Start: Below an overhanging crack in the white rock at the top of the cliff to the right of Black Fly. The crack is most easily spotted from the carriage road.

Pitch 1: Scramble up to the crack and follow it to the top. (30 feet)

FA 1975: Ron Matous

11. SHORT JOB 5.4 G

Start: At the left edge of a 14-foot-high right-facing corner, which is below a broken yellow corner capped by an overhang, 125 feet right of Black Fly.

Pitch 1: Climb up broken rock to the left of the slab and step right into the yellow corner. Continue up about 10 feet and then move left and up to a bushy ledge. (40 feet) 5.4 G

Pitch 2: Walk and scramble up right 20 feet and follow a ramp diagonally up left to its top. Then go right and climb up past a crack to the top. (70 feet) 5.3

FA 1958: Gardiner and Mary Perry, and Carol Maken

12. 69 5.3 G

Start: On a slab directly below a ceiling, 18 feet right of Short Job.

THE TRAPPS

Pitch 1: Climb the slab and the left side of a nose to the ceiling. Traverse right around the ceiling and continue up to a comfortable belay ledge. (50 feet) 5.3 G

Pitch 2: Rappel or scramble up right on broken rock to the top. Why not? This was the year they were married.

FA 1969: Dick and Marilyn DuMais

13. NO PICNIC   5.4   G

Start: At a slab below a short, white left-facing corner formed by a block, just after the trail drops and 55 feet right of Short Job.

Pitch 1: Climb up the slab and corner, and continue straight up through the overhangs and some bulging rock to a pine tree at the top. (80 feet)

FA 1950s: Willie Crowther and Gardiner Perry

14. SHIT OR GO BLIND   5.8   G–PG

Start: On the face 10 feet right of No Picnic.

Pitch 1: Climb the face past a bulge to a stance below the first overhang. Step right and climb through the overhang to a stance below the second overhang. Step right again, pass this overhang at a pointed block, and then move up to a belay. (50 feet) 5.8 G–PG

Pitch 2: Continue up the face to an overhang with a steep nose. Then climb the overhang and the face above to the top. (50 feet)

FA 1974: Joe Ponte and Ivan Rezucha

15. SUDORIFEROUS   5.2   G

Start: At a small cave below a broken left-facing corner, 32 feet right of No Picnic.

Pitch 1: Climb the face and corner to a large ledge with a tree. (40 feet)

Pitch 2: (V1) Climb straight up past an overhang and continue 25 feet beyond, staying right of the nose. Then diagonal left under another overhang and move up past its left side to the top. (60 feet)

Variation 1:   5.9 Step left, climb through the overhangs, and continue up the face to the top.

FA 1975: John D'Arcy, Bruce Miller, and Rich Kast

16. HEEL, HOOK, AND HACK-IT 5.10−   R−X
Start: On top of the Dirty Gerdie block, at an overhang 8 feet right of a broken right-facing corner, behind the uppermost tree.
Pitch 1: Clear the overhang to reach a stance (no pro) and then continue up to the top.   (50 feet)
FA 1987: Michael Emelianoff, Brian Anderson, and Jerry Grupo

17. HERDIE GERDIE 5.8 PG
Start: At a ramplike left-facing corner with a crack that leads up right, 8 feet left of Dirty Gerdie.
Pitch 1: Follow the corner and crack until they end and continue up the face to the top of the block.   (50 feet)
FA 1965: Dick Williams and Dick DuMais

18. DIRTY GERDIE 5.9− PG ★
Start: At a short vertical fracture at ground level, in the center of the white face of the huge block that is 20 feet off the carriage road, 60 feet right of No Picnic.
Pitch 1: (V1) Climb up the center of the face 15−20 feet, move right, and continue to the top.   (50 feet)
Variation 1: Dogs in Heat 5.11 PG Climb past two vertical seams on the right side of the white face (without using the outside corner) and finish on Dirty Gerdie. Height-related—harder if shorter.
FA 1963: Thom Scheuer and Jim Andress
FFA 1964: John Hudson
FA (Variation 1: Toprope) 1975: Rich Ross
FA (Variation 1: Lead) 1975: Rich Ross

19. RED CABBAGE 5.9−   G
Start: At a crack 2−3 feet around the corner from Dirty Gerdie, on the right wall of the huge block.
Pitch 1: Climb the crack until it ends, exit left, and continue up the face to the top.   (50 feet)
FFA 1969: Joe Kelsey and Dick DuMais

20. RED CABBAGE RIGHT   5.10   PG
Start: At a vertical fault just right of the Red Cabbage crack.

Pitch 1: (V1) Follow the fault to a small jutting overhang. Climb past this on the right, and zigzag up and right to a short crack. Climb the crack, move back left, and finish up a short crack and steep face to the top.   (50 feet)

Variation 1:   5.10   Start on the right side of the face, and move up and left to join the regular route.

FA: early 1970s

21. FRIDAY THE 13TH   5.8   R
Start: At a vertical seam or fault, 16 feet right of the Dirty Gerdie block.

Pitch 1: Follow the seam to a ledge and continue up white rock to another ledge.   (50 feet)   5.7

Pitch 2: Climb 10 feet up the large left-facing corner, traverse right onto the face, and continue up and right to the top.   (50 feet)   5.8   R

FA 1982: Joe Bridges and Faith Aubin

22. FANCY IDIOT   5.6   PG
Start: On the face, 8 feet left of Bunny (or in the slot just to the right, directly behind a large tree).

Pitch 1: Climb the face to the base of a small crescent-shaped right-facing corner. Move up the corner for a few feet and then diagonal up left (or follow the crescent corner up right—5.8) to a ledge. Continue up and then move left to a ledge below a large overhanging left-facing corner.   (60 feet)   5.6   PG

Pitch 2: Climb the corner (or diagonal up right through the overhangs) to the top.   (60 feet)   5.4

FA 1955: Ann Church and Krist Raubenheimer

23. BUNNY   5.4   G   ★
Start: At an open book that leads to an overhang, 55 feet right of the Dirty Gerdie block.

Pitch 1: Follow the open book to an overhang, and step up left past a bulge to a ledge. Traverse right 15 feet and move up to a stance. Then continue up a corner and the short face above to a small ledge below a chimney. (70 feet) 5.4 G

Pitch 2: Climb the chimney and the face on the left to a large ledge. Walk right 20 feet and then scramble up an easy face to the top. (70 feet) 5.1

If you can get off the ground, you've got it made!

FA 1955: Ann Church and Krist Raubenheimer

24. RETRIBUTION 5.10 G ★★

Start: At a right-facing corner with an overhang 25 feet up, just right of Bunny.

Pitch 1: Follow the corner past the overhang until the corner ends. Move left and work up past a bulge to easier rock. Then diagonal up right to a crack and continue to the top. (120 feet)

FA 1958: Art Gran and Peter Himot
FFA 1961: Jim McCarthy

25. NO SOLUTION 5.12 X

Start: Midway between Retribution and Nosedive.

Pitch 1: Climb the face and overhang midway between Retribution and Nosedive.

Popular as a toprope climb before it was led, and likely to remain so. No wandering or you'll be off route.

FA (Toprope) 1976: Kevin Bein
FA (Lead) 1988: Sebastian Schwertner

26. NOSEDIVE 5.10 G ★★

Start: At a left-facing corner, 13 feet right of Retribution.

Pitch 1: Follow the corner to a stance below the bulge. Climb straight up the crack (or avoid the first part by traversing right a bit, climbing up, and then moving back left—easier) past the bulge and continue straight up the face to the top. (110 feet)

FA 1956: Ted Church and Krist Raubenheimer
FFA 1961: Jim McCarthy

MENTAL BLOCK

This huge block has many short climbs that are quite popular. It is located across from Nosedive and Double Chin, and just left (south) of the main

access trail that goes from Route 44–55 to the carriage road near the Überfall. The climbs are described from left to right, starting on the relatively low-angle south face.

a. 5.4 Start on the left side of the face, a few feet down from the carriage road. Follow a broken, sickle-shaped crack to the top.

b. MENTAL BLOCK 5.11 (Toprope) Start at some vertical seams on the south face, just right of center. Climb the seams to a thin horizontal crack, pass the crack, and continue up the face, following the left of two vertical seams to the top.
FA (Toprope) 1963: Dick Williams

c. THE DENT 5.8 Start at some vertical seams on the right side of the face. Follow the seams to the top, using the outside corner.
FA (Toprope) 1963: Dick Williams
FA (Lead): Unknown

d. SONJA 5.10 Start at the crack on the far left side of the overhanging east face. Follow the crack to the top.
FA (Toprope) 1964: Dick Williams
FA (Lead): Unknown

e. STUPID CRACK 5.12− PG−R Start at the crack 8 feet right of Sonja. Climb the crack past a bulging overhang and a short chimney to the top.
FA (Toprope) 1977: Kevin Bein
FA (Lead) 1984: Kim Carrigan

f. 5.10 R Start at the off-width crack 12 feet right of Sonja. Climb the crack past a pinched section to the top.
FA (Toprope): Unknown
FA (Lead): Unknown

g. 5.9 Start at a thin crack, 6 feet right of the off-width. Follow the crack (which widens and contains a flake) to the top.

FA (Toprope): Unknown
FA (Lead): Unknown

h. 5.8 Start at an off-width crack system, 4 feet right of the 5.10 off-width and 13 feet left of the right edge of the face. Follow the crack system past a large jutting flake to the top.
FA (Toprope): Unknown
FA (Lead): Unknown

i. 5.10+ Start on the face midway between the 5.8 crack system and the right edge of the face. Climb the face to the top.
FA (Toprope): Unknown
FA (Lead): Unknown

27. DOUBLE CHIN   5.5   G   ★
Start: At a crack below a prominent right-facing corner with two overhangs, directly across from the Mental Block boulder and just right of Nosedive.
Pitch 1: Climb the corner past both overhangs to a ledge.   (80 feet)   5.5   G
Pitch 2: Continue up the corner and the face on the right to the top.   (60 feet)   5.3
Always awkward!
FA 1954: Norton Smithe and Doug Kerr

28. SOMETHING SCARY   5.10   PG–R
Start: On the face 8 feet right of Double Chin, below an incipient crack that starts at the lip of the overhang.
Pitch 1: Climb the face past double overhangs to a blocky left-facing corner. Continue past the corner and through the ceiling (10 feet left of the pointed block on Double Clutch) to the top. (110 feet)
FA 1979: Hardie Truesdale and Chris Monz

29. EYEBROW   5.6   PG
Start: At a short crack directly across from the northwest corner of the Mental Block boulder, 22 feet right of Double Chin.

THE TRAPPS

Pitch 1: Climb the crack and the face above until below an overhang, and move up to a stance. (60 feet) 5.5

Pitch 2: Climb up past a bulge to a small overhang and traverse right 20 feet to a left-facing corner, which is at the right edge of a large overhang. Then follow the crack above to the top. (70 feet) 5.6 PG

FA 1959: Gary Hemming and Claude Suhl

30. DOUBLE CLUTCH   5.9+   G   ★

Start: Same as Eyebrow.

Pitch 1: Climb up to the horizontal crack, traverse right about 15 feet, and move up through a cleft in the overhang. Then continue straight up to the Eyebrow belay. (60 feet) 5.9+   G

Pitch 2: Climb past a bulge and traverse left until below an orange V-shaped block stuck under the overhang (V1). Step up right to a small corner under the overhang, climb past the overhang to a ledge, and then scramble to the top. (50 feet) 5.8+

Variation 1:   5.10   PG Climb straight up past the V-shaped block to the top.

The first-pitch crux is only 5.9 if you do it dynamically; otherwise, it's much harder. The route also can be started by bouldering directly up to the cleft in the overhang.

FA 1964: Dick Williams, John Hudson, and Pete Geiser

31. GILL'S BOULDER PROBLEM   5.12−   R

Start: On the face 5 feet right of the Double Clutch direct start.

Pitch 1: Climb straight up through the ceiling and finish 8 feet right of the Double Clutch cleft.

FA 1969: John Gill

32. RALPH'S CLIMB   5.8   PG, A3

Start: On the face 15 feet left of Doug's Roof.

Pitch 1: Climb the face past the break in the first overhang to the roof. Clear the roof at its widest point (where there is a foot-long incipient crack or seam at the lip) and continue up the face to a pine tree. Move up right to a short, thin crack that starts at a small overhang. Then continue up through the next set of overhangs to the top, staying to the right of Eyebrow. (120 feet)

Will this ever go free?
FA 1964: Ralph Worstfold

33. DOUG'S ROOF 5.11+ G
Start: At a crack that runs up to and out through the roof, 47 feet right of Eyebrow.
Pitch 1: (V1, V2) Climb the crack, clear the roof with a very long reach, and gain a stance. Then continue up to a small ledge with a pine tree on the left. (50 feet) 5.11+ G
Pitch 2: Rappel or continue up right from the ledge past the right edge of the overhang above. Then continue up to the top. (80 feet)
Variation 1: Lower Eaves 5.9 G Start at a blocky, 12-foot-high right-facing corner, 20 feet right of the regular route. Climb the corner to a comfortable square ledge. Diagonal up left to the nose and work up the face to a stance. Then continue up left to join the regular route.
Variation 2: Eaves 5.8 R Use the Lower Eaves start and continue up past the square ledge to a stance under the roof. Traverse left to the nose and move up to a stance, where Lower Eaves is rejoined. The start is well protected, but there is a long runout above.

Beware of the piton (placed on the first ascent) at the lip of the roof—no telling how good it is. Height-related—easier if taller.
FA 1954: Doug Kerr and Stan Gross
FFA 1972: Bob Jahn

34. BRIDLE PATH 5.7 PG
Start: At a short, broken incipient crack, midway between Lower Eaves and Horseman.
Pitch 1: Climb straight up the face to the roof, walk right, and join Horseman for about 15 feet to the first horizontal crack that goes out left. Traverse left to the nose and then, staying close to the nose, continue up the face to the optional belay on Horseman. Step left and move up. Then step left again to the right side of a small but long overhang, move up, and continue to the top. (120 feet)

The traverse out left and up to Horseman was most likely an old

THE TRAPPS

variation to Horseman; also, old pitons were found on the last 10 feet of the climb.

FA 1988: Joe Bridges and Dick Williams

35. HORSEMAN   5.5   G   ★★★

Start: At a thin crack directly below the huge right-facing corner at the right end of the roof, 50 feet right of Doug's Roof.

Pitch 1: Climb the thin crack and the corner to its top (V1). Traverse left around the corner to a stance (some parties belay here). Then step up and right to a crack, which is followed through an overhang to the top.   (150 feet)

Variation 1: Climb straight up to rejoin Horseman.

This old classic is probably the nicest route in this section of the cliff. As the story goes, a horseman came by and said to the first ascent party, "Is this the way to Minnewaska?"

FA 1941: Hans Kraus and Fritz Wiessner

36. PONY EXPRESS   5.6−   PG

Start: At a very faint vertical fracture in the face, 10 feet right of Horseman.

Pitch 1: Climb 20 feet up the face to the higher of two horizontal cracks. Traverse left to the Horseman crack and continue up to the base of the corner. Then diagonal up right past a small right-facing corner to two steep cracks, which are followed past a bulge to a ledge.   (80 feet)   5.6−

Pitch 2: Move down and left to a right-facing corner. Climb the corner and step up left to a flaring chimney that leads to the top. (70 feet)   5.6−

FA 1957: Ted Church and Krist Raubenheimer

37. APOPLEXY   5.9   PG   ★★

Start: Same as Pony Express.

Pitch 1: Climb straight up the face to a small right-facing corner. Continue up through the overhangs to a flaring chimney that leads to the top.   (90 feet)

Beware of the small, loose flake 25 feet up—groundfall is possible if it were to fail.

FA 1960: Jim McCarthy

38. CORONARY 5.10 R
Start: At the tree between Pony Express and Dirty Chimney.
Pitch 1: Follow a faint crack directly in line with the tree to a ledge. Then finish up the small right-facing corner just right of Apoplexy to the top.   (90 feet)
FA 1973: Jim Kolocotronis

39. DIRTY CHIMNEY 5.0 G
Start: At the left-hand of two trees at the base of a large, dirty left-facing corner, 18 feet right of Horseman.
Pitch 1: Climb up the corner to the blocks, step around right, and continue up to a large ledge with a pine tree.   (50 feet)   5.0
Pitch 2: Scramble up the gully to the top.   (50 feet)   5.0
Well named, this route is frequently used as an approach for setting up topropes on neighboring climbs.
FA 1957: Krist Raubenheimer and friend

40. JUNIOR 5.9+ R
Start: On the face midway between Dirty Chimney and Laurel.
Pitch 1: Climb straight up the face past a bulge, step left, and continue up a short crack and the face above to some ledges.   (50 feet)   5.9+   R
Pitch 2: Scramble to the top.
FA early 1960s: Bob Gilmore

41. LAUREL 5.7 G ★
Start: At a thin crack with a ledge 20 feet up, 10 feet right of Dirty Chimney.
Pitch 1: Climb the crack to its top.   (50 feet)   5.7   G
Pitch 2: (V1) Rappel, scramble up the blocks above, or finish on Dirty Chimney.
Variation 1: Walk to the back of the ledges, climb up some faces, and go past an overhang to the top.   (60 feet)
The boulder problem at the start of this climb has stopped many a trooper and has been given grades as high as 5.9—the taller you are, the easier it will seem. The climbing above this first move is 5.6, the original rating.

THE TRAPPS

FA early 1950s: Thornton Read, Norton Smith, and Lester Germer

42. CLOVER 5.7 G–PG
Start: On the face 9 feet right of Laurel.
Pitch 1: (V1) Climb to the first ledge, step to the right of the tree, and continue to the top. (95 feet)
Variation 1: 5.5 Start 3 feet left of Rhododendron, go up a diagonal ramp, and join the regular route.
FA 1974: Paul Rubin and Marc Cassler

43. RHODODENDRON 5.6– G ★
Start: At a crack, 19 feet right of Laurel.
Pitch 1: Follow the crack to a ledge with a tree, and either rappel or continue to the top. (80 feet)
FA: early 1950s

44. BIRCH 5.10+ PG–R
Start: At a vertical seam, 5 feet right of Rhododendron.
Pitch 1: Climb the seam and continue past the overhang and the face above to the top. (80 feet)
The tree that sticks out of Das Wiggles can be used for protection.
FA 1984: Russ Clune and Jeff Gruenberg

45. DAS WIGGLES 5.3 PG
Start: At the base of a chimney in the back of a left-facing corner, just right of Rhododendron.
Pitch 1: Climb the chimney past the chockstone to the top. (75 feet)
An enjoyable chimney that is sometimes used as a descent route.
FA 1946: Hans Kraus and Dick Hirschland

46. SHITTY MITTY 5.11– PG–R
Start: At a crack on the overhanging face midway between Das Wiggles and Walter Mitty.
Pitch 1: Follow the crack to an overhang (V1) and move left.

Then continue up the overhanging face and cracks above to the top.   (75 feet)

   Variation 1:   Mitty Mouse   5.8+   PG   Traverse right to the nose and continue up to the top.

   FA 1973: George Willig and Jim Thompson

47. WALTER MITTY   5.8   PG

   Start: On the face just around the corner to the right of Shitty Mitty.

   Pitch 1: Climb up and right past a crack to an overhang. Clear the overhang and continue straight up the face to the top.   (70 feet)

   FA 1963: Steve Larsen and Dick Williams

48. LOW EXPOSURE   5.10+   G

   Start: At a nose at the left edge of what used to be the "frog pond," just right of Walter Mitty and below a jamcrack that breaks an overhang.

   Pitch 1: Climb the nose, work out the jamcrack, and belay on the big ledge above.   (20 feet)   5.10+   G

   Pitch 2: Step left and climb up the face 3 feet left of Walter Mitty and 3 feet right of a left-facing corner.   (20 feet)

   You've heard the phrase, "Life is a pitch." Well, this pitch is a bitch, especially if you're not used to jamming cracks.

   FA 1969: John Stannard

49. SQUIGGLES   5.4   G–PG   ★

   Start: At a crack that leads to a left-facing corner, 25 feet right of Low Exposure and around the corner from a very small frog pond.

   Pitch 1: Climb about 10 feet up to a ramp and move up right around the right edge of an overhang. Then continue up the face to the left edge of a boulder at the top of the cliff.   (50 feet)

   Like on many of the climbs in this area, whether leading or following, chances are you'll get lots of annoying advice.

   FA 1959: Peter Himot and Bill Meyer

THE TRAPPS

50. DISLOCATION 5.9 R
Start: On the face 5 feet right of Squiggles.
Pitch 1: Climb directly up to a ramp below the Squiggles overhang and continue straight over the overhang above to the top.

Jim Thompson dislocated his shoulder just after the crux—what a predicament!

FA 1973: Jim Thompson

51. SQUIGGLES DIRECT 5.10 R
Start: Directly below a thin crack that begins 6 feet above the ground, below the right edge of the Squiggles overhang.
Pitch 1: (V1) Follow the crack to the top. (50 feet)
Variation 1: Squiggles Redirect 5.11 Start 5 feet farther right and climb up to join the regular route.

FA 1963: Dick Williams and John Hudson
FFA 1963: Dick Williams

52. DEVINE WIND 5.12− (Toprope)
Start: At the lowest part of the face midway between Squiggles Direct and Jacob's Ladder.
Pitch 1: Climb straight up the face and finish a few feet left of the Jacob's Ladder ramp.

FA (Toprope) 1985: Barbara Devine

53. JACOB'S LADDER 5.10 X
Start: At a dirty ramp that leads up right to a broken corner.
Pitch 1: (V1) From the ramp, just before the base of the corner, climb up left along a small ramp and past a tiny overhang. Then continue straight up to the top. (50 feet)
Variation 1: Climb directly up to the upper part of the small ramp and join the regular route.

Originally done on the lead, this is now a well-known toprope problem that can be done in several ways. It was the first 5.10 in the Gunks (and unprotected at that!) and was originally rated 5.8. Aren't you glad you weren't a budding 5.8 leader in 1960? Or maybe you were!

FA 1960: Phil Jacobus

54. CROWBERRY RIDGE 5.6 PG
Start: On some blocks below a short nose that can be reached by walking up right on the ramp below Jacob's Ladder or by scrambling straight up from below.
Pitch 1: Follow your nose to the top.   (60 feet)
FA 1981: Todd Swain

THE ÜBERFALL

The Überfall is the main meeting spot in the Trapps and, depending on the weather, is often the scene of much confusion, fun, and fiasco. Here, climbers gather together to laugh, shout, boulder, show off, make fun of each other, and sometimes even climb, although climbing is rarely done without it becoming a major epic.

The area is bounded on the left by a spring and on the right by the Susie A block. Midway between the two is the main descent route for this end of the cliff, a short 4th-Class scramble down through broken rock that is slippery and requires some care. Also in the area is a bulletin board, trash can, Stokes litter, and first-aid box.

The Überfall acquired its name, according to Fritz Wiessner in a 1960 Appalachia *article, from "the method used in the descent of letting oneself, with outstretched arms, fall across the four-foot gap between the massif and a huge block [the Susie A block] above the road."*

55. HUDSON'S BOULDER PROBLEM 5.11 – PG
Start: Under a low roof behind the first-aid box, 35 feet right of the Überfall descent route and 55 feet right of Crowberry Ridge.
Pitch 1: (V1, V2) Climb up to the beginning of the obvious undercling (V3), step left, reach out to the lip, and continue a few more feet to the finish.
Variation 1: **5.11+** **(Toprope)** Climb straight up to the end of the undercling and join the regular route.
Variation 2: **5.11 –** **(Toprope)** Start on the face below the right side of the roof, and climb up and left to almost meet Variation 3.
Variation 3: **5.12 +** **(Toprope)** Climb straight out the roof at its widest point to a bucket with a twig and continue to the top.
FA (Toprope) 1965: John Hudson

THE TRAPPS

FA (Lead): Unknown
FA (Variation 2: Toprope) 1973: Steve Wunsch
FA (Variation 3: Toprope) 1981: Dick Cilley

56. SUSIE A   5.10+   R–X
Start: At the big detached block just right of Hudson's Boulder Problem.
Pitch 1: Climb the left side of the main face of the block and finish up right along a diagonal seam on the main face above. (50 feet)

This is rarely led for a variety of reasons: hard, scary, and an unaesthetic line. The first half of the climb is a very popular boulder problem, and there are several others on the block as well.
FA 1958: Roddy Miller and Jim Andress
FFA 1975: Rich Romano

57. THE FLAKE   5.1   PG
Start: At a chimney formed by a huge flake, 10 feet right of the Susie A block.
Pitch 1: Follow the chimney to the top of the flake and finish up the face above.   (50 feet)

58. KEN'S CRACK   5.7   G   ★★
Start: On a boulder below a clean crack, 8 feet right of The Flake.
Pitch 1: Climb the crack to the top.   (50 feet)

Gunks climbers in particular used to be afraid of this climb because jamming techniques would actually have to be used.
FA 1951: Ken Prestrud and Lucien Warner

59. PHOEBE   5.10   R–X
Start: On a block below a bolt, 12 feet left of Boston.
Pitch 1: Climb past the bolt to a tiny overhang (V1). Step right and continue up past a very small overhang to the top.   (50 feet)
Variation 1:   5.10−   Continue straight up to the top.
FA (Toprope) 1963: Dick Williams
FA (Lead) 1963: Dick Williams

60. BOSTON 5.5− PG
Start: At a crack that widens to a chimney containing an overhang, 35 feet right of Ken's Crack.
Pitch 1: Climb the crack and chimney past the overhang to the top. (50 feet)
Named for the following incident: After the climb, Bonnie Prudden, seated, was indicating locations in eastern Massachusetts using her thigh as a map. Dick Hirschland remarked, "I wish I were in Boston."
FA 1950: Dick Hirschland and Bonnie Prudden

61. CHARIE 5.10− (Toprope)
Start: On the face 3 feet right of Boston.
Pitch 1: Climb the face without using any holds on Boston.
FA (Toprope) 1963: Dave Craft

62. FITSCHEN'S FOLLY 5.8 R−X
Start: On the face midway between Boston and some stacked blocks to the right.
Pitch 1: Climb directly up the face to the obvious flake, move left, and continue to the top. (50 feet)
A nice face climb, though not a recommended lead, especially if you're just beginning to break into the 5.8 grade—better to toprope it.
FA 1961: Joe Fitschen

63. ALPHABET ARÊTE 5.10+ PG
Start: On top of three stacked blocks immediately right of Fitschen's Folly.
Pitch 1: Climb past a short corner and an overhang to the left side of a small ledge. Then move up and climb the arête past a piton to the top. (50 feet)
FA (Toprope) 1986: Todd Swain
FA (Lead) 1986: Todd Swain and Bob Hostettler

64. D.D. ROUTE 5.10 R
Start: On the right side of the stacked Alphabet Arête blocks.
Pitch 1: Climb to the top of a thin crack that diagonals up right.

THE TRAPPS

Continue up past the right side of a small ledge, move left at a horizontal crack, and then work up past a bulge to the top. (50 feet)
FA (Toprope): 1985
FA (Lead): 1985 or later

65. C.C. ROUTE 5.7− PG
Start: At the base of a large left-facing corner that contains a large crack in the back and another on the right face, 35 feet right of Boston.
Pitch 1: Climb the corner and the crack in its back to the roof. Then traverse left and exit up to the top. (60 feet)

John Turner was a member of the Climbers Club, hence the name. Al Alvarez on the other hand. . . .
FA 1955: John Turner and Al Alvarez

66. THE STAR ROUTE 5.4 G
Start: At the base of the crack in the right wall of the C.C. Route corner.
Pitch 1: Climb the crack to a ledge on the right (V1). Then go right around the corner to another crack and follow it to the top. (75 feet)
Variation 1: 5.8 G Continue up the crack until it is possible to exit right to join the regular route.

67. CRIMSON CORNER 5.0 G
Start: At the base of a low-angle rib or nose, a short walk around right from C.C. Route, past some low-angle rock.
Pitch 1: Follow the rib to the top. (40 feet)

68. YALE 5.3 PG
Start: On top of the left side of a large block, 23 feet left of the Harvard boulder.
Pitch 1: Cross over to the main face and climb up right to the top of a large block. Then follow the cracks and the face above to the top. (40 feet)
FA: Unknown

69. EYESORE 5.6 G
Start: Same as Harvard.

Pitch 1: From the top of a boulder, climb past the overhang and a left-facing corner to a large ledge on the right (some parties belay here on both this route and Harvard). Then traverse out left to a crack, and climb this and the face above to the top. (100 feet)

FA: Unknown

70. HARVARD 5.2 G
Start: At a large boulder leaning against the face, just below an overhand with a crack above, 105 feet right of the edge of the C.C. Route corner.

Pitch 1: From the boulder, squeeze up the chimney behind the overhang to a ledge and continue up a left-facing corner to a large ledge (some parties belay here), or follow Eyesore to the ledge. Continue up the chimney on the right to the top of the protruding flake. Then step up right to a ledge, move back left, and follow the chimney to the top. (80 feet)

FA 1953: George Evans and Robert Graef

71. TRAPPED LIKE A RAT 5.7 G
Start: At a block just right of a large but short left-facing corner capped by an overhang, 17 feet right of Harvard.

Pitch 1: From the right side of the block, step onto the face and use a crack to move up right to the left side of the overhang. Follow the crack and corner system above to a ledge (some parties belay here). Then move right and continue up through an overhang, following a crack and corner to the top. (30 feet)

FA: early 1970s

72. CILLEY DICKIN' 5.12− PG ★
Start: On top of a large boulder, 10 feet right of Trapped Like a Rat. The right side of the boulder drops 15 feet to the ground, and above the boulder is a left-arching open book that begins 15 feet up.

Pitch 1: Climb broken rock to the nose on the right. Then move

THE TRAPPS   83

up the nose and step back left into the open book, which is followed to a ledge. (40 feet) 5.12−   PG
Pitch 2: Rappel or finish on a nearby climb.
FA (Toprope) 1981: Dick Cilley
FA (Lead) 1981: Hugh Herr

73. STIRRUP TROUBLE 5.10 PG ★★★
Start: At a crack in a shallow 10-foot-high open book, below a smooth white face and on top of the huge block to the right of Harvard.
Pitch 1: Climb the crack and vertical fracture past a horizontal crack. Traverse left and work up the crack to the overhang. Then go left and follow the corner through the overhang to the top. (60 feet)
Now that everyone's wearing lycra tights, this name has new meaning.
FA early 1960s: Bill Goldner
FFA 1973: John Stannard

74. THE MOHEL 5.12− (Toprope)
Start: On the face between Stirrup Trouble and P38.
Pitch 1: Climb the face.
FA (Toprope) 1985: Jeff Gruenberg

75. P38 5.10 G ★★
Start: Below a crack on the steep face, 13 feet right of the Stirrup Trouble block.
Pitch 1: Climb to the top of the crack, move left, and continue up to the top. (40 feet)
Originally named P38 because 38 pitons were used, this route was incorrectly named in the 1972 guidebook, and many climbers still refer to it as Shady Lady—a much nicer name.
FA 1962: Dave Craft and Jim Andress
FFA 1964: Dick Williams

76. RADCLIFFE 4th Class
Start: At the base of a gully that leads up left and has a tree in it, 30 feet right of P38.

Pitch 1: Climb up the gully and a short chimney to a ledge. Walk left and up to a large pine tree and then walk back up the gully to the top. (80 feet)

Often used as a descent route, this climb contains some nice climbing, but the fact that Badcliff is so close detracts greatly.

FA: early 1950s

77. BADCLIFF 5.10− PG
Start: At a large tree, 15 feet up the Radcliffe gully.

Pitch 1: Climb a shallow, broken right-facing corner to a vertical seam and follow the seam to a small ledge. Move left to a small tree and continue up the face past a series of faults and bulges to a large ledge. (100 feet) 5.10− PG

Pitch 2: Finish up the obvious fault or walk off to the left. (40 feet)

FA 1981: Todd Swain and Patty Lanzetta

78. DENNIS 5.5 G ★
Start: At the base of a nose below an overhang and directly behind the southernmost of the two huge boulders next to the carriage road, 20 feet right of Radcliffe. (The northernmost boulder is known as the Chockstone Boulder.)

Pitch 1: Climb up past the overhang, step left, and continue up low-angle rock and boulders to a ledge. Then work up the steep face and right-facing corner above to a second ledge. (80 feet) 5.5 G

Pitch 2: Climb past a triangular overhang to an open book, which is followed to the top. (60 feet) 5.4

FA 1960: Gardiner and Mary Perry, and Ann Buffin

CHOCKSTONE BOULDER
About a minute and a half walk north along the carriage road from the Überfall are two huge boulders beside the road, between which the Belly Roll crack can be seen.

The right or northernmost one is known as the Chockstone Boulder because it is split by a squeeze chimney containing a chockstone. It has some excellent boulder problems on it, some of which can be considered equal to many of the so-called new routes because of their length (30−40 feet).

THE TRAPPS

Climbers will often be found testing their skills here. The various routes are described from left to right, starting on the relatively low-angle south face between the blocks.

a. 5.10 (Toprope) Start just left of Pebbles on the south face. Follow a crack past a scoop and continue to the top.
FA (Toprope) 1964: Jim McCarthy

b. PEBBLES 5.7 PG–R Start on the pebbly face between two boulders, near the right outside corner. Climb up right on the face to the outside corner, and follow the corner and the left face to the top.
FA 1965: Doug Tompkins

c. GIRDLE TRAVERSE 5.13 – Starting at Pebbles, traverse around the corner to the right and continue to the far right end of the main face, staying close to the ground.
FA 1986: Lynn Hill

d. TWEEDLEDUM 5.11 – PG Climb the crack system on the left side of the main (east) face to the top.
FA 1964: Steve Larsen and Dick Williams

e. CHOCKSTONE CHIMNEY 5.4 PG Climb the squeeze chimney in the middle of the main face.

f. TWEEDLEDEE 5.11 – PG Follow the crack system just right of Chockstone Chimney to the top.
FA 1964: Steve Larsen and Dick Williams

79. BELLY ROLL 5.4 PG ★

Start: At a broken crack that widens to a left-slanting chimney about 25 feet up, just right of Dennis. (The crack can be seen from the carriage road when looking past the left side of the Chockstone Boulder.)
Pitch 1: Climb the crack and chimney, and continue up to a ledge. (50 feet) 5.4

Pitch 2: Climb up the steep left-facing corner above to a ledge. (20 feet) 5.4

Pitch 3: Scramble up left to an overhang, move around this to the right, and climb to the top of the grooves above. Then traverse left and continue to the top. (80 feet) 5.4

A popular route. The reason for its name will become quite apparent when it is climbed.

FA 1955: Doug Kerr and Norton Smithe

80. RODDEY 5.2 PG

Start: At a tree below a large, ugly right-facing corner, 17 feet right of Belly Roll.

Pitch 1: (V1) Climb the corner and exit up left to a ledge. Continue up a groove to an overhang, step right, and move up to a dirty ledge. (70 feet) 5.2 PG

Pitch 2: Follow the corner above to the top. (40 feet) 5.1

Variation 1: Slightly Roddey 5.10 R–X Climb the face to the ceiling (V2), hand traverse left and move up past the lip to a ledge. (Often toproped because of its difficulty and lack of protection—a piton is gone.)

Variation 2: 5.11+ (Toprope) Move left under the ceiling 3 feet and climb straight over the lip on small holds just left of Variation 1.

FA 1958: Roddey Miller and Jim Andress

FA (Variation 1) 1959: Marguerite Baumann, Bill Kemsley, and Bill Goldner

FFA (Variation 1) 1969: Kevin Bein

FA (Variation 2: Toprope) 1978: Kevin Bein

81. DAYDREAM 5.8 PG

Start: At some huge boulders that lean right against a large, broken, 30-foot-high left-facing corner.

Pitch 1: Walk over the boulders and climb up to a ledge to the left of Jackie. Climb the overhang above and diagonal up left to a flake. Then traverse left to a left-facing corner and continue up to a belay ledge. (80 feet) 5.8 PG

Pitch 2: Finish on a nearby climb.

FA 1976: Rich Ross and Mike Robin

82. JACKIE 5.5 G ★★

Start: At a low point on the face below a shallow right-facing corner, 40 feet right of Roddey.

Pitch 1: Climb the face and corner to a small tree. Traverse left to a stance below an overhang. Go right around the overhang and work up a crack to a second crack. Move up right, continue straight up past an overhang, and follow cracks and grooves to a notch in the large overhang above. Then climb through the notch to a ledge with a tree. (90 feet) 5.5 G

Pitch 2: Rappel, or diagonal up left around the corner and climb the face to the top. (50 feet) 5.3

FA 1952: Jack Taylor and Lester Germer

83. CLASSIC 5.7 PG ★★

Start: At the remains of a dead tree that leans out from the cliff at the base of the Pink Laurel corner.

Pitch 1: Climb up 10 feet (V1) and traverse left to a left-facing groove. Work up the groove, step left, and follow a crack to its top. Then traverse left about 10 feet and continue up past a notch in an overhang to a ledge with a tree. (100 feet) 5.7 PG

Pitch 2: Rappel, or step left and follow an open book to the top. (60 feet) 5.4

Variation 1: Classy 5.8 PG Continue up to a left-facing corner, and follow it and the face to the ceiling. Then traverse left to join the regular route.

The first move is pretty serious if you fall—many people have injured their feet or ankles here—so don't fall and miss the enjoyable climbing above.

FA 1960: Mike Borghoff and Brownell Bergen

84. PINK LAUREL 5.9 G ★★

Start: At the first left-facing corner to the right of Jackie.

Pitch 1: Climb the corner to a short chimney and overhang. Exit left and continue up a crack and over a bulge to a corner. Follow the corner and then diagonal up left to a belay ledge under the ceiling. (120 feet) 5.9 G

Pitch 2: Follow a long flake up to the ceiling (V1, V2, V3).

Traverse right about 20 feet to a corner, move up the corner past a second overhang, and then follow a nose to the top. (70 feet)

Variation 1: 5.6 Move left and climb up past the overhang to the top.

Variation 2: 5.10 Climb directly over the ceiling above the flake and continue to the top. (Beware of loose rock.)

Variation 3: 5.9 Move right and then climb back up left through the overhangs to the top.

The rock on this climb has changed considerably due to rockfall in the spring of 1971—certainly not the 5.6 it used to be.

FA 1955: Ted and Ann Church

85. A-GAPE 5.11− PG

Start: On top of a large boulder, 23 feet right of Pink Laurel and 15 feet left of Ape Call.

Pitch 1: Climb a short crack to an overhang and a bulge. Move right and go past the bulge to lower-angle rock. Then work up the left-facing corner above to an overhang and move right to the Ape Call belay stance. (80 feet) 5.9

Pitch 2: Traverse left and move up 15 feet to some flakes in a large overhang. Climb the overhang, continue straight up past a smaller overhang, and then follow a nose to the top. (100 feet) 5.11− PG

The loss of an important hold has increased the grade from its original 5.10−. *Agape* (ah-gah-pay) is a Greek word meaning *love*, but the name has more than one meaning.

FA 1973: Dave Loeks and Joe Bridges

86. APE CALL 5.8 PG–R ★

Start: On a slab just left of a flaring bombay chimney, 38 feet right of Pink Laurel.

Pitch 1: (V1) Climb up the face into a left-facing corner and continue up to a good stance below the ceiling. (80 feet) 5.8

Pitch 2: Work up to the ceiling, move left, and climb through a notch in the ceiling to a big ledge. (90 feet) 5.8

Pitch 3: Follow the last pitch of RMC to the top. (80 feet) 5.4

Variation 1: Bumwad 5.9 PG Climb up into the right side of the bombay chimney, traverse left, and exit up past an overhang to join the regular route.

FA 1962: Jim McCarthy, Jim Andress, and Ants Leemets
FA (Variation 1) 1961: Dick Williams and Dave Craft

87. APE AND ESSENCE   5.9+   PG

Start: On the steep face to the right of the bombay chimney, 10 feet right of Ape Call.

Pitch 1: Climb 15 feet up the face to a crack on the outside of the chimney. Move up right and then continue up past a small ledge to a belay in the corner above.   (50 feet)   5.9+   PG

Pitch 2: Continue straight up some left-facing corners to a large ledge.   (80 feet)   5.4

Pitch 3: Continue to the top.

FA 1973: Jim McCarthy and Laura Brant

88. JANE   5.8   PG–R

Start: At the right hand of two crack systems just left of RMC.

Pitch 1: Follow the right crack to a ceiling and traverse around right, following a crack to a steep face. Then continue straight up the face to a belay ledge.   (130 feet)   5.8   PG–R

Pitch 2: Climb straight up to the top.

FA 1973: Jim Kolocotronis and Tom Rosecrans

89. RMC   5.5–   G   ★

Start: At a large blocky left-facing corner, 32 feet right of Ape Call.

Pitch 1: Scramble up the boulders on the right to a chimney. Climb the chimney and face to a crack that leads to an overhang. Then traverse left about 10 feet to a pine tree and continue up the face to a ledge.   (50 feet)   5.4

Pitch 2: Step left, climb up past a bulge, and follow a small right-facing corner to an overhang. Then go around the overhang on the right and move up to a dirty ledge.   (70 feet)   5.5–   G

Pitch 3: Walk left past the dirty corner and traverse left to the center of the white face. Climb straight up the white face to the top.   (80 feet)   5.3

RMC stands for the Rensselaer Mountain Club.
FA 1948: Ralph Clapp and Grant Oakley

90. RAUBENHEIMER SPECIAL   5.7 –   PG   ★
Start: At a nose, 20 feet right of RMC.
Pitch 1: Climb directly up the nose past an overhang to a thin vertical fracture on the white face. Then continue straight up past a bulge and the low-angle rock above to a ledge.   (75 feet)   5.7 – PG
Pitch 2: Continue straight up broken rock to a nose on the left, which is followed to the top.   (80 feet)   5.3
Height-related—harder if shorter.
FA circa 1958: Krist and Wally Raubenheimer

91. BETTY   5.3 –   G   ★
Start: At the base of an 8-inch-wide crack, 18 feet right of Raubenheimer Special.
Pitch 1: Follow the crack past a block, step right, and continue up broken rock to a ledge.   (60 feet)   5.3 –
Pitch 2: Climb the chimney on the right to a ledge, walk right, and move up to another ledge (V1). Go right to the base of a second chimney and work up the left face of this to the top.   (100 feet)   5.3 –
Variation 1: Traverse left and climb the nose and the face above to the top.
Don't be misled by the grade—this is not a good beginner's climb because of the wide crack and long reaches.
FA 1941: Betty Woolsey and Fritz Wiessner

92. THE BLACKOUT   5.8   R   ★
Start: At a bulge, 20 feet right of Betty.
Pitch 1: Go up about 20 feet (V1), move left, and continue up to a belay ledge at some blocks in the corner.   (50 feet)   5.5
Pitch 2: Climb the corner, traverse right 10 feet to a nose, and follow some cracks to a ledge with a tree.   (50 feet)   5.7
Pitch 3: Climb up to another ledge, step right, and work up orange-red rock to an overhang. Then traverse right, climb past a

notch, and continue up the face above to the top. (50 feet) 5.8 R

Variation 1: 5.8 Continue straight up to the belay ledge. (50 feet)

The bolt on the last pitch was *not* placed by the first ascent party.

FA 1968: Dick Williams, Dave Craft, and Dick DuMais

93. LATE SHOW   5.12−   PG–R

Start: On the face 7 feet past the right-facing corner that is just right of The Blackout.

Pitch 1: Climb past a small overhang to the right side of a smooth overhang and follow a thin crack to the Matinee belay. (This pitch is often toproped.) (40 feet) 5.11−   PG–R

Pitch 2: Step right and climb past a vertical seam (the original Matinee aid line) to an overhang. Pass this overhang and diagonal up right to the Matinee corner, which is followed to its top. Then step left, climb out the crack in the ceiling, and continue up the face above to join Matinee. (80 feet) 5.12−   PG–R

Pitch 3: Rappel or finish on a nearby climb.

Before the crux hold on the second pitch broke in 1987, the route was graded 5.11−.

FA 1971: Steve Levin and Kevin Bein

94. MATINEE   5.10+   G   ★★★

Start: Same as Big Chimney.

Pitch 1: Follow a shallow corner to the roof, traverse left, and then move up and left to a big ledge. (60 feet) 5.10 PG

Pitch 2: (V1) Move back right and climb up past an overhanging corner to a stance at the base of a large left-facing corner. Continue up to a ceiling, exit right around the corner, and work up the face to another ceiling. Go left past this ceiling and climb up to a ledge with a pine tree. (80 feet) 5.10+   G

Pitch 3: Rappel or finish on a nearby climb.

Variation 1: Kinky Claw   5.11   R   Walk left 10 feet to a rusty orange streak below double overhangs. Climb up past the overhangs to a third overhang, move left to a shallow open book, and follow this to a fourth overhang. Then traverse left and finish up the Blackout cracks.

A wonderful variety of climbing.
FA 1961: Yvon Chouinard and Jim Andress
FFA 1963: Jim McCarthy and John Hudson
FA (Variation 1) 1983: Hugh Herr and Russ Clune

95. CREATURE FEATURES 5.11 PG
Start: Same as Big Chimney.
Pitch 1: Follow Big Chimney to a ledge inside the second chimney. Move up to horizontal holds and traverse left to a corner. Follow the corner past a stance to a ceiling (V1). Traverse left to the lip of the outside corner, climb up and right onto the face, and then continue up to join Matinee. (150 feet) 5.11 PG
Pitch 2: Rappel or finish on a nearby climb.
Variation 1: 5.9 Exit right and climb up the face to join Matinee. (This is a popular escape from the regular route.)
FA (Toprope) 1975: Kevin Bein
FA (Lead) 1976: Kevin Bein and Mark Robinson

96. BIG CHIMNEY 5.5 PG
Start: At a chimney on the right face of a large left-facing corner, 45 feet right of Betty. The chimney can be seen from the carriage road.
Pitch 1: Follow the chimney to an overhang and work right to the base of a second chimney (some parties belay here). Then move up the second chimney to a broken left-facing corner that leads to a large, dirty ledge. (130 feet) 5.5 PG
Pitch 2: (V1) Climb a loose, blocky right-facing corner to the top. (50 feet) 5.4
Variation 1: 5.7 Traverse left and climb up to a right-facing corner and an overhang. Then continue through the overhang and finish up the face above.
Originally known as Double Chimney.
FA 1942: Fritz Wiessner and Ann Gross

97. MISS BAILEY 5.6 PG
Start: Same as Big Chimney.
Pitch 1: Follow Big Chimney to the base of the second chimney. (40 feet) 5.5 PG

THE TRAPPS

Pitch 2: Diagonal up left across the face and climb a small right-facing corner to an overhang. Then step right, pass the overhang, and continue to the top. (100 feet) 5.6 PG

FA 1950s: Dave Noyes and Eric Schiffman

98. FETUS 5.9+ PG–R
Start: Same as Baby.

Pitch 1: Scramble up left past some blocks to the base of a right-facing flake. Climb up the flake and then either go straight up (harder) or traverse right 5 feet (the original line) and continue straight up to a huge, dirty ledge area. (90 feet) 5.9+ PG–R

Pitch 2: Finish on a nearby climb.

FA 1959: John Lomont and Francis Coffin
FFA 1965: Dick Williams

99. BABY 5.6 G-PG ★★★
Start: At a small cave beneath a crack, 30 feet right of the Big Chimney corner.

Pitch 1: Follow the crack system to a big ledge. (80 feet) 5.6

Pitch 2: Climb the prominent left-facing corner directly above to an overhang, step right, and continue to the top. (60 feet) 5.6

A good climb and a fine tribute to the first ascent party.

FA 1941: Fritz Wiessner, Mary Cecil, and Betty Woolsey

100. TWISTED SISTER 5.8 G
Start: At a blocky corner on the left side of a large boulder pile, 15 feet right of Baby.

Pitch 1: Climb the corner and the face below a short arching right-facing corner that is 2–4 inches deep. Then continue up the face between Baby and Easy Overhang to a big ledge. (80 feet) 5.8 G

Pitch 2: Walk left and uphill 20 feet to a face below an overhang. Climb past the overhang and continue up the face just left of a left-facing corner to another overhang. Diagonal up left past this overhang and work up and right to a left-facing corner capped by a ceiling formed by a huge block. Follow the corner to the ceiling, exit right, and continue to the top. (60 feet) 5.6 PG–R

FA (Pitch 2) 1960: Art Gran and Dave Craft
FA 1984: Ivan Rezucha and Annie O'Neill

101. EASY OVERHANG   5.2   PG   ★★

Start: On top of the large boulder pile to the right of Baby and directly below the right edge of a flake at the base of the right edge of the obvious chimney.

Pitch 1: Climb up to the chimney and follow it (V1) for about 40 feet. Then step left onto the face and continue up to a very large, dirty ledge. (Be careful of loose rock.)   (60 feet)   5.2

Pitch 2: Walk right about 15 feet and diagonal up right to an overhang in a left-facing corner (V2). Move up right past the overhang (V3) and continue about 35 feet up to another overhang. Traverse right to a small ledge around the corner (some parties belay here). Then, either climb straight up to the top or traverse right about 15 feet to an easy corner, which is followed to the top. (70 feet)   5.2

Variation 1:   5.3   Halfway up the chimney, step out left onto the face and climb up to the regular routine.

Variation 2:   Easy Baby   5.6   Continue straight up the corner and the one above to an overhang, and then diagonal up left to the top.

Variation 3:   Indecent Exposure   5.3   Traverse out right about 30 feet (exposed) to the main face and continue up to join the regular route near the top.

The belay ledges are covered with many loose pebbles and rocks, so be extra careful and watch where your ropes run.

FA 1941: Hans Kraus and Susanne Simon
FA (Variation 3) 1955: Ted Church

102. QUEASY O   5.10−   R−X

Start: At a steep polished face, 5 feet right of Easy Overhang and just left of Son of Easy O.

Pitch 1: Climb up the face to some left-facing flakes and follow these to the Son of Easy O belay.   (90 feet)   5.10−   R−X

Pitch 2: Continue up Easy Overhang until below a left-facing corner, which is then followed to the top.   (60 feet)   5.6

THE TRAPPS

FA (Pitch 1: Toprope) 1960s: John Stannard
FA (Lead) 1981: Russ Raffa, Dick Williams, and Russ Clune

103. SON OF EASY O 5.8 G ★★★

Start: At a thin crack on the smooth face 10 feet right of Easy Overhang.

Pitch 1: Follow the crack past a small, short, broken left-facing corner until it ends and continue up to a belay ledge. (80 feet) 5.8

Pitch 2: Climb up right to the large overhanging left-facing corner above and continue past an overhang. Then step right around the corner and work straight up the face to join Easy Overhang near the top. (80 feet) 5.8

FA 1962: Jim McCarthy and Al DeMaria

104. HEATHER 5.9 R–X

Start: On the polished face 15 feet right of Son of Easy O.

Pitch 1: Climb the face to a small ramp and diagonal up right to a stance. Then step left and continue up past a bulge and a small tree to a belay ledge. (80 feet) 5.9 R–X

Pitch 2: Continue up steep rock past a small overhang to a large overhang split by a crack at its widest part. Climb past the overhang and finish up the face above. (80 feet) 5.8

This route is less dangerous if protection is used on Pas de Deux.

FA 1974: Henry Barber, Pete Ramins, and Rick Hatch

105. PAS DE DEUX 5.8 PG ★★

Start: At a short left-facing corner, 40 feet right of Easy Overhang.

Pitch 1: (V1) Step right onto the face and move up to better holds. Traverse left and step up and across the main crack to a small ledge. Then follow the crack to its top, and angle up and right to a good ledge. (80 feet) 5.8 PG

Pitch 2: From the ledge, go up right around the overhangs above. Step up left to a right-facing corner and climb the corner to its top. Then move diagonally up and left to the beginning of the GT Ledge. (80 feet) 5.7

Variation 1: 5.10 PG Climb the obvious crack-fault system straight up to the traverse on the regular route.

FA 1959: Jim McCarthy and Jack Hansen, after placing protection on rappel

FFA 1959: Jim Geiser

106. CITY LIGHTS 5.7 G–PG ★★

Start: At a large tree below a crack that has a jog in it 15 feet up, 18 feet right of Pas de Deux.

Pitch 1: Climb the crack to a small ledge and move left to a right-facing flake. Pass the flake and continue up the face to the Pas de Deux belay ledge. (80 feet) 5.7 G–PG

Pitch 2: Climb up and slightly left to a right-facing corner, which is followed to its top. Step left, move up a few feet, step back right, and work up to a stance. Then continue up the easier face above to the top. (90 feet) 5.6

FA 1965: Dick Williams and Art Gran

107. FROG'S HEAD 5.6− G ★★★ '

Start: At a 12-foot-high crack on a white block, 25 feet right of City Lights.

Pitch 1: Follow the crack over the block and past a bulge, and continue up a small left-facing corner to a ledge. (90 feet) 5.6− G

Pitch 2: Work up steep rock for 20 feet and move right to a thin crack, which is followed to a large overhanging right-facing corner. Climb about halfway up the corner (V1), exit left around the outside corner onto the face, and continue up to the GT Ledge (V2). Finish by walking off left. (90 feet) 5.5

Variation 1: Continue up the corner to the GT Ledge.

Variation 2: 5.6 Climb directly over the large overhang above and finish up a short face.

If you look carefully, you might find the frog's head on the second pitch.

FA 1941: Fritz Wiessner and Lorens Logan

THE TRAPPS

108. MARIA 5.6+ PG ★★
Start: Same as Frog's Head.
Pitch 1: (V1, V2) Follow Frog's Head until just past the bulge, traverse right about 50 feet, and then climb up and right to a belay ledge in a large left-facing corner. (80 feet) 5.5
Pitch 2: Follow the corner to the GT Ledge. (90 feet) 5.6
Pitch 3: Continue up the corner above to the overhang at its top. Then step left and climb the crack through the overhang to the top. (The less ambitious can avoid the last overhang by traversing right below it and finishing up an easy cleft.) (50 feet) 5.6+ PG
Variation 1: Maria Direct 5.9 G Climb the face and small right-facing corner 10 feet left of Maria Redirect and join the regular route at the belay ledge.
Variation 2: Maria Redirect 5.11− R Climb a thin crack system directly up to the belay ledge in the large left-facing corner above. (Often toproped.)
FA 1946: Maria Millar and Fritz Wiessner
FA (Variation 1) circa 1956: John Turner
FA (Variation 2) 1968: Ants Leemets

109. SUNDOWN 5.8+ PG
Start: On the right side of the Frog's Head block.
Pitch 1: Climb the chimney behind the block, move left, and continue up past orange-colored rock and a short vertical fault to a ledge. (90 feet) 5.8+
Pitch 2: Move right a few feet and climb up the face past some blocks and an overhang to a ledge. (90 feet) 5.7
Pitch 3: Climb past the right side of the overhang above to the top. (30 feet)
FA 1984: Ivan Rezucha and Annie O'Neill

110. KAMA SUTRA 5.12− R
Start: On the steep face 15 feet right of Frog's Head and 5 feet left of a very thin crack that starts at a small overhang 7 feet above the ground.
Pitch 1: Climb the face to small horizontal holds at the overhang and move right to bigger holds on the lip. Work up to a stance (at

this point most climbers diagonal up right to the Maria corner and rappel, or traverse off left and downclimb Frog's Head) and continue up to a belay ledge. (70 feet) 5.12− R

Pitch 2: Move right and work up past a small ledge and tree. Then traverse left about 20 feet, climb up past an overhang, and continue up to the GT Ledge. (140 feet) 5.8

Pitch 3: Continue up the center of the face above to the top. (40 feet)

FA 1964: Ants Leemets and Dick Williams
FFA 1974: John Stannard

111. SULTANA 5.8 PG

Start: At a right-slanting corner that ends at an overhang 10 feet off the ground, 55 feet right of Frog's Head.

Pitch 1: Climb up around the right edge of the overhang and continue up to a grassy ledge. Step right until below a flake and work up the steep face to a large overhang. Then traverse left and climb up through the overhang to a belay. (100 feet) 5.8 PG

Pitch 2: Continue up the face past a small right-facing corner to the overhangs. Then follow some left-facing flakes and climb up to the GT Ledge. (90 feet) 5.7

Pitch 3: Finish on Maria.

Oh! Sultana—if you only knew! (She probably did.)

FA 1963: Dick Williams and John Hudson
FFA 1964: Dick Williams

112. SCUNGILLI 5.7 PG

Start: At a tree on top of some boulders and below a crack, 33 feet right of Sultana.

Pitch 1: Follow the crack for about 15 feet to a stance. Continue up and left past some right-facing flakes, traverse left for about 15 feet to a crack, and work up to an overhang. Climb the overhang (or traverse right around it—easier) and then diagonal up right to a belay on a protruding ledge. (100 feet) 5.7 PG

Pitch 2: Continue up the face to the GT Ledge. (80 feet)

Pitch 3: Finish on a nearby climb.

FA 1958: Art Gran and Jack Hansen

THE TRAPPS

113. JEAN 5.9 PG ★
Start: Same as Scungilli.

Pitch 1: Climb the crack and traverse right along a ramp to an orange left-facing corner, which is followed to an overhang. Climb the overhang and belay on a small stance on the left. (70 feet) 5.9 PG

Pitch 2: Move left and climb a corner. Then move back right and continue up to a groove that leads to the GT Ledge. (80 feet) 5.6

Pitch 3: Continue up the face past an overhang and then diagonal up right to the top. (40 feet) 5.6

FA 1960: Art Gran, Phil Jacobus, and John Hudson
FFA 1964: Dick Williams

114. PRECARIOUS PERCH 5.9 PG
Start: Same as Scungilli and Jean, or at a broken face and small left-facing corner 10 feet farther right.

Pitch 1: Either follow Jean or use the alternate start to reach the overhang 10 feet right of Jean. Then climb past the overhang to a ledge. (60 feet) 5.9 PG

Pitch 2: Rappel or continue up the face between Jean and Sixish to the GT Ledge. (90 feet) 5.8

Pitch 3: Finish on a nearby climb.

FA 1981: Rich Perch and Mike Sawicky

115. SIXISH 5.4+ G ★★★
Start: On top of some boulders below a large right-facing corner, 50 feet right of Scungilli.

Pitch 1: Climb a small, steep left-facing corner to good holds and move left to the large right-facing corner (or climb directly up to this corner—5.6). Continue up the corner and some flakes to the overhangs, and then move around left to a small belay spot. (50 feet) 5.4+ G

Pitch 2: Climb around left past some small overhangs and move back right to a crack. Then continue up the crack and the face above to the GT Ledge. (90 feet) 5.3

Pitch 3: (V1) Move left and climb the face on the outside of the corner to an overhang. Then move right a bit and continue straight up to the top. (50 feet) 5.4

Variation 1: 5.10 PG · Climb the face to the right of the huge pine tree, traverse left beneath the ceiling, and continue to the top. (This was the original line—the present third pitch was once a variation.)

FA 1951: Hans Kraus and Dick Hirschland
FFA (Variation #1) 1962: Dick Williams

116. ONE BLUNDER AND IT'S SIX FEET UNDER 5.10 X

Start: At a short left-facing corner, 5 feet right of Sixish; or at a steep bulging face, 5 feet left of Drunkard's Delight.

Pitch 1: Using either start, climb the steep face between Sixish and Drunkard's Delight to a belay on Drunkard's. 5.9− X

Pitch 2: At the broken corner on the left, move left and climb the face to the GT Ledge. (80 feet) 5.6

Pitch 3: Finish on a nearby climb.

FA 1985: Todd Swain, Matt Jasinski, and John Goobic

117. DRUNKARD'S DELIGHT 5.8− PG ★★

Start: At a right-slanting crack at the end of a drop in the trail, 25 feet right of Sixish.

Pitch 1: Diagonal up right to a crack system 15 feet above the ground and follow this until it ends. Then work up left to a ledge below a large overhang. (100 feet) 5.8−

Pitch 2: Climb out over the overhangs at the break, move left, and continue up to the GT Ledge. (80 feet) 5.8−

Pitch 3: Walk right to a large right-facing corner, and climb this and the face on the right to the top. (80 feet) 5.4

Highly recommended, but not with a hangover!

FA 1959: Jim Andress and Jim McCarthy

118. FIVE TENDONS 5.10+ R

Start: At the most logical spot on the face about midway between Drunkard's Delight and Morning After.

Pitch 1: Climb the face to a belay under the ceiling. (100 feet) 5.10

Pitch 2: Continue up (just touching Morning After) to the ceiling, clear it, and climb up to the GT Ledge. (80 feet) 5.10+ R

Pitch 3: Finish on a nearby climb.
FA (Pitch 1) 1984: Felix Modugno
FA (Pitch 2) 1981: Will Chen

119. MORNING AFTER 5.8− PG ★
Start: Same as Rusty Trifle.
Pitch 1: Climb up to a small right-facing corner that starts about 30 feet above the ground. At the top of the corner, diagonal up left to some right-facing flakes that lead to a ledge. Then traverse right and belay at some bushes below a left-facing corner. (90 feet) 5.8−
Pitch 2: Move up right around the corner and continue up the face to the GT Ledge. (90 feet) 5.7
Pitch 3: Climb up to a small overhang and move around it on the right. Continue up to a layback crack in a white groove, which then leads to the top. (70 feet) 5.8−
FA 1964: Jim Andress and Doug Tompkins

120. BLOODY MARY 5.6 PG
Start: Same as Rusty Trifle.
Pitch 1: Climb the obvious crack for about 30 feet and traverse left to a small right-facing corner. Work up the corner, move left, and continue up past some flakes and another small right-facing corner to a belay directly below a large overhang. (70 feet) 5.6
Pitch 2: Step left and move up to another large overhang. Traverse right about 10 feet and climb up to a stance (some parties belay here). Then continue straight up to the GT Ledge. (90 feet) 5.6
Pitch 3: (V1) Move left to the first short right-facing corner, which is 8 feet high. Climb the corner, step left past a large ledge, and continue straight up the face past a bulge to the top. (90 feet) 5.5
Variation 1: 5.8 Walk right about 20 feet to the first right-facing corner and follow this to the top.
FA 1972: Walter Baumann, Dick Williams, and Cherry Merritt

121. RUSTY TRIFLE 5.5 G ★

Start: At a 15-foot-high left-facing corner formed by large blocks, 40 feet right of Drunkard's Delight.

Pitch 1: Climb up the corner and blocks for about 30 feet. Traverse right across the face (5.5) to a ledge. (The traverse can be avoided by starting on a ledge farther right, at the base of the huge Bloody Bush corner—5.3.) Continue up a low-angle right-facing corner, step up left, and then move up and back right to a short left-facing corner. Follow this corner and the one above to a dirty ledge with a pine tree. (100 feet) 5.5 G

Pitch 2: Diagonal up right to a large block and then work back up left to a right-facing corner. Above the corner, go straight up to the overhangs and then diagonal up left to the GT Ledge. (60 feet) 5.3

Pitch 3: From the top of some blocks, step up over a low overhang, work up right, and then climb back up and left to a white right-facing corner below a tree. Continue up the corner and finish up the face above. (90 feet) 5.3

FA 1950: Hans Kraus and Bonnie Prudden

122. ARC OF A DIVER 5.9 G

Start: At a crack or vertical fault, 16 feet right of Rusty Trifle.

Pitch 1: Follow the crack past a tree and the Rusty Trifle traverse to a short left-facing corner below an overhang. Continue up the corner and then climb past the overhang to a ledge. (60 feet) 5.8

Pitch 2: Continue up a small left-facing corner past a double-tiered overhang and diagonal up left to the GT Ledge. (60 feet) 5.7

Pitch 3: Climb the obvious right-facing corner past a large overhang to the top. (60 feet) 5.9 G

FA 1985: Ray Dobkin and Joe Ferguson

123. ROCK AND BREW 5.9 PG–R

Start: At a steep face below a small overhang that is 10 feet above the ground, 40 feet right of Rusty Trifle and 25 feet left of Bloody Bush.

Pitch 1: Climb up to the overhang, move left, and work up to a good stance in a small, short left-facing corner. Diagonal up right past a thin crack to a small overhang or bulge, traverse left about 10 feet, and then continue up the face past a small overhang to a ledge. (110 feet) 5.9 PG–R

Pitch 2: Step right and continue up past a bulging overhang to the GT Ledge. (50 feet)

Pitch 3: Climb past a bulge and work up the face to a crack system that leads to a pine tree. Then finish up the steep face above. (80 feet)

FA 1973: Dick Williams and Dave Loeks

124. MAKE HASTE OR TOMATO PASTE   5.10   PG–R

Start: On the face 8 feet right of Rock and Brew.

Pitch 1: Climb the face and go past an overhang at a vertical fault. Then move right and continue up past a bulge to a belay on the Rusty Trifle traverse. (30 feet) 5.10 R

Pitch 2: Continue up the face to the left of Rusty Trifle to the GT Ledge. (80 feet)

Pitch 3: Finish on a nearby climb.

FA 1985: Todd Swain and Neil Harvey

125. TRUSTY RIFLE   5.9   G

Start: Same as Bloody Bush and the alternate Rusty Trifle start.

Pitch 1: Starting at a thin seam, climb the face left of the outside corner to the GT Ledge. (100 feet) 5.9 G

Pitch 2: Go left about 20 feet and climb up the face about 10 feet right of a flake, past a short left-facing corner, to the top. (50 feet) 5.8 G

FA 1984: Todd Swain, Dave Saball, and Andy and Randy Schenkel

126. BLOODY BUSH   5.7   G

Start: At the huge right-facing corner to the right of Rusty Trifle (same as the alternate Rusty Trifle start).

Pitch 1: (V1) Climb the face and the varying off-width crack in the corner (V2) to the GT Ledge. (100 feet) 5.7 G

Pitch 2: Climb straight up and then diagonal up right around some overhangs past a right-facing corner. Then go left to another right-facing corner and continue up to the top. (100 feet) 5.5 G

Variation 1: Rusty Jam 5.9 G Start at a crack 7 feet right of Make Haste or Tomato Paste. Climb the crack to join the regular route.

Variation 2: From a ledge on the right, exit left around the corner and traverse left to the pine tree belay on Rusty Trifle.

The second pitch was originally known as Easy Street.
FA (Pitch 1): 1950s
FA (Pitch 2) 1972: Dick DuMais and John Stannard
FA (Variation 1) 1975: Rick Cronk, Matt Muchnik, Kevin Bein, John Bragg, and Rich Perch

127. UNCLE RUDY 5.8 PG
Start: On the pebbly face 20 feet right of Bloody Bush.
Pitch 1: Climb the face past an overhang and some small ledges and trees to a large ledge with a tree. (60 feet) 5.8
Pitch 2: Continue up past an overhang to the GT Ledge. (60 feet) 5.8
Pitch 3: Climb up to a small overhang, move left, and work up to a large overhang to the right of a right-facing corner. Climb over the overhang and follow a crack to a small overhang split by another crack. Then continue past this overhang to the top. (80 feet) 5.8
FA 1975: Mike and Pete Werner

128. WRIST 5.6 G ★
Start: At a prominent crack, 130 feet right of Rusty Trifle and 20 feet left of Invitation to Hell.
Pitch 1: Climb the crack and face to a loose, broken ledge below a left-facing corner that contains a wide crack. (60 feet) 5.3
Pitch 2: Climb the wide crack and then continue up and slightly right to the GT Ledge. (70 feet) 5.5
Pitch 3: Climb the right-facing corner above to a ceiling, traverse out left, and move up to a ledge (some parties belay here). Continue up the face, moving right and then back up left to the top. (100 feet) 5.6 G
FA 1953: Bonnie Prudden and Hans Kraus

129. INVITATION TO HELL   5.10+   PG

Start: At the right-facing corner on the left side of the prominent arch.

Pitch 1: Climb up the corner to within 10 feet of its top, occasionally using the outside edge and face to the left. Then move left around the corner and work up the face to a horizontal crack and a white bulge. Continue past the bulge (or traverse right and go around it—easier) to the GT Ledge.   (140 feet)   5.8

Pitch 2: Walk left about 25 feet and belay at a tree below a roof.

Pitch 3: Work up to the roof at a bush and traverse right 5-10 feet along a reddish flake to a break in the ceiling. Then climb past the break and continue to the top.   (80 feet)   5.10+   PG

The first half of the first pitch has loose rock and poor protection—better to start on the first half of Arch and then join the regular route.

FA 1984: Mike Steele and an acquaintance, after the second pitch was inspected, cleaned, and protected on rappel

130. ARCH   5.5−   PG   ★

Start: At a small overhanging right-facing corner that ends at an overhang 20 feet up, directly below the center of the prominent arch.

Pitch 1: Climb the small arête formed by the right-facing corner for about 15 feet, using some flakes and the face to the left. Move right to the center of the arch (this spot can be reached directly from below by climbing the small overhang on the right). Then continue up the face to near the top of the arch (V1) and traverse around right to a ledge.   (100 feet)   5.5−   PG

Pitch 2: Climb up and left to a crack or gully that leads to broken rock and the GT Ledge.   (70 feet)   5.4

Pitch 3: Climb up right past a notch in the overhang. Then move left and diagonal up right to a left-facing corner (V2), which is followed to the top.   (80 feet)   5.4

Variation 1:   Wick's Banana   5.9   PG   Climb straight up past the crack in the roof at the apex of the arch and rejoin the regular route at the large ledge above.

Variation 2:   5.5   Climb through the overhangs on the left and continue to the top.

FA 1953: Hans Kraus and Bonnie Prudden
FA (Variation 1) 1962: Dick Williams and Bill Goldner

131. BILLY SHEARS   5.9−   PG
Start: At the huge left-facing corner that forms the right side of the prominent arch.
Pitch 1: Follow the corner past an overhang, and continue past several bushes and across the Arch traverse to the crack in the overhang below and just right of the apex of the arch. Then climb through the overhang to the large ledge above.   (90 feet)   5.9− PG
Pitch 2: Continue straight up to the GT Ledge.   (40 feet)   5.3
Pitch 3: Walk right about 20 feet to a right-facing corner, which is followed to a second corner and an overhang. Then exit left and move up to the top.   (70 feet)   5.8
FA 1982: Ray Dobkin, Joe Ferguson, and Max Strumia

132. VICIOUS RUMORS   5.11+   PG
Start: At the crack on the right face of the arch, just right of the Billy Shears corner.
Pitch 1: Follow the crack up the face past an overhang, diagonal up right around the corner to a ledge, and rappel.   (50 feet)
FA 1985: Darrow Kirkpatrick and Frank Minunni

133. RIBLESS   5.6   PG
Start: Same as Ribs.
Pitch 1: Climb the face and arête on the left to a ledge.   (70 feet)   5.6
Pitch 2: Rappel, climb up left to join Arch, or step right to join Ribs.
FA: 1980s

134. RIBS   5.4   PG
Start: At the base of the arête on the right side of the prominent arch.
Pitch 1: Go right around the corner and continue up the face past a crack to a ledge. Diagonal up right to a tree on another

ledge and then climb up the flaky right-facing corner on the left to a very loose ledge. (110 feet) 5.4

Pitch 2: Continue straight up the steep rock above to the GT Ledge. (60 feet) 5.4

Pitch 3: Finish on a nearby climb.

FA 1953: Hans Kraus and Bonnie Prudden

135. CALISTHENIC 5.7 PG

Start: At a steep, bulging face that starts 4–5 feet above the ground, 34 feet right of the Ribs arête and 30 feet left of Gorilla My Dreams.

Pitch 1: Climb straight over the overhang at the bottom and continue straight up to some small, dirty ledges. (70 feet) 5.7 PG

Pitch 2: Continue up the face to the GT Ledge. (60 feet)

Pitch 3: Walk left to a short left-facing corner with a crack. Climb the crack and corner to an overhang, step right, and continue to the top of the corner. Then exit left and follow the last 20 feet of Gaston to the top. (80 feet) 5.7

FA 1962: Phil Jacobus and John Hudson

136. GORILLA MY DREAMS 5.7 PG

Start: At a dirty right-facing corner that begins 5 feet above the ground, 30 feet right of Calisthenic.

Pitch 1: Climb up the corner, continue past a grassy ledge, and work up a small corner and the face on the right to a small ledge. (70 feet) 5.7 PG

Pitch 2: Climb up the face and then diagonal up right to a bush in a large left-facing corner. Then continue up right past some blocky overhangs to a ledge. (100 feet) 5.6

Pitch 3: Walk left to the left-facing corner on the third pitch of Gaston and follow the corner through the overhangs to the top. (60 feet) 5.4

An ape-pealing climb.

FA 1966: Dick Williams, Ants Leemets, and Jim McCarthy

137. SPLASHTIC 5.9− PG–R ★
Start: On the face just left of a right-facing corner, 10 feet right of Gorilla My Dreams.

Pitch 1: Climb up the face to a small ledge. Traverse right about 10 feet and continue up to another small ledge. (70 feet) 5.8

Pitch 2: Climb up to the corner in the white rock above the overhang. Then step down and traverse around the corner to a belay on the face just below an overhang. (70 feet) 5.9− PG–R

Pitch 3: Diagonal up right to the overhang, climb up through a notch, and continue up to a ledge. (60 feet) 5.7

Pitch 4: Finish on the last pitch of Strictly from Nowhere. (50 feet) 5.4

FA 1966: Dick Williams and Ants Leemets

138. GASTON 5.8 PG
Start: At a steep ramp that rises 10 feet, midway between Splashtic and Travels with Charley.

Pitch 1: (V1) Follow the ramp to a bulge, diagonal up right over the bulge, and then work back up left to a thin face. Continue up to a belay below a long inside corner which curves up to the left. (Height-related—easier if taller.) (80 feet) 5.8−

Pitch 2: Climb the corner and the face on the left, and continue up to a large ledge. (100 feet) 5.8 PG

Pitch 3: Climb the left-facing corner above until below the overhangs. Then traverse left (V2) about 40 feet past the end of the overhangs and continue to the top. (90 feet)

Variation 1: Oscar's Variation 5.7 Climb the large orange left-facing corner just right of the regular start.

Variation 2: 5.10 G Traverse left about 10 feet and climb through the overhangs to the top.

Just when you think you're past the crux, you're at it!

FA 1952: Ken Prestrud and Lucien Warner

139. TRAVELS WITH CHARLEY 5.8− R
Start: At the large orange left-facing corner to the right of Gaston (same as Oscar's Variation).

Pitch 1: Climb the corner and face to a belay at the base of an arching left-facing corner. (80 feet) 5.7+

Pitch 2: Climb up past some white flakes to a large overhang. Traverse out right onto the face and continue up a small right-facing corner to the overhangs above. Work up through the right side of the overhangs and then continue up to a large ledge at a pine tree. (80 feet) 5.8− R

Pitch 3: Climb past the overhangs at a notch immediately above and continue to the top. (50 feet) 5.7

Because of poor protection this route was never very popular when it was originally rated 5.6; now, at 5.8−, even though it is still poorly protected despite the advances in hardware, it has become quite popular.

FA 1968: Dave Ingalls and Charlie Bookman

140. STRICTLY FROM NOWHERE 5.7 PG ★★

Start: Directly below a small overhang that is 10 feet above the ground, 17 feet right of Travels with Charley.

Pitch 1: Climb up to the overhang and pass it on the right. Then work up and slightly left on the face to a good ledge at a right-facing corner. (75 feet) 5.6

Pitch 2: Climb steep rock to a left-facing corner at the overhangs above and then climb out right around the overhangs to a ledge with a pine tree. Go back up left past a small overhang and then diagonal up right over another overhang to the large vegetated belay ledge just beyond. (100 feet) 5.7 PG

Pitch 3: Traverse left to a left-facing corner, and climb the corner and the face above to the top. (50 feet) 5.4

FA 1959: Art Gran and Jim Andress

141. EPICLEPSY 5.10 X

Start: On a face with a broken crack, 20 feet right of Strictly from Nowhere.

Pitch 1: Climb up the middle of the face to a belay ledge. (60 feet) 5.8−

Pitch 2: Continue up the steep face and climb through the overhang above at the widest point. Then step 5 feet left to a belay at a pine tree. (30 feet) 5.10 X

Pitch 3: Continue up the face, move diagonally up right, and climb through the overhangs at a crack on the right. Belay on a ledge above. (70 feet) 5.9+

Pitch 4: Continue to the top. (50 feet)

FA (Toprope) 1972: Kevin Bein

FA (Lead) 1976: Kevin Bein, Mark Robinson, Barbara Devine, and Roy Kligfield

142. SHOCKLEY'S CEILING   5.6   G   ★★★

Start: In the large, blocky right-facing corner to the right of Strictly from Nowhere.

Pitch 1: (V1) Scramble out left and up to the top of the boulders above. Follow a chimney behind a flake to a ledge. Then traverse right and move up to a ledge with several small trees. (80 feet) 5.4

Pitch 2: Step back left and climb the overhang and the right-facing corner above to a point where it is easy to move left around onto the face. Diagonal up the ramps to the left and work up the face for about 40 feet. Then traverse right and climb up to a belay in broken rock below a ceiling. (110 feet) 5.5

Pitch 3: (V2, V3) Traverse right to a crack, follow it through the overhang, and continue to the top of the corner above. Then step out right around the corner, climb over a second overhang at a crack, and finish up the face above. (80 feet) 5.6 G

Variation 1:   5.7   Climb the large right-facing flake to the right of the blocky corner, move left to a tree, and continue up to the ledge above the chimney on the regular route.

Variation 2: Shockley's Without   5.3   R   Diagonal up left to a crack in a pleasant-looking white face. Follow the crack to a ledge and then climb another crack in a short left-facing corner to the top. (70 feet)

Variation 3: Shockley's Within   5.6   PG   Midway between the regular route and Shockley's Without, climb the overhang, move slightly right, and continue to the top. (65 feet)

One of the best-known and most popular routes in the Trapps, Shockley's often attracts crowds on the hairpin turn below. Much to the surprise of one crowd in 1965, it was the scene of an all-nude ascent by a party of Vulgarian males.

THE TRAPPS

FA 1953: Bill Shockley and Doug Kerr
FA (Variation 1) 1960: Raivo Puusemp

143. MISTER TRANSISTOR   5.10−   PG
Start: At a large right-facing flake (same as Variation 1 on Shockley's Ceiling), just left of P.R.
Pitch 1: Follow Variation 1 on Shockley's to the ledge above the Shockley's chimney. Work up past a crack and a fault, and pass the overhang above on the right. Then continue up to a belay under a ceiling. (80 feet)   5.10−   PG
Pitch 2: Climb up the face and over the ceiling 10 feet left of the Shockley's corner. Continue up a left-facing corner, and then go up and right to another ceiling. Climb over this ceiling on the right and belay on the ledge above.   (80 feet)   5.8
Pitch 3: Finish on a nearby climb.
This route is mostly a combination of old variations.
FA 1984: Ivan Rezucha and Todd Swain

144. P.R.   5.11+   R   ★
Start: On the face below a very thin crack, 20 feet right of Shockley's Ceiling.
Pitch 1: Climb past the crack to a stance and continue up the steep face past a bulge to the first Shockley's Ceiling belay. (60 feet)   5.11+   R
Pitch 2: Continue up the face past a small overhang to a ledge. (50 feet)
Pitch 3: Work up the steep face through a notch in the overhang above, step up right, and continue to the top.   5.9 or 5.10
You'll need more than good public relations to get up this one.
FA 1972: Skip King
FA (Pitch 3): Jim McCarthy and Sandy Bill
FFA 1974: John Stannard

145. GRIM-ACE FACE   5.9   PG   ★★
Start: On the steep face just before a short, blocky left-facing corner, 35 feet right of Shockley's Ceiling.
Pitch 1: Climb up the face past a bulge to the first High Corner belay ledge.   (80 feet)   5.8   R

Pitch 2: (V1) Walk right a few feet to a tree, and climb loose rock to an overhang. Step right and continue up past another overhang to the GT Ledge below an imposing ceiling. (120 feet) 5.8+ R

Pitch 3: Work up and left, clear the ceiling at a short left-facing corner, and continue up the face to the top. (90 feet) 5.9 PG

Variation 1: 5.10 R–X Climb straight up some frail rock past a small overhang and continue up the steep face above to the GT Ledge.

FA 1966: Jim McCarthy and Royal Robbins
FA (Variation 1) 1982: Pete Thexton and Dick Williams

146. NO BELLE PRIZE 5.10 R–X
Start: Same as High Corner.
Pitch 1: Climb the first pitch of High Corner and continue up a blocky corner and a steep face to the GT Ledge. (150 feet) 5.7

Pitch 2: Walk about 15 feet left, and climb past a right-facing corner and some overhangs just right of P.R. to the top. (80 feet) 5.10 R–X

FA 1984: Ivan Rezucha

147. HI CORONER! 5.9 PG
Start: At a crack on the left wall of the High Corner corner.
Pitch 1: Climb the crack and the obvious squeeze chimney, and then continue directly up the steep face above to the GT Ledge. (This used to be a variation to High Corner.) (150 feet) 5.8

Pitch 2: Climb the imposing left wall of High Corner, following a shallow corner system to the top. (60 feet) 5.9 PG

FA 1984: Todd Swain, Pat Barlow, and Ray Dobkin

148. HIGH CORNER 5.5 PG
Start: At a crack in a large right-facing corner that has a blocklike flake and a grassy ledge at its top, 80 feet right of Shockley's Ceiling.
Pitch 1: Climb the crack and the corner, and then diagonal up left to a tree near the first Shockley's Ceiling belay. (75 feet) 5.3

Pitch 2: Continue up the right-facing corner and the face on the right to a large ledge at the base of a long corner.   (100 feet) 5.5

Pitch 3: Follow the long corner until about 20 feet below the top. Then traverse awkwardly out left and climb to the top.   (70 feet)   5.5

FA 1942: Fritz Wiessner and Roger Wolcott

149. GLYPTOMANIAC   5.8+   PG

Start: On the face 15 feet right of High Corner.

Pitch 1: Climb the face past a grassy ledge and a broken fault-crack system to a large blocky ledge below a right-facing corner. (50 feet)

Pitch 2: Follow the corner past some overhangs and continue up the face to the GT Ledge.   (90 feet)

Pitch 3: Climb the face about 10 feet to the right of High Corner and move right past an overhang to the top.   (50 feet)

FA 1982: Ivan Rezucha, Don Lauber, and Annie O'Neill

150. GLYPTODON   5.8   PG   ★

Start: At a right-facing corner that contains overhangs 25 feet above the ground, 35 feet right of High Corner.

Pitch 1: Climb the corner, go left at the first overhang, and work up the face to the right edge of another overhang. Follow an open book for a few feet, move left onto a steep face, and continue up right to a grassy ledge.   (100 feet)

Pitch 2: From the left end of the ledge, climb the overhang and continue up the face to the GT Ledge.   (50 feet)   5.8   PG

Pitch 3: Follow a crack that diagonals up right to the top.   (80 feet)   5.6

FA 1970: Helmut Microys and Eric Marshall

151. NEMESIS   5.10−   PG

Start: At a thin vertical fracture on the face, 10 feet right of the Glyptodon corner.

Pitch 1: Follow the fracture past a small left-facing flake to a ledge (or follow the Glyptodon corner to the overhangs and go right around them to the ledge).   (60 feet)   5.10−   PG

Pitch 2: Climb up the flaky right-facing corner above and then diagonal up left to an overhanging right-facing corner. Follow this corner to a tree and a small ledge on the left. Diagonal up left to a notch in the overhangs and continue up to a ledge.   (110 feet) 5.8

Pitch 3: Work up the face to a broken diagonal crack, which is followed to a large ledge. Then climb up under an overhang, traverse out right, and continue to the top.   (60 feet)

FA 1966: Steve Larsen, Dick Williams, John Hudson, Jim McCarthy, and Phil Jacobus

152. MIDNIGHT COWBOY   5.9+   R   ★

Start: At a thin crack, 22 feet right of Nemesis.

Pitch 1: Climb up about 15 feet and step up right past a bulge to a grassy ledge.   (60 feet)   5.9+   R

Pitch 2: Step left, climb up to a small ledge, and continue up the face past a bulge to the GT Ledge.   (140 feet)   5.8+

Pitch 3: Climb up until beneath a ceiling, traverse right around the corner onto the face, and continue up to the top.   (60 feet) 5.9

FA 1968: Richard Goldstone and Dick Williams

153. GLYPNOD   5.8   PG   ★

Start: At a crack in a slightly overhanging right-facing corner that has a tree at its base, 52 feet right of the Glyptodon corner.

Pitch 1: Climb to the top of the crack and corner, and scramble up left to a large ledge.   (40 feet)   5.7   PG

Pitch 2: Climb the face to the right of the large right-facing corner and continue past some unstable-looking rock to a ledge. Then diagonal up left to a good belay below the obvious right-facing corner.   (100 feet)   5.4   R–X

Pitch 3: Follow the corner to a ceiling, clear the ceiling, and continue past an overhang. Then exit left around the corner and climb to the top.   (70 feet)   5.8   PG

FA circa 1956: John Wharton and Dave Isles

FFA circa 1956: John Turner and Craig Merrihue

THE TRAPPS

154. YESTERDAY'S LEMONADE 5.10− PG−R
Start: On the face 13 feet right of Glypnod.

Pitch 1: Climb the face to an overhang. Step right, clear the overhang, and reach a short left-facing corner. Then continue up the undulating face, moving left and right as necessary, to the GT Ledge. 5.10− PG−R

Pitch 2: Finish on a nearby climb.

FA 1970s: Charlie Rollins and John Stannard

155. ANGUISH 5.8 PG
Start: Below a left-pointing flake that is just below a short left-facing corner, 40 feet right of the Glypnod corner.

Pitch 1: Climb up past the flake and corner to a ledge, and walk right about 15 feet to another left-facing corner. Work up this corner and the face above until below an overhang. Then move left and climb up to a ledge. (80 feet) 5.5−

Pitch 2: Climb up the face and then diagonal up right on easier rock to a big ledge below some large overhangs. (60 feet) 5.5−

Pitch 3: Continue up the face to a corner in the overhangs, diagonal up left through the overhangs, and finish up the face above. (50 feet) 5.8 PG

Named for Burt Angrist who, on the first ascent, managed to hit his thumb, drop a piton, lose his glasses, and fall, all in one incredibly deft motion.

FA 1965: Jim McCarthy and Burt Angrist

156. RUBY SATURDAY 5.9− PG
Start: Beneath a vertical fracture that begins 6 feet above the ground, 20 feet right of Anguish.

Pitch 1: Climb straight up the face about 20 feet, traverse right, and move up to a ledge. Then follow a blocky right-facing corner and the face on the left to the first Simple Ceilings belay. (80 feet) 5.8

Pitch 2: Step up left to an overhang and traverse back right just above the belay spot until the overhang can be climbed. Then follow a faint groove up the steep face above to the GT Ledge. (90 feet) 5.9− PG

Pitch 3: Finish on the last pitch of Anguish. (50 feet) 5.8 PG

FA 1966: Jim McCarthy and Ants Leemets

157. RASPBERRY SUNDAE 5.9+   PG
Start: On the broken face 10 feet left of Three Pines.

Pitch 1: Climb up to a tree-covered ledge and continue up the face. Then move right a bit past some overhangs (which are even with a big pine on the right), and continue up broken rock to the GT Ledge. (150 feet) 5.9 R

Pitch 2: From the top of the Three Pines corner, climb up left past a ceiling and continue to the top. (80 feet) 5.9+ PG

FA 1982: Ivan Rezucha, Don Lauber, and Annie O'Neill

158. SIMPLE CEILINGS 5.5 PG
Start: Same as Three Pines.

Pitch 1: Climb up and left to a ledge. Follow a corner for about 40 feet, and then go out left and move up to a ledge. (70 feet) 5.5

Pitch 2: Traverse left along the ledge and climb a flake. Then move left again and climb up to the second Glypnod belay. (90 feet) 5.5

Pitch 3: Starting at the pine tree a little past the Glypnod corner, work up to the overhangs above and move left past them. Climb directly up the steep face above to another large ledge (some parties belay here). Then follow the corner above to a white face on the left, traverse left across this, and continue up to the top. (130 feet) 5.3

FA 1957: Willie Crowther and Gardiner Perry

159. THREE PINES 5.3 G ★★★
Start: At a 15-foot-high, block-filled right-facing corner that contains a jutting block, directly below a left-facing corner with a pine tree at its top, 20 feet right of Ruby Saturday.

Pitch 1: Scramble up to a ledge below a crack. (V1) Climb up left and then diagonal up right to a large left-facing corner, which is followed to a ledge and a large pine tree. (60 feet) 5.3

Pitch 2: Continue up the corner to the GT Ledge. Walk right over boulders and past another large pine until below the first large left-facing corner. (50 feet) 5.3

Pitch 3: Climb up 20 feet to a small ledge in the main corner, following either of two smaller corners that converge at the ledge. (V2) Traverse out right (exposed) past a crack (which can be climbed directly—5.6) to a large ledge. Walk right and up to the base of a white face with a crack. (50 feet) 5.3

Pitch 4: Follow the crack for about 30 feet to a ledge. Then walk right about 35 feet and scramble back up left to the top (or finish directly up some thin cracks on the short white face above the ledge—5.5). (50 feet)

Variation 1: 5.4 Climb straight up the crack to the huge left-facing corner and rejoin the regular route.

Variation 2: The Dangler 5.9 G Continue up the main corner, hand traverse out right along the lip of the roof, and finish up the face above.

FA 1941: Hans Kraus, Roger Wolcott, and Del Wilde

160. SOMETHING BORING 5.9 X

Start: On the face midway between Three Pines and Something Interesting.

Pitch 1: Climb up the face to a small tree and diagonal up left to a small ledge. Traverse right 5 feet and then continue straight up to the second Three Pines belay ledge. (110 feet) 5.7 R

Pitch 2: Continue up the face past a small overhang to the GT Ledge. (60 feet) 5.9 X

Pitch 3: Follow a right-facing corner past an overhang to a stance. Then diagonal up the overhanging left face to a tree on the nose, step left around the nose, and continue straight up to the top. (80 feet) 5.8

Boring? That'll be the day!

FA 1971: Walter Baumann, Jim McCarthy, Laura Brant, Beth Stannard, and Christian Leroyer

161. SOMETHING OR OTHER 5.10− R

Start: On the face about 7 feet left of Something Interesting.

Pitch 1: Climb the face between Something Boring and Something Interesting to the GT Ledge. (100 feet) 5.7

Pitch 2: Start of the left-facing corner of Something Interesting and climb through the ceiling above at a flake just right of center. Then continue up the face to the top. (50 feet) 5.10− R

FA 1982: Russ Raffa, Steve Beccio, and Russ Clune

162. SOMETHING INTERESTING 5.8 G ★★★

Start: At a short right-facing corner below a long crack, 30 feet right of Three Pines.

Pitch 1: Climb the corner and follow the crack past a bulge to a stance (some parties belay here—70 feet). Continue up the crack past a small corner and then work up the face to the GT Ledge. (120 feet) 5.8 G

Pitch 2: Climb the left-facing corner directly behind the pine tree until it is possible to swing around onto the face to the right. Continue up a few moves and traverse left to a large right-facing corner. Follow the corner to a grassy ledge and then scramble to the top. (90 feet) 5.7

FA 1946: Hans Kraus, Ken Prestrud, and Bonnie Prudden

FFA 1950s: Art Gran

163. HIGHER STANNARD 5.9− PG ★★

Start: At a 2-inch-deep, 4-foot-high left-facing corner that arches up left on the face, behind a tree 10 feet right of Something Interesting.

Pitch 1: Climb up and right to a vertical fracture just above a short, shallow ramp 20 feet up. Follow the fracture for 10 feet, traverse right a few feet, and diagonal up right to another shallow ramp. Continue up left to a right-facing corner (V1), which is followed up past an overhang to a small belay stance. (80 feet) 5.9− PG

Pitch 2: Rappel, or traverse right around the outside corner and continue up to the GT Ledge. (80 feet) 5.5

Pitch 3: Finish on a nearby climb.

Variation 1: 5.5 **PG** Traverse left, climb up through the break in the overhang, and then traverse back right to the regular route at the small belay stance.

FA 1967: Jim McCarthy and John Stannard

THE TRAPPS

164. BIRDIE PARTY 5.10− PG ★★
Start: Below a thin crack that leads to a long, narrow grassy ledge, 40 feet right of Something Interesting.

Pitch 1: Climb the crack and continue up the face, following more thin cracks and a short, shallow right-facing corner, to a large flake that protrudes left. Then, either hand traverse right to the M.F. belay or climb on top of the flake and traverse right (scary) to a belay stance. (90 feet) 5.8+

Pitch 2: Diagonal up left to a horizontal crack, traverse right, and climb up past an overhang, about 20 feet before traversing left. Then step left to a belay in the right-facing M.F. corner. (80 feet) 5.10− PG

Pitch 3: Finish on the last pitch of M.F. or diagonal up left to Three Pines and the GT Ledge, and finish on a nearby climb.

Kevin thought he was on M.F. when he inadvertently freed the route!

FA 1959: Jim McCarthy and Doug Tompkins
FFA 1966: Kevin Bein

165. INTERSTICE 5.10+ R ★★
Start: On the face below the left side of a 6-inch overhang that arches up left below a thin crack, 20 feet right of Birdie Party.

Pitch 1: Climb up the face past the overhang and crack to a ledge. Continue up to some pointed or jutting rock at the base of an arching left-facing corner. Follow the corner until about halfway up, exit right, and move up and left to the large protruding Birdie Party flake. Then hand traverse right and climb up to the M.F. belay. (80 feet) 5.10− PG

Pitch 2: Climb up and left to a cleft in the ceiling just left of Birdie Party. Go through the cleft and continue up steep rock to easier climbing and the GT Ledge. (100 feet) 5.10+ R

Pitch 3: Finish on a nearby climb.

FA 1975: John Stannard and associates

166. MOTHER'S DAY PARTY 5.10 PG ★★
Start: At an arching left-facing corner, 8 feet left of M.F.

Pitch 1: Climb 10 feet up the corner to a shallow, 4-inch-deep left-facing corner. Follow this to a small stance and work up a seemingly blank face to a ledge. Continue up bulging orange rock just left of a greenish corner, and then climb up and right into the corner (above greenish munge). Move up right onto the face and continue up to the M.F. belay. (90 feet) 5.10

Pitch 2: Diagonal up right to a notch in the ceiling, climb through the ceiling, and continue up the face to the GT Ledge. (90 feet) 5.10

Pitch 3: Finish on a nearby climb.

FA 1973: Jim Kolocotronis and Herb Laeger

167. M.F. 5.9 PG ★★★

Start: Below a thin crack that is below a large but short left-facing corner, 40 feet right of Birdie Party.

Pitch 1: Follow the crack to a small ledge 20 feet up, move left and up, and then step back right to a crack in a bulge. Continue up to the overhanging left-facing corner and swing around right onto the face. Then climb up past a bulge to a belay ledge. (90 feet) 5.9 PG

Pitch 2: Traverse right past a corner, climb up through an overhang, and step right. Continue up the steep face above until it is possible to traverse off left to a ledge at the base of a loose right-facing corner. (80 feet) 5.9

Pitch 3: Climb the corner and face to a ledge, and scramble to the top. (50 feet)

A great climb—a classic.

FA 1960: Jim McCarthy, Roman Sadowy, and Claude Suhl

168. WATER KING 5.10+ R

Start: On the face midway between M.F. and Men at Arms.

Pitch 1: Climb the face between M.F. and Men at Arms to the notch in the ceiling. Clear the ceiling, continue up the face past an overhang, and join Men at Arms. (70 feet)

FA 1981: John Meyers and Mike Freeman

169. MEN AT ARMS 5.9 PG ★

Start: Same as Try Again.

Pitch 1: Follow Try Again to the ledge above the corner, and then climb up and left, following some fractures until they end.

THE TRAPPS

(V1) Traverse right and move up to the Try Again stance. Then traverse back left about 15 feet to a small ledge above the overhang. (100 feet) 5.9

Pitch 2: Climb straight up past a vertical seam and steep face to a small ledge. Then continue up past the left side of some overhangs to the GT Ledge. (100 feet) 5.9

Pitch 3: Continue up the face past the left side of another overhang to the top. (50 feet)

Variation 1: 5.10 PG Climb straight up to the small ledge above the overhang and rejoin the regular route.

Williams was being shot at with Chinese rockets by Art Gran when the first pitch was being led.

FA 1966: Jim McCarthy and Dick Williams
FA (Variation 1) 1970s: Henry Barber

170. TRY AGAIN 5.10 PG ★★

Start: On the face below a left-facing corner that begins 15 feet above the ground, 35 feet right of M.F.

Pitch 1: Climb the face and corner to a ledge on the right. Continue up the face past a short right-facing corner to a stance at the base of another but smaller right-facing corner. Work up this corner, clear the overhang, and move right and up on the steep face above to a ledge. (100 feet) 5.10 PG

Pitch 2: Rappel or continue up two inside corners to the GT Ledge. (80 feet)

Pitch 3: Finish on a nearby climb.

If you don't succeed the first time....

FA 1955: Jim McCarthy and Hans Kraus
FFA 1967: Richard Goldstone, Jim McCarthy, and Raymond Schrag

171. FLY AGAIN 5.11+ PG

Start: At a broken left-facing corner, 10 feet right of Try Again.

Pitch 1: Climb the corner and continue up the bulging face to a ledge. Walk right a few feet to a thin vertical seam, and work up this and the bulging face to a vertical fracture in the overhang. Then climb past the overhang to the Coexistence belay. (100 feet) 5.11+ PG

Pitch 2: Rappel or finish on a nearby climb.
Height-related—easier if taller.
FA (Toprope) 1983: Kevin Bein
FA (Lead) 1983: Russ Clune and Mike Law

172. COEXISTENCE   5.10+   PG   ★★★
Start: At a large tree stump below the left end of a small overhang that is 10 feet above the ground and about 20 feet right of Try Again.
Pitch 1: Climb straight up past overhang to a ledge. Move right to a thin crack and follow it to a short right-facing corner. Then move up, hand traverse left a bit, and continue up past an overhang and a bulge to a ledge.   (100 feet)   5.10+   PG
Pitch 2: Rappel, or continue up some corners and the face to the GT Ledge.   (90 feet)   5.5
Pitch 3: Climb easy rock to the top.   (40 feet)
FA 1962: Jim McCarthy, Phil Jacobus, John Hudson, and Peter Armour
FFA 1967: Richard Goldstone and Jim McCarthy

173. STAR ACTION   5.10   PG   ★★
Start: At the first broken 10-foot-high left-facing corner to the right of Coexistence.
Pitch 1: Climb the corner and a vertical fault or seam, move left, and work up to a ledge. Continue up past a tiny left-facing corner, climb through the overhangs above, and move left to a right-facing corner. Follow the corner to an overhang, step left, and move up to a stance. Then traverse left to the Coexistence belay.   (100 feet)   5.10   PG
Pitch 2: Rappel or climb a very small left-facing corner above the right side of the ledge. Continue up the face (following a thin crack), go past an overhang, and work up the right-facing Overhanging Layback corner to the GT Ledge.   (100 feet)
Pitch 3: Move right about 10 feet to a left-facing corner beyond the ceiling and continue to the top.   (50 feet)
FA 1974: Bob Richardson, Dick Saum, and Ivan Rezucha

174. DON'T SHIFT   5.11+   (Toprope)
Start: On the face just left of Graveyard Shift.

Pitch 1: Climb the face just left of the Graveyard Shift crack, move up and right (crossing Graveyard), and continue up (where Graveyard moves left) to join Tough Shift (at its 5.8 move). Then continue straight up through the overhang above.

FA (Toprope) 1986: Kevin Bein

175. GRAVEYARD SHIFT   5.10+   PG–R   ★★★
Start: On the face below a very thin black crack, about 4 feet right of Star Action.

Pitch 1: Climb straight up to the crack and continue up the steep face to the right of the crack until the crack ends. Then move left and work up to easier rock. Continue up to an overhang and a left-facing corner, move left, and climb up to another overhang. Go past this overhang and diagonal up right past a third overhang. Then traverse off right to Overhanging Layback and rappel.   (130 feet)

FA 1978: Russ Raffa and Rich Ross

176. TOUGH SHIFT   5.10   R   ★★
Start: At a thin crack, 12 feet right of Star Action and 22 feet left of Overhanging Layback.

Pitch 1: Follow the crack to a ledge on the right. Continue up a small right-facing corner past steep orange rock to an overhang. Traverse left around the corner and onto the face, and move up to a stance. Climb up and left to a fault in the overhang, clear the overhang, and continue up the face about 10 feet. Then traverse right to Overhanging Layback and rappel.   (130 feet)

FA 1961: Jim McCarthy and Ants Leemets

177. OVERHANGING LAYBACK   5.7   PG
Start: At a right-facing corner with a flake at its top that forms an overhang, 22 feet right of Tough Shift.

Pitch 1: Climb the corner and chimney to the flake, move out right a few feet (V1), and diagonal up left to a belay stance in the right-facing corner above.   (80 feet)   5.7   PG

Pitch 2: Continue up the corner until good holds lead out left around the outside corner onto the face. Follow a smaller right-facing corner up and left, and then angle back up right until below an overhang. Traverse around the overhang on the right and continue up to the GT Ledge. (150 feet) 5.5

Pitch 3: Take the easiest route up the short cliff band above to the top. (40 feet)

Variation 1: Continue right, underclinging to the right edge of the flake, and then diagonal up left to rejoin the regular route.

FA 1946: Fritz Wiessner and Bill Shockley

178. NO EXISTENCE   5.9   R–X

Start: At a triangular block that is 4 feet above the ground, 15 feet right of Overhanging Layback.

Pitch 1: Climb up the face and then diagonal up left to a stance in the Overhanging Layback corner. (80 feet) 5.8 R

Pitch 2: Continue up left to a large right-facing corner. Follow the corner, clear the overhang above at a notch, and continue up to the GT Ledge. (120 feet) 5.9 R–X

Pitch 3: Continue basically straight up to the top. (40 feet)

FA 1964: Jim McCarthy and Sam Streibert

179. SCENE OF THE CLIMB   5.11–   PG   ★★★

Start: Below a small overhang, just left of Land's End.

Pitch 1: Climb up to the overhang and traverse left to a vertical seam, which is often wet. Continue up past the seam and a bulge to easier rock that leads to a point about 15 feet below the right side of an overhang. Diagonal up left and pass the overhang. Then, either traverse off left to Overhanging Layback and rappel (as most parties do), or continue up the face to a belay stance. (120 feet) 5.11– PG

Pitch 2: Climb up to the overhangs above, traverse left, and then diagonal up right through the overhangs to the GT Ledge. (80 feet) 5.10

Pitch 3: Finish on the last pitch of No Existence.

FA 1976: Kevin Bein and Ron Sacks

180. LAND'S END 5.9− PG

Start: On a smooth greenish face below some yellow overhangs that are about 20 feet above the ground, 40 feet right of Overhanging Layback.

Pitch 1: Climb the face to an overhanging right-facing corner, and continue up past a right-facing flake and a smaller overhang to a small stance. Traverse right to a ramp that goes up right (this can be very exciting for the second) and follow it to about the halfway point. Then move up, diagonal up right to a stance, and continue up to a belay. (80 feet) 5.9− PG

Pitch 2: Rappel or continue up past a right-facing corner (V1) to an overhang with a crack. Climb the overhang and follow an arching right-facing corner to the GT Ledge. (90 feet)

Pitch 3: Continue to the top. (40 feet)

Variation 1: From the right-facing corner, traverse out left and continue up easy rock to the GT Ledge.

FA 1960: Art Gran and Jim McCarthy

181. THE JANE FONDA WORKOUT FOR PREGNANT WOMEN 5.12 (Toprope)

Start: Below the overhang 10 feet right of Land's End.

Pitch 1: Climb the overhang.

FA (Toprope) 1985: Russ Clune

182. ORGANIC IRON 5.12+ R

Start: At a large, flaky, broken left-facing corner, 48 feet right of Land's End.

Pitch 1: Follow the corner (or climb the crack and flakes 10 feet farther right) to the tiered ceiling. Clear the ceiling and reach easier rock. Then diagonal up right to the Impenetrable Ceilings belay. (80 feet) 5.12+ R

Pitch 2: Rappel or climb up to a right-facing corner and exit left. Work up past an overhang and then continue up the face above to the GT Ledge. (60 feet)

Pitch 3: Continue to the top. (40 feet)

FA 1982: Ivan Rezucha

FFA 1984: Lynn Hill and Russ Raffa

183. IMPENETRABLE CEILINGS 5.11 PG

Start: On a block-covered ledge just left of a left-facing corner, 25 feet right of Organic Iron and 30 feet left of Dry Martini.

Pitch 1: Follow the corner to a ledge and move left to a crack that leads to a double-tiered ceiling. Climb through the ceiling past some flakes and a small notch, and then continue up the face to a belay. (80 feet) 5.11 PG

Pitch 2: Continue up to join Scotch on the Rocks near the ceiling. (60 feet)

Height-related—harder for shorter climbers.

FA 1978: Ivan and Paul Rezucha

184. SCOTCH ON THE ROCKS 5.10+ PG

Start: Same as Dry Martini.

Pitch 1: Follow the large left-facing corner to an overhang, where a thin crack at the lip goes diagonally up left. Climb past the overhang and continue straight up past more overhangs to the face above. Then traverse left to broken rock and follow a right-facing corner to a ledge. (100 feet) 5.10+ PG

Pitch 2: Climb up left to a ceiling with a crack that goes diagonally up left. Follow the crack system to the GT Ledge. (60 feet)

Pitch 3: Continue to the top. (40 feet)

Watch out for loose rock.

FA 1974: Ivan Rezucha and Paul Potters

185. DRY MARTINI 5.7 PG

Start: Below a large left-facing corner capped by a ceiling, 30 feet right of Impenetrable Ceilings and just right of some large orange blocks that lean against the face.

Pitch 1: Climb up to the corner (V1), go out right around the outside corner, and traverse right about 40 feet until below a ledge in a right-facing corner. Then climb up to the ledge and belay. (This ledge can also be reached from directly below—5.6.) (80 feet) 5.6

Pitch 2: Go left around the outside corner, climb up past a bulge with an old bolt, and then diagonal up right past a corner to a ledge. (90 feet) 5.7 PG

Pitch 3: Step back left and work up to a V-shaped chimney-trough, which is followed to its top. Then climb the corner above until it is easy to step out left and continue up to the GT Ledge. (120 feet)

Pitch 4: Climb easily up the face to the top. (40 feet)

Variation 1: Climb up and right around the overhanging outside corner, traverse right to the bulge with the old bolt, and rejoin the regular route.

FA 1955: Hans Kraus, Bonnie Prudden, and Lucien Warner

186. TEQUILA MOCKINGBIRD 5.7+ PG

Start: On top of a block, 20 feet right of Dry Martini.

Pitch 1: Climb orange-white rock to a ledge below an overhang, clear the overhang, and diagonal up right and then back left to the first Dry Martini belay. (This was an old variation to Dry Martini.) (50 feet) 5.6 G

Pitch 2: Follow the large right-leaning, right-facing corner above to a ceiling, exit left, and climb up to the Dry Martini belay. 5.6 G

Pitch 3: Follow Dry Martini for about 15 feet and then diagonal right to a loose, blocky right-facing corner which is followed to the GT Ledge. 5.7+ PG

Pitch 4: Finish on Dry Martini.

FA 1975: Rich Perch and Ivan Rezucha

187. P.T. PHONE HOME 5.10+ PG

Start: Below a crack that begins at an overhang 30 feet above the ground and which is below a short right-facing corner capped by another overhang, 65 feet right of Dry Martini and 20 feet left of Co-Op.

Pitch 1: Climb up the face past the overhang and the corner to a ledge. Diagonal up right to a short left-facing corner. Then step right around the corner, traverse right until it is possible to clear the bulging overhang, and continue up the face to a ledge. (V1) (100 feet) 5.10+ PG

Pitch 2: Climb the steep face above to an overhang. Clear the overhang at a short right-facing corner, traverse a little left, and continue to the top. (80 feet) 5.8

Variation 1: Tits Like Orange Fireballs 5.11 PG Continue up past the ceiling at a fixed piton and up the face.

FA 1981: Russ Raffa, Russ Clune, Pete Thexton, and Jeff Gruenberg

FA (Variation 1) 1988: Jeff Morris and Jim Damon

188. CO-OP 5.9 − PG

Start: Below the left side of a block that is sitting on a ledge 10 feet above the ground, 85 feet right of Dry Martini and 40 feet left of Welcome to the Gunks.

Pitch 1: Climb up past the block and the bulge above to an overhang (V1). Traverse left about 20 feet and continue up past another bulge to a long, narrow ledge. Then traverse right about 30 feet and belay. (100 feet) 5.6

Pitch 2: Climb up the face past an overhang to easier rock and a belay ledge (some parties continue up and right to a pine tree and rappel). (50 feet) 5.9 − PG

Pitch 3: Climb up, diagonal up left a few feet, and continue up to an overhang. Then work up right to a right-facing corner and follow it to the top. (100 feet)

Variation 1: 5.10 − PG Climb through the overhang and rejoin the regular route.

FA 1954: Jim McCarthy and Dave Bernays
FFA 1960s: Art Gran

189. FALL TO GRACE 5.11 PG

Start: Below a 4-foot-high right-facing corner that begins on a moss covered ledge 8 feet above the ground, 15 feet left of Welcome to the Gunks.

From the corner, climb straight up past buldging rock at some small right facing flakes to meet an incipient crack (white) that breaks 2 small tiered overhangs. Step right to a larger left facing flake then work your way past the buldging, pinkish rock to some right facing flakes beneath the overhang. Clear this overhang, following a broken crack to a jutty flake and the next overhang. Step left, move up and back right then climb past two overhangs

(about 5 ft. left of Co-op) and face above to easier rock. Diagonal up right to a ledge and pine tree belay and rappel station.
  FA 1990: Dick Williams and Tom Spiegler

190. WELCOME TO THE GUNKS   5.10   PG–R   ★★★
  Start: Below an overhang, 30 feet right of Co-Op.
  Pitch 1: Work up the face past two horizontal fractures to the overhang. Move left a few feet to an obvious fault and climb past the overhang to a small ledge. Continue up bulging orange rock past another overhang (watch out for a loose block). Then continue up the face past a short left-facing corner and more overhangs to a belay at a tree.   (140 feet)   5.10   PG–R
  Pitch 2: Rappel or continue up to the GT Ledge.   (70 feet)
  Pitch 3: Continue to the top.   (40 feet)
  One good move after another—a fine climb.
  FA 1973: Jim Kolocotronis and Andy Cairns

191. LAUGHING MAN   5.11   PG
  Start: Same as Welcome to the Gunks.
  Pitch 1: Climb up the face to some flakes under the ceiling. Hand traverse right until it is possible to surmount the ceiling. Continue up the face above to a left-facing corner broken by a triangular overhang. Climb to the top of the corner and diagonal up right to a right-facing corner. Then go past an overhang and continue up to the first Credibility Gap belay.   (80 feet)   5.11   PG
  Pitch 2: Rappel or follow a ramplike right-facing corner up left past an overhang and a fault system to the large Credibility Gap ledge with the tree.
  Pitch 3: Rappel or follow Credibility Gap to the top.
  FA 1970s: Rick Pleiss and friend

192. TREE'S A CROWD   5.9   G
  Start: At some broken orange and white blocks on a ledge just above the ground, 20 feet downhill to the left of the Asphodel corner.
  Pitch 1: Climb up to a short, wide corner and follow this until it is possible to hand traverse left to a tree. Using the tree to get onto

the face, climb up and right to an overhang, and go past this to a right-facing corner. Then continue up to the Credibility Gap belay. (50 feet) 5.9 G

Pitch 2: Rappel or finish on Credibility Gap.

FA 1980: Ivan Rezucha and Don Hamilton

193. CREDIBILITY GAP 5.6 PG

Start: At the left-hand of two cracks on the left face of the Asphodel corner.

Pitch 1: Climb the crack to its top, diagonal up left to a ramplike right-facing corner, and belay below a large overhang. (80 feet) 5.6

Pitch 2: Diagonal up right and clear the overhang on the left. Work up the face to a large ledge with a tree (some parties rappel from here) and then continue up to the GT Ledge. (90 feet) 5.6

Pitch 3: Continue to the top.

FA 1968: Jim McCarthy, Joe Kelsey, and Dick Williams

194. ASPHODEL 5.5 G

Start: At a huge yellow right-facing corner, 100 feet right of Co-Op.

Pitch 1: Follow the corner to its top and diagonal up left across dirty, gritty rock to a ledge with a tree. (90 feet) 5.5 G

Pitch 2: Climb up left, diagonal back up right, and continue up to the GT Ledge. (100 feet) 5.4

Pitch 3: Continue to the top.

FA 1953: Hans Kraus and Bonnie Prudden

195. BEATLE BROW BULGE 5.9+ PG

Start: At the highest point of some boulders, on a grey face with grassy ledges 20 feet above, 70 feet right of Asphodel.

Pitch 1: Climb up past the grassy ledges to a broken right-facing corner, which is followed to a ledge below an overhang. (50 feet) 5.7 R–X

Pitch 2: Climb the overhang and continue up to a left-facing corner that leads to a ledge. (60 feet) 5.9+ PG

THE TRAPPS

Pitch 3: Step right and climb the face to the GT Ledge. (80 feet)

Pitch 4: Continue up to a left-facing corner with an overhang and follow the corner to the top. (50 feet)

FA 1966: Jim McCarthy, Matt Hale, and Jim Alt

FFA 1973: John Stannard and Henry Barber

196. BLUEBERRY WINE 5.10+ R

Start: On the face 22 feet right of Beatle Brow Bulge and 15 feet left of Blueberry Ledges.

Pitch 1: Climb up the face to a ramp, follow the ramp up left to its top, and continue up to a tree and obvious ceiling. Clear the ceiling on the right, climb up past the next overhang, and continue up the face to a ledge. (80 feet) 5.10+ R

Pitch 2: Rappel or finish on a nearby climb.

FA 1970s: John Stannard

197. BLUEBERRY LEDGES 5.5− G

Start: At a clump of trees, 27 feet right of Beatle Brow Bulge and 10 feet left of a block that forms a left-facing corner.

Pitch 1: Climb up to a ceiling, traverse right, and continue up to a short left-facing corner. Climb the corner, move around right, and work up to a ledge. Then go left 20 feet to a belay. (120 feet) 5.5− G

Pitch 2: From the left end of the ledge, climb a corner, go up and left to another corner, and then continue up to the GT Ledge. (70 feet) 5.2

Pitch 3: Finish up the right-facing corner off to the left. (70 feet) 5.2

FA 1958: Willie Crowther and Gardiner Perry

198. SELDOM MUSTARD, NEVER RELISH 5.10 G

Start: Same as Blueberry Ledges. Scramble up right to a large ledge that is about 20 feet below a left-facing corner, 26 feet left of Beginner's Delight.

Pitch 1: Climb the face and the corner to a ledge just left of some grass and trees. Continue past bulging, overhanging rock to the face above, and climb up and left (avoiding Beginner's Delight) to the GT Ledge. (140 feet)

Pitch 2: Start 10 feet left of the prominent left-facing corner. Climb up the face and continue past a ceiling to the top. (60 feet) 5.10 G

FA 1979: Steve and Cory Jones

199. BEGINNER'S DELIGHT 5.3 PG ★★★

Start: At the base of some dirty ramps that lead up right to a large ledge, 25 feet right of Blueberry Ledges.

Pitch 1: Scramble up right to a tree on the ledge or (nicer) climb straight up to the tree from the short inside corners directly below. Then, either follow the corner directly above to a belay ledge, or step out right around the corner and climb a series of left-facing corners to the belay. (30 feet) 5.2

Pitch 2: Follow the main corner for about 40 feet and traverse left across the face to the second small corner (or follow the main corner to its top and then traverse left—slightly harder). Climb up to some ledges that lead back right (or continue 5 feet farther left to a third corner and climb up to the ledges). Work up the ledges and traverse left to a right-facing corner (some parties belay here). Then continue up to the GT Ledge (loose rock) below a ceiling, step left, and belay in some boulders. (120 feet) 5.3

Pitch 3: Climb the white left-facing corner above, going right to pass the overhang. Continue up to a right-facing corner, move left at its top to avoid the overhang, and then continue straight up to the top. (70 feet) 5.3

FA 1948: Hans Kraus and Roger and Del Wolcott

200. OCTOBERFEST 5.9− R−X

Start: Below a hand and finger crack that begins 10 feet above the ground, 10 feet right of the alternate start to Beginner's Delight and 40 feet left of Snooky's Return.

Pitch 1: Climb the crack system to a ledge (V1), diagonal up right 15 feet to a broken left-facing corner, and follow the corner to another ledge. 5.7

Pitch 2: Climb up left and follow a left-facing corner (just right

THE TRAPPS

of the huge Beginner's Delight corner) to the GT Ledge. 5.9− R−X

Pitch 3: Climb the right face of the large corner above and hand traverse out right. Then climb past an overhang to the left of Minty Overhang and continue up the face to the top. (40 feet)

Variation 1: Continue up the face past a short left-facing corner and rejoin the regular route.

FA 1979: Alan Long, Al Rubin, and Paul Ledoux

201. SNOOKY'S RETURN 5.8 PG ★★

Start: At a very thin crack with a tiny overhang 10 feet up, 45 feet right of the Beginner's Delight corner.

Pitch 1: (V1) Climb the crack and the face above to a ledge. (100 feet) 5.8

Pitch 2: Climb a left-facing corner to the overhang. Traverse left 10 feet, work up a steep face, and step right. Then continue up and left along a groove to the GT Ledge. (80 feet) 5.8

Pitch 3: Walk left to a large left-facing corner. Climb the face to an overhang, exit right, and continue to the top. (50 feet) 5.7

Variation 1: 5.7+ R Climb the face to the right, past a small, short right-facing corner, and join the regular route.

FA 1958: Jim McCarthy and Dave Craft

202. FRIENDS AND LOVERS 5.9 PG

Start: On the face below a small right-facing corner, 20 feet right of Snooky's Return and 5 feet left of a hairline crack that rises to a small overhang 25 feet above the ground.

Pitch 1: Climb the face past the corner to the overhang, move right, and continue up the steep face past some flakes and a white overhang to a ledge. (110 feet) 5.9 PG

Pitch 2: Walk left 30 feet to the start of the second pitch of Beginner's Delight.

Pitch 3: Follow the Beginner's Delight corner for about 30 feet, move out right onto the face, and continue up to the GT Ledge. (70 feet) 5.6

Pitch 4: Climb the large left-facing corner above, go past an overhang, and continue up the face to the top. (70 feet) 5.6

FA 1978: Ron Sacks, Anne Dubats, Mike Sawicky, and Rick Cronk

203. MINTY 5.3 G ★★
Start: Below a small 20-foot-high right-facing corner and above a large block leaning against the face at a ledge, 55 feet right of Snooky's Return.
Pitch 1: Climb the corner and walk left about 15 feet. Then work up the face and a right-facing corner past a pine tree, and continue up to a ledge below another right-facing corner. (50 feet) 5.3
Pitch 2: Climb the outside edge of the corner, and continue up the face and a crack to a ledge with a pine tree below a chimney. Go up the chimney, move left, and continue up to the GT Ledge. (130 feet) 5.3
Pitch 3: (V1) Follow the left-facing corner on the right to an overhang, exit right, and continue up and left to the top. (50 feet) 5.2
Variation 1: Minty Overhang 5.5 PG Climb through the double overhang 20 feet left of the corner and continue up the face to the top.
FA 1941: Fritz Wiessner, Minty Warren, and Betty Woolsey

204. BAG'S END 5.8+ PG
Start: On the face about midway between Minty and Tipsy Trees.
Pitch 1: Climb the face past a small overhang and tree, and continue up to a pine tree growing horizontally out from the cliff. (80 feet) 5.8+ PG
Pitch 2: Continue up the face past an overhang to a blocky overhang. Go past this overhang to a short left-facing corner and then work up past more overhangs to the GT Ledge. (80 feet)
Pitch 3: Climb out on the right side of the overhang above and continue up the face past another overhang to the top. (40 feet)
FA 1982: Ivan Rezucha and Annie O'Neill

205. TIPSY TREES 5.3 G
Start: At the base of a left-facing pile of blocks, 20 feet right of Minty.

THE TRAPPS

Pitch 1: Climb broken rock and the easy face to a ledge with a pine tree, and belay on the left side of the ledge. (90 feet) 5.3

Pitch 2: Move left to a long, blocky inside corner and follow it to its top. Then move right, work back up left, and continue up to a good ledge. (130 feet) 5.3

Pitch 3: Step right, climb up the face, and follow the prominent corner to its top. Then go out right and finish up the face above. (50 feet) 5.3

FA 1958: Gardiner and Mary Perry

206. THE WOMB STEP 5.7 PG

Start: At a crack that is 3–5 inches wide and 20 feet long, 30 feet right of Tipsy Trees.

Pitch 1: Climb the crack past lower-angle rock and trees to a ledge below a right-facing corner. (70 feet)

Pitch 2: Climb to the top of the corner and then make a long traverse (V1) diagonally up left to join Tipsy Trees. (140 feet) 5.7 PG

Variation 1: Womb for Went 5.9 PG About midway along the traverse, belay below an orange overhang. Climb past the overhang and continue up a right-facing corner to its top. Then diagonal up right to a fault in the ceiling, climb through the ceiling, and continue up the steep face above, past some final overhangs, to the top. (150 feet)

FA 1954: Jim McCarthy and Bob Larson
FA (Variation 1): 1970s

207. CHIMANGO 5.9+ PG

Start: On the face midway between The Womb Step and Hawk.

Pitch 1: Climb the face and low-angle rock to the first Hawk belay ledge (at the base of a large right-facing corner). (70 feet) 5.3

Pitch 2: Climb to the top of the corner, exit right, and diagonal up left to an overhang. Climb the overhang at the fault, and continue up and slightly left to another overhang. Clear this overhang and work up the face to the GT Ledge. (80 feet) 5.9

Pitch 3: Climb the ceiling above the tree and continue to the top. (60 feet) 5.9+ PG

FA 1980: Ivan Rezucha and Bill Ravitch

208. HAWK 5.4+ PG ★

Start: At a thin crack tht leads to a ledge on a low-angle face, 55 feet right of Tipsy Trees.

Pitch 1: Follow the crack up the broken face to a large ledge below a large left-facing corner. (80 feet) 5.3

Pitch 2: Go up the corner until it is possible to move out around it to the right. Angle up and right to a second corner, move up and right around this one, and then continue up and right once again to a small ledge. (75 feet) 5.4+ PG

Pitch 3: Climb up to a large ledge and follow the large white left-facing corner above to its top. Then step right onto the face and continue to the top. (70 feet) 5.4

FA 1958: Willie Crowther and Gardiner and Mary Perry

209. PEREGRINE 5.8 PG

Start: On the face 25 feet right of Hawk.

Pitch 1: Climb up the face past a grassy ledge and a small left-facing corner. Then continue past a tree to a belay below the second left-facing corner of Hawk. (80 feet)

Pitch 2: Continue up the face past an overhang to the corner and exit right just above the point where Hawk goes right. Then climb up to a left-facing corner, which is followed past an overhang to the GT Ledge. (80 feet)

Pitch 3: Climb the crack to the right of the tree and continue to the top. (50 feet)

FA 1980: Ivan Rezucha and Bill Ravitch

210. REACH OF FAITH 5.10− PG

Start: Same as Southern Pillar.

Pitch 1: Climb up the face to a belay ledge between Hawk and Southern Pillar. (70 feet)

Pitch 2: Wander up the face, moving right and then back left, and climb up through an overhang at a break. Continue up the

THE TRAPPS

face to the GT Ledge, walk right about 20 feet, and belay below a corner and an overhang. (100 feet)

Pitch 3: Walk back left 20 feet, climb up past an overhang to a diagonal flake (V1), and continue up through a large overhang to the top. (40 feet)

Variation 1: 5.10− Traverse left, climb up into an overhanging left-facing corner, and continue to the top.

FA 1980: Ivan Rezucha

211. SOUTHERN PILLAR 5.2 G ★

Start: At a small 20-foot-high left-facing corner formed by a flake and some blocks, 52 feet right of Hawk. High above it on the right is a large left-facing corner.

Pitch 1: Climb the corner to a ledge on the right. Walk right across the ledge to a short step that leads to a good ledge at the base of the main corner. (60 feet) 5.2

Pitch 2: Either climb about 20 feet up the main corner and traverse out left about 30 feet, or traverse left 30 feet and then climb 20 feet up the face at a thin crack. Continue up a small black corner to a larger, grungy left-facing corner. Traverse out right around this corner and then follow a small groove up to a ledge at the base of a huge block. (90 feet) 5.2

Pitch 3: Climb up the outside of the block (or work up behind it) to its top. (V1) Then follow the small corner and chimney above to a ledge (V2), and walk out right and belay. (60 feet) 5.2

Pitch 4: Scramble easily to the top.

Variation 1: Continue up the right face of the main corner all the way to the top.

Variation 2: 5.7 Climb straight up the corner above, past a large overhang, to the top.

FA 1941: Hans Kraus and Roger and Del Wolcott

212. COLUMBIA 5.9− G

Start: At a diagonal crack, 15 feet right of Southern Pillar.

Pitch 1: Climb up the crack and the face past a bulge to a ledge with a block. (50 feet) 5.8

Pitch 2: Climb straight up the face above the block to a pink and white left-facing corner. Follow the corner until it leans back and belay in a depression on the right face. (80 feet) 5.9– G

Pitch 3: (V1) Climb the right face of the inside corner to the GT Ledge. (60 feet)

Pitch 4: Finish on Southern Pillar.

Variation 1: 5.10 PG Diagonal up right to a small triangular overhang, climb over the point of the overhang, and continue up to the GT Ledge.

If you want something a lot more challenging than Harvard, go to Columbia.

FA 1969: Roy Kligfield, Dave Ingalls, and Jim Driscoll
FFA 1969: Joe Kelsey
FA (Variation 1): 1970s

213. MADAME GRUNNEBAUM'S WULST   5.6   G   ★★★

Start: On top of some boulders, 45 feet right of Southern Pillar.

Pitch 1: Climb the face to a tiny ledge, traverse left about 15 feet, and move up left to a tree at a short left-facing corner. (70 feet) 5.4

Pitch 2: Climb up and right to a prominent yellow dihedral and follow it to its top. Traverse right about 10 feet (V1), diagonal up left to an overhang, and then move back right to a belay stance. (70 feet) 5.6 G

Pitch 3: Continue up steep rock past a bulge with a crack and traverse left to a nose. Climb the nose to the base of a 2-inch crack. Then, either continue up past the crack to the top, or traverse 25 feet right to a left-facing corner and follow the corner to the top. (70 feet) 5.6 G

Variation 1: 5.4 Climb directly up to the belay stance.

FA 1943: Hans Kraus and Harry Snyder

214. MADAME GRUNNEBAUM'S SORROW   5.8–   PG

Start: Same as Madame Grunnebaum's Wulst.

Pitch 1: Climb the first pitch of Madame Grunnebaum's Wulst.

Pitch 2: Follow Madame Grunnebaum's Wulst to the top of the yellow corner. Traverse right and up across the face to its right edge. Then step around the corner to the second Northern Pillar belay ledge. (90 feet) 5.6

FRITZ WIESSNER atop MADAME GRUNNEBAUM'S WULST
Dick Williams

Pitch 3: Climb up about 10 feet, traverse left on steep, loose rock above the overhangs at the top of Le Teton, and continue up to the top. (50 feet) 5.8– PG
FA (Toprope) 1958: Jim McCarthy
FA (Lead) 1958: Jim McCarthy and a belayer

215. LE TETON 5.9 G ★★
Start: At a gully just left of Northern Pillar, directly below a large right-facing corner at the top of the cliff.
Pitch 1: Scramble up the gully to a shallow cave at the base of a broken, overhanging corner. (80 feet)
Pitch 2: Climb the corner and the face on the left to a stance at the base of a white wall split by an inch-wide crack, which is just left of the second Northern Pillar belay ledge. (50 feet) 5.7
Pitch 3: Step out left and climb the crack to its top. Then traverse left around the corner to a small belay spot. (40 feet) 5.9 G
Pitch 4: Follow the steep nose above to the GT Ledge and then scramble to the top. (50 feet) 5.7
Don't bother with the first two pitches; instead, follow Northern Pillar to the ledge below the belay at the end of its second pitch.
FA 1955: Jim McCarthy and Stan Gross
FFA 1965: Art Gran and Lito Tejada-Flores

216. NORTHERN PILLAR 5.2 G ★★
Start: At the left edge of a grey face and directly below a large right-facing corner at the top of the cliff, 100 feet right of Southern Pillar.
Pitch 1: (V1) Climb up the face for about 35 feet to good holds that lead right. Traverse right about 25 feet until just before a small tree and then continue up to a ledge. (80 feet) 5.1
Pitch 2: Follow a groove for about 30 feet to its top. Step left to a steep 10-foot-high step. Climb this and the one above it, and continue up to a tree on a good-sized ledge. Then traverse left to a broken corner and work up to a fine belay at the base of the large right-facing corner. (100 feet) 5.1
Pitch 3: (V2) Follow the corner to the GT Ledge, and scramble left and up to the top. (50 feet) 5.2 G

THE TRAPPS

Variation 1: Finger Locks or Cedar Box 5.5 G Start at a finger crack 15 feet left of Hyjek's Horror. Climb the crack past a bulge and a tree, and continue up the face to the ledge with the tree on the regular route.

Variation 2: Cemetery Wall 5.8 PG Climb the crack on the left wall of the corner.

FA 1941: Hans Kraus and Susanne Simon
FA (Variation 2) 1958: Art Gran

217. HYJEK'S HORROR   5.8−   PG   ★

Start: On a smooth face below a thin, almost vertical seam that begins 10 feet above the ground and leads to a small overhang, 65 feet right of the Le Teton gully and 15 feet past the Finger Locks or Cedar Box crack.

Pitch 1: Climb the face and seam to the overhang, step left, and continue directly up the smooth face to a ledge.   (60 feet)   5.8− PG

Pitch 2: Climb straight up to a ledge with a tree. Continue up and right through some overhangs to ledges and easier rock that lead to the top.   (140 feet)   5.4

FA 1963: Mike Hyjek and John Lomont

218. TWIN OAKS   5.3   PG

Start: At a rounded nose directly below a wide crack that slants up left, 20 feet right of Hyjek's Horror.

Pitch 1: Climb up to the crack and follow it to a ledge with a tree.   (50 feet)   5.3

Pitch 2: Climb the short face above at a broken section, and then work up and left to a belay ledge.   (80 feet)   5.3

Pitch 3: Move up and left over bulging rock to some loose flakes that form a left-facing corner below an overhang. Then climb up and right over the flakes (avoiding the overhang) to the top.   (70 feet)   5.3

FA 1957: Gardiner and Mary Perry

219. TRIPLE BULGES   5.5   PG

Start: Same as Twin Oaks.

Pitch 1: Climb the first pitch of Twin Oaks.

Pitch 2: Climb the second pitch of Twin Oaks and belay at the second ledge above the broken section. (90 feet) 5.3

Pitch 3: Work up past a bulge to a small overhang. Climb over the overhang near its left end and diagonal up right to a large overhang just below the top. Go directly over this overhang and scramble to the top. (130 feet) 5.5 PG

FA 1959: John Lomont and Francis Coffin

220. DELUSIONS OF GRANDEUR 5.9+ PG
Start: On the face below a ceiling, 10 feet right of Twin Oaks.

Pitch 1: Climb up to the ceiling, clear it, and continue up the face to a ledge with a tree (same belay as Triple Bulges and Willie's Weep). (50 feet) 5.9+ PG

Pitch 2: Traverse left 20 feet (crossing Twin Oaks and Triple Bulges) to a left-facing corner. (20 feet)

Pitch 3: Climb up the corner (crossing Twin Oaks) and continue up the face to the top.

FA 1983: Chris Monz and Mike Sawicky

221. WILLIE'S WEEP 5.2 G
Start: At the right edge of some boulders, 40 feet right of Twin Oaks and 15 feet right of a large broken right-facing corner.

Pitch 1: Climb up the face until good holds lead left to the corner and the first Twin Oaks-Triple Bulges belay ledge. (80 feet)

Pitch 2: Diagonal up right to a small left-facing corner, and then continue up and slightly right to the GT Ledge. (70 feet)

Pitch 3: Follow the right-facing corner above to some ledges, go over a small overhang, and continue up a short face to the top. (80 feet)

FA 1953: George and Herbert Evans, and Robert Graef

222. DON'T SHOOT 5.6 G
Start: On the face just left of a right-facing corner, 15 feet right of Willie's Weep.

Pitch 1: Climb the face, moving slightly right to a bushy left-facing corner that begins about 25 feet above the ground. Follow

THE TRAPPS

the obvious crack to its top and then step left 5 feet to a small pine tree 10 feet below an overhang. (90 feet)

Pitch 2: Climb the face above the pine tree until just beneath the overhang. Traverse left a few feet to a bush in a very small right-facing corner. Go over the overhang at this point and then walk left along a ledge to another pine tree (same belay as Willie's Weep). (40 feet)

Pitch 3: Climb the flakes in the shallow inside corner above and continue to the top. (110 feet)

The first ascent party called this climb an unpleasant, unaesthetic, dull, and cowardly route—see if you agree!

FA 1965: Dave Ingalls and Vin Hoeman

223. LAT-ON THE SEASON 5.7 PG

Start: On the slimy low-angle face 15 feet right of Don't Shoot, directly below the right edge of an overhang 10 feet off the ground.

Pitch 1: Climb up past the right side of the overhang to a bushy ledge. Walk left about 15 feet and continue up a whitish, pebbly face to a small ledge. Then traverse right about 20 feet to a belay below a short left-facing corner capped by the right side of a long overhang. (110 feet)

Pitch 2: Climb up past the corner onto the face. Continue up to the overhanging corner above (V1), move up right past some overhangs, and diagonal up left to a pile of blocks on a large ledge (some parties belay here). Work up through the notch in the overhang above and then continue up the face to the top. (140 feet) 5.7 PG

Variation 1: 5.6 PG Traverse left 20 feet to join Gleet Street at the short flaky right-facing corner capped by the overhang.

FA 1964: Art Gran and unknown belayer

224. GLEET STREET 5.8 R

Start: At the short low-angle face immediately left of Funny Face, directly below a very thin crack that goes through an overhang.

Pitch 1: Follow the crack to a grassy ledge and pine tree, go left about 5 feet, and climb up to another ledge. Angle up right past a small right-facing corner and then diagonal up left to the small ledge on Lat-On the Season that is 20 feet below the center of the long overhang. (90 feet) 5.8 R

Pitch 2: Climb a fault system and go through the overhang at a notch. Continue up past a tree to a short, flaky, right-facing corner capped by an overhang. Then move left and climb up to join Lat-On the Season at the pile of blocks on the ledge. (80 feet) 5.6 PG

Pitch 3: Walk right about 15 feet, climb through an overhang at some left-facing flakes, and continue to the top. (40 feet) 5.5 R

FA 1986: Keith Mercer and Jeff Street

225. FUNNY FACE 5.5 – PG

Start: At a left-facing corner (the first of two) with an overhang 10 feet up, 40 feet right of Don't Shoot.

Pitch 1: Climb up past the overhang on the right and diagonal up right past grassy ledges to a small left-facing corner. Follow the corner to its top and then continue staight up to a ledge. (90 feet) 5.5 –

Pitch 2: Diagonal up left to some corners and flakes, and follow these to a large ledge (some parties belay here) (V1). Then continue up the corner above to the top. (120 feet) 5.5 –

Variation 1: Climb up, work out left under the ceilings to the face, and continue up to the top. 5.5

FA 1954: Jim McCarthy and Tim Mutch

226. SON OF BITCHY VIRGIN 5.6 PG

Start: At a broken right-facing corner with an overhang at its top, 28 feet right of Funny Face.

Pitch 1: Climb the corner and step left around the overhang onto the face (or climb the flakes on the left through the cleft in the overhang). Then continue up the face to the first Bitchy Virgin belay. (100 feet) 5.4

Pitch 2: Climb straight up over some bulges to the GT Ledge. (110 feet) 5.6 PG

Pitch 3: Climb easier rock to the top. (40 feet)

THE TRAPPS

Before Tri-cams, Friends, and TCUs were invented, this climb was poorly protected (R).

FA 1967: Jim McCarthy and John Reppy

227. IMMACULATE CONCEPTION 5.6 PG

Start: On the face between Son of Bitchy Virgin and Bitchy Virgin, just right of a right-facing corner.

Pitch 1: Climb up the face past an overhang and some bulges, and continue up the face just left of an arête to the first Bitchy Virgin belay. (100 feet) 5.6 G

Pitch 2: Climb the face between Son of Bitchy Virgin and Bitchy Virgin to the top. (110 feet) 5.6 PG

FA 1986: Todd Swain and John Thackray

228. BITCHY VIRGIN 5.6 R ★

Start: At a large right-facing corner at the back of a gully formed by a huge block leaning against the face, 20 feet right of Son of Bitchy Virgin.

Pitch 1: Climb to the top of the corner and step left to a small ledge. (100 feet) 5.6

Pitch 2: Traverse up to the right, following the path of least resistance, to a stance below some loose blocks. Then, either step around to the right and diagonal up left to a tree on the GT Ledge, or climb straight up over the blocks to the tree. (110 feet) 5.6

Pitch 3: Climb easier rock to the top. (30 feet)

Some claim that with the subtle use of modern equipment this climb is decently protected—unlike in 1954, when it was a bold first ascent.

FA 1954: Hans Kraus and Bonnie Prudden

229. UNNAMED 5.2 G

Start: On the left face of the huge 60-foot-high block that forms the Bitchy Virgin gully.

Pitch 1: Climb the left side of the block to the ledge on its top (or climb the corner on the right side of the block, which is called the Lemon Squeezer). (40 feet) 5.2

Pitch 2: Climb up and a bit right to a large left-facing corner.

Then work up the corner and the face on its left to the GT Ledge. (110 feet)   5.2

Pitch 3: Climb easier rock to the top.   (40 feet)

Most parties use the Lemon Squeezer start.

FA 1942: Fritz Wiessner, Betty Woolsey, and Mary Cecil

230. DAT MANTEL   5.10   PG

Start: On the main face of the Dis-Mantel block, just around the corner from Unnamed and 10 feet left of Dis-Mantel.

Pitch 1: Climb the face past an overhang to the top of the block. (60 feet)

FA 1976: Rich Perch, Kevin Bein, Barbara Devine, and Rich Ross

231. DIS-MANTEL   5.10   G

Start: On the main face of the huge detached block, at a short crack that ends at a horizontal crack, 15 feet from the left edge.

Pitch 1: Climb up to the horizontal crack, move right, and go through an overhang at a notch. Then work past another overhang and continue up the face to the top of the block.   (80 feet)   5.10   G

Pitch 2: Step left and climb up left to an overhang. Pass the overhang and continue straight up to the GT Ledge.   (120 feet) 5.7

Pitch 3: Continue to the top.

Originally rated 5.8 until a handhold broke off in 1987.

FA 1973: Joe Strutt, Roy Kligfield, and Jack Hunt

232. KERNMANTLE   5.8   PG

Start: On the right side of the main face of the Dis-Mantel block.

Pitch 1: Climb the right side of the face past two overhangs, move around right and up, and then go back left and up to a tree on top of the block.   (70 feet)

FA 1976: Rich Ross and Dave Sweet

233. HIGH TIMES   5.9+   PG–R

Start: On the face 5 feet left of Stop the Presses, Mr. Williams.

Pitch 1: Climb up the face to a ceiling, traverse right 5 feet, and clear the ceiling at a right-facing corner. Then continue up to a pine tree on the left.   (50 feet)   5.9+   PG–R

Pitch 2: Rappel, or climb the face to a left-facing corner and exit right. Diagonal up and right, and then continue up the face past some overhangs to the GT Ledge.   (130 feet)   5.8   G

Pitch 3: Scramble to the top.

FA 1976: Rich Ross and Mike Sawicky

234. STOP THE PRESSES, MR. WILLIAMS   5.8+   PG

Start: On the face below a small left-facing corner that leads to an overhang, 10 feet left of Gory Thumb.

Pitch 1: Climb the face and corner to the overhang. (V1) Step right, pass the overhang, and continue up the steep face above, past a small right-facing corner, to a large ledge with a pine tree.   (50 feet)   5.8+   PG

Pitch 2: Step left, work up the face, and move right over a bulge. Then diagonal up left past an overhang (at a corner) and continue past the GT Ledge to the top.   (130 feet)   5.7

Variation 1:   5.6   Traverse right 10 feet to a crack, follow it to a ledge, and rejoin the regular route.

FA 1972: Roman Laba and Roy Kligfield

235. GORY THUMB   5.8+   G–PG   ★

Start: On the left end of a narrow, grassy ledge, 50 feet right of the huge Dis-Mantel block, at the point where the trail descends 35 feet.

Pitch 1: (V1) Traverse right on the ledge and climb up to a white face below a thin crack. (V2) Continue past the crack to a ledge and then traverse left to a large pine tree on a ledge.   (50 feet)   5.8+   G–PG

Pitch 2: Traverse back right, and climb up left past a bolt and over a bulge. Then traverse about 35 feet right (V3) past a small corner and continue up to a small belay stance below an overhang.   (100 feet)   5.6

Pitch 3: Climb the overhang and continue up the face past the GT Ledge to the top.   (80 feet)   5.7

Variation 1:   5.9   Climb the unprotected face 5 feet right of Wild Horses (or the right-facing corner immediately to the right or the face just right of the corner) and join the regular route on the grassy ledge.

Variation 2:   5.8   PG   Climb the face to the right of the crack and rejoin the regular route.

Variation 3:   5.8   PG   Climb past a loose orange block to the left of the corner and continue up the steep face to the GT Ledge.

FA 1954: Jim McCarthy and Dave Bernays
FFA 1964: Dick Williams
FA (Variation 2) 1960s: Art Gran
FA (Variation 3) 1983: Stan Hayes and Gail Toby

236. RAUNCHY   5.8   PG   ★

Start: At the first of two short right-facing corners below the right end of the Gory Thumb ledge.

Pitch 1: Climb up the corner, go past the Gory Thumb ledge, and continue up into a smaller right-facing corner. Step left onto the face and climb up 10 feet. Then move back right and work up to the large ledge with the Gory Thumb pine tree.   (70 feet)   5.8−   G

Pitch 2: Climb up to a large overhang (5.3, X) below a left-facing corner. Traverse left and follow the corner to the GT Ledge. Then continue straight up to the top.   (130 feet)   5.8   PG

FA 1963: Jim McCarthy and Bill Goldner

237. WILD HORSES   5.9   R   ★

Start: On the face 10 feet right of Raunchy.

Pitch 1: Climb up the face past the Gory Thumb ledge to a crack. Follow the crack until it ends and continue up the face past a bulge to a ledge. Then walk left to the Gory Thumb pine tree and belay.   (60 feet)   5.8   PG–R

Pitch 2: Diagonal up right to the top of the left-facing corner above and step right. Then climb straight up the steep face past the GT Ledge to the top.   (130 feet)   5.9   R

FA 1975: Dick Williams, Roy Kligfield, Al Rubin, and Ivan Rezucha

238. BADFINGER 5.9+ PG

Start: On the face below the vertical section of a very large right-facing corner capped by a ceiling, about midway between Wild Horses and Help!

Pitch 1: Climb the face and the corner (V1) until a few feet below the ceiling. (V2) Move up right and clear the ceiling at the break. Then continue up the face above, traverse all the way left to the Gory Thumb pine tree, and rappel. (80 feet)

Variation 1: Sort of Damocles 5.7+ G Start at the bush on the ledge to the left. Go left to a crack near the corner, and follow the crack to rejoin Variation 2 and the regular route.

Variation 2: Sword of Damocles 5.9+ PG Escape left and climb up the face to rejoin the regular route.

FA 1982: Ivan Rezucha and Don Lauber
FA (Variation 1) 1984: Todd Swain and Andy Schenkel
FA (Variation 2) 1983: Stan Hayes

239. HELP! 5.11+ R

Start: On the face just left of a low right-facing corner and directly below a large yellowish flake under a roof, 55 feet right of Raunchy.

Pitch 1: Climb up the face and a ramp to the left edge of the flake. Go past the flake and the ceiling, and continue up the face above. Then traverse left 10 feet and work up to a belay below some overhangs. (90 feet) 5.11+ R

Pitch 2: Diagonal up left past the overhangs and climb up the face past a steep bulge. Then continue up and slightly left, past an overhang on the right, to the GT Ledge. (100 feet) 5.9+

Pitch 3: Scramble to the top.

Height-related—harder for shorter climbers.

FA 1965: Dick Williams and Joe Kelsey
FFA 1973: John Stannard and John Bragg

240. PLEH! 5.11+ R

Start: On the right side of some large blocks that lean against the face, below the right side of an overhang that is below the right side of the large yellowish Help! flake.

Pitch 1: Climb up past a short right-facing corner and the overhang to a stance under the obvious roof. Traverse left to the Help! flake and go past the roof at a left-facing flake at the lip. Then continue up and right to a belay at a left-facing corner below an overhang. (100 feet) 5.11+ R

Pitch 2: Climb basically straight up to the GT Ledge and continue to the top. (100 feet)

Also known as Scum of Sam.

FA 1985: Jim Damon and Mick Avery

241. V-3 5.7 G ★★

Start: At a crack directly below a large V-shaped notch at the right end of a long ceiling, 50 feet right of Help!

Pitch 1: Follow the crack to a left-facing corner (V1), step left, and move up to a stance below another left-facing corner. Climb up right past the V-shaped notch in the ceiling to a flaring chimney. Then, either continue straight up the chimney to a belay ledge, or move out left and go up the face to the ledge. (100 feet) 5.7 G

Pitch 2: (V2) Climb the face and corner above to the GT Ledge. (120 feet) 5.1

Pitch 3: (V3) Walk right and follow a right-facing corner to the top. (30 feet) 5.2

Variation 1: Galactic Hitchhikers 5.9+ PG Exit right and climb up past an overhang to a belay. Then, either rappel from Country Roads or finish on a nearby climb.

Variation 2: 5.2 PG Traverse left and join the second pitch of Gory Thumb. (40 feet)

Variation 3: 5.7 G Climb past the ceiling above to the top. This is a classic.

FA 1954: Hans Kraus, Ken Prestrud, and Bonnie Prudden

FA (Variation 1) 1985: Todd Swain, Tad Welch, Dave and Marie Saball, Brad White, and Dick Peterson

242. CITY STREETS 5.10 PG

Start: On the face halfway between V-3 and Country Roads.

Pitch 1: Climb up the face to a ledge, move right, and diagonal up left through the ceiling to a large but short left-facing corner.

Then continue up to the first Country Roads belay stance and rappel. (60 feet)
FA 1976: Ivan Rezucha, Joe Bridges, and Dick Saum

243. COUNTRY ROADS 5.10 PG ★
Start: Same as Commando Rave.
Pitch 1: Follow the thin crack to a small ledge. Step right and diagonal up left to a large overhang below the right side of a large hanging block. Climb the notch on the right side of the block and belay on top of the block at a pine tree. (60 feet) 5.10 PG
Pitch 2: Rappel or climb to the GT Ledge. (150 feet)
Pitch 3: Continue to the top. (60 feet)
FA: 1950s
FFA 1971: John Stannard and Pat Milligan

244. COMMANDO RAVE 5.9 PG ★
Start: At a thin crack marked by a small right-facing corner halfway up, 30 feet right of V–3.
Pitch 1: Climb 20 feet up the crack to a long but narrow ledge. Traverse right about 30 feet, climb up to ceiling, and then traverse around right to a belay stance. (70 feet) 5.9 PG
Pitch 2: Climb directly up the face to the GT Ledge. (130 feet) 5.7
Pitch 3: Continue to the top.
Despite the bravado suggested by the name, you are advised to think about the moves before attacking.
FA 1963: Jim McCarthy and John Hudson

245. METROPOLIS 5.11+ PG–R ★
Start: On the face to the left of a huge block that leans against the cliff, 15 feet right of Commando Rave.
Pitch 1: Climb up to the polished, bulging overhang. Continue up and right through the ceiling above (at a major fault) to a small left-facing corner at the lip. Follow the corner past another ceiling and belay at a tree on the face above. 5.11+ PG–R
Pitch 2: Rappel, or continue up the face and a left-facing corner to the GT Ledge.

Pitch 3: Continue to the top.
FA 1981: Russ Raffa and Ivan Rezucha

246. BEYOND THE FRINGE 5.9 R
Start: Below a right-facing corner that begins 10 feet above the ground, which is below the point where the ceiling starts to rise, 85 feet right of Commando Rave.

Pitch 1: Follow the corner past an overhang and move up until below a roof. Then traverse left to a ledge at the lip of the roof, and continue up to a belay ledge and tree. (80 feet) 5.9 R

Pitch 2: Climb the crack and face above to the GT Ledge. (120 feet) 5.6

Pitch 3: Continue to the top.

Originally known as Un-Appealing Ceiling.
FA 1963: Bill Goldner and Pete Ramins
FFA: Doug Tompkins and Jim McCarthy

247. BALROG 5.10 G–PG ★
Start: At a small, short right-facing corner at the left edge of a huge boulder pile, 30 feet right of Beyond the Fringe.

Pitch 1: Climb the corner and crack to a small triangular overhang, step left, and continue up the crack to a ceiling. Move up and left onto the face, and then work up to a ledge with a pine tree. (80 feet) 5.10 G–PG

Pitch 2: Continue up the face to join Dry Heaves and Alley Oop, and follow them to the GT Ledge. (120 feet)

Pitch 3: Continue to the top.
FA 1967: Jim McCarthy and Richard Goldstone

248. BULLFROG 5.12– PG–R
Start: Same as Balrog.

Pitch 1: Follow Balrog to the small triangular overhang and continue up a crack to the arching right-facing corner. Work up the corner until it is possible to reach up left to the lip of the ceiling. Move up into the next overhanging corner. Exit up and left (beware of loose rock) onto the face, and continue up to a belay at a pine tree. (80 feet) 5.12– PG–R

Pitch 2: Rappel or climb up the face to the GT Ledge, moving to the right and crossing Dry Heaves and Alley Oop on the way. (90 feet)

Pitch 3: Continue to the top.

FA 1984: Felix Modugno and Jim Damon

249. BLIND ALLEY 5.8 PG

Start: Same as Dry Heaves.

Pitch 1: Follow the Dry Heaves corner to the overhang and work straight up to orange rock. Continue up the face, rejoin Dry Heaves, and follow it to its first belay. (80 feet) 5.8 PG

Pitch 2: Climb up and right, and cross Alley Oop. Then follow a left-facing corner to the GT Ledge. (90 feet) 5.6

Pitch 3: Continue up past a bulge to the top. (40 feet)

FA 1979: Alan Long, Al Rubin, and Paul Ledoux

250. DRY HEAVES 5.8 PG

Start: At the base of a short right-facing corner capped by an overhang, 12 feet left of Alley Oop.

Pitch 1: Climb to the top of the corner and undercling right to the end of the obvious flake. Continue up a small right-facing crack and corner system until it is possible to traverse left to a short corner and an overhang. Move up to a notch below the Alley Oop notch. Then move left and up a few feet to a belay. (80 feet) 5.8 PG

Pitch 2: Climb up the face to the left of Alley Oop, which is eventually joined and followed to the GT Ledge. (120 feet)

Pitch 3: Follow Alley Oop to the top.

FA 1976: Mark Robinson, Sandy Stewart, and Grant Calder

251. ALLEY OOP 5.7 PG ★

Start: At the highest point on the huge boulder pile, 5 feet right of a tree and below a tiny arching right-facing corner that is 2 inches deep. There is a faint vertical fault above the corner.

Pitch 1: Diagonal up right past the corner to some right-facing flakes. Climb the flakes and work back left to a right-facing corner. Follow the corner to an overhang, traverse out left, and then continue up to a belay ledge. (80 feet) 5.7 PG

Pitch 2: Climb straight up the face, move left, and follow a slimy left-facing corner to the GT Ledge. (90 feet) 5.4

Pitch 3: Continue straight up the face to the top or finish up the corner on the right.

The first ascent party used a wild three-man shoulder stand to get started.

FA 1956: Jim McCarthy, Hans Kraus, and Stan Gross
FFA late 1950s: Art Gran

252. CHEAP THRILLS 5.10 PG ★

Start: At a vertical seam just left of a tree, 25 feet right of Alley Oop. An alternate start that is commonly used begins 10 feet downhill from Alley Oop and diagonals up right to the original line.

Pitch 1: Climb past the seam to a short, rounded left-facing corner (grassy on top) and a left-facing flake. Continue up and left to orange rock, and work up past a short right-facing corner to a double-tiered ceiling. Then climb through the ceiling at another short right-facing corner and belay on a stance above. (120 feet) 5.10 PG

Pitch 2: Traverse left to Dry Heaves and Alley Oop, and rappel; or move left and climb a left-facing corner (or the face on its right) to the GT Ledge. (100 feet)

Pitch 3: Climb the obvious right-facing corner and exit left to the top.

High-class thrills would be more like it.

FA 1972: Kevin Bein and Roy Kligfield

253. DEEP CHILLS 5.11+ R–X

Start: At the Cheap Thrills seam or on the face 10 feet farther right, on top of a block and just right of a tree.

Pitch 1: Climb the face to some right-facing flakes under the first overhang. Continue up to a small overhang. Move left, and work up past orange and white rock to another overhang. (V1) Then diagonal up right to a final overhang, clear this to the left of a flake, and belay above. (80 feet) 5.11+ R–X

Pitch 2: Traverse right to Cakewalk and rappel, or climb the face between Cheap Thrills and Cakewalk to the GT Ledge. (100 feet)

Pitch 3: Continue to the top.

Variation 1: Continue a few feet left and clear the ceiling at its widest point.

FA 1982: Russ Raffa, Bob D'Antonio, Russ Clune, and Hugh Herr

254. CAKEWALK 5.7 PG ★

Start: At a large pine tree 30 feet above the ground, 35 feet right of the huge Alley Oop boulder pile. Scramble up dirt- and block-covered ledges to the tree.

Pitch 1: Step left to a crack, move up, and step back right to a right-facing flake. Climb the flake and diagonal up left to a large corner. Follow the corner, step left onto the face, and then move up to a belay ledge. (90 feet)   5.7   PG

Pitch 2: Continue up the face to a ledge, move up right to a long gully, and follow this up left to the GT Ledge. (140 feet)   5.4

Pitch 3: Scramble to the top.

FA 1956: Jim McCarthy and Hans Kraus

255. NURDLAND 5.10 R

Start: Same as Cakewalk.

Pitch 1: Climb up the bulging face and intersect Turdland. Then diagonal up left and continue up the face to a belay stance. (90 feet)   5.10   R

Pitch 2: Traverse left to Cakewalk and rappel, or continue up the face between Cakewalk and Turdland, and follow the diagonal gully up left to the GT Ledge. (90 feet)   5.7   PG

Pitch 3: Scramble to the top.

FA 1981: Mike Sawicky

256. TURDLAND 5.10+ PG ★

Start: Same as Cakewalk.

Pitch 1: Diagonal up right to a bolt (V1), move up left, and continue up to the right side of a small overhang and another bolt. Work up to a small, very short right-facing corner and a small overhang. (V2) Then climb straight up past a third bolt to a stance and traverse left to the Cakewalk belay ledge. (100 feet)   5.10+ PG

Pitch 2: Rappel, or traverse back right and climb the face to the left-slanting Cakewalk gully, which is followed to the GT Ledge. (150 feet)

Pitch 3: Continue to the top.

Variation 1:   **5.10+**   **PG**   Climb straight up past the bulge above and rejoin the regular route.

Variation 2:   **5.9**   **PG**   Move right and climb up to rejoin the regular route.

FA 1959: Jim McCarthy and Jack Hansen
FFA 1966: Dick Williams

257. TRIANGLE   5.9−   PG

Start: Same as Cakewalk or at a large right-facing flake-corner 30 feet to the right.

Pitch 1:   (V1)   Follow the wide, slanting crack up right or the flake-corner up left to the overhang. Then clear the overhang and move up a few feet to a belay. (100 feet)   5.9−   PG

Pitch 2: Traverse right to the gully, downclimb to the Never Never Land tree, and rappel; or continue up the face to the gully, which is followed to the GT Ledge.

Pitch 3: Scramble to the top.

Variation 1:   **5.9**   **PG**   Climb the center of the triangular face to the overhang, move left, and then diagonal up right to the regular route.

FA 1954: Hans Kraus, Bonnie Prudden, and Ken Prestrud
FFA 1960: Art Gran and Al DeMaria
FA (Variation 1) 1978: Bruce Meneghin

258. NEVERMORE   5.10   PG−R

Start: At the large right-facing flake-corner of Triangle.

Pitch 1: Climb about 15 feet up the flake-corner and traverse right to a short left-facing ramp. Follow the ramp past two short left-facing corners and work up the steep face above, going left and then right to some small right-facing flakes. Then continue past these and a ledge to the Never Never Land belay tree, and rappel. (80 feet)

Height-related—harder for shorter climbers.
FA 1982: Russ Clune and Rich Ross

259: NEVER SAY NEVER 5.10 R–X
Start: At a small broken fault that leads up left for about 15 feet, 13 feet left of Never Never Land.

Pitch 1: Climb the fault, step right, and continue straight up the face past a bulge to the Never Never Land belay ledge and tree. Rappel. (80 feet)

The name of this route will have meaning to anyone over 30— it did to the first ascent party. The final bulge is an old variation to Never Never Land.

FA 1971: Dick Williams and Jim McCarthy

260. NEVER NEVER LAND 5.10− PG ★★★
Start: At the low point on the face, directly below a thin vertical seam that starts 8 feet above the ground, 70 feet right of Cakewalk.

Pitch 1: Climb the thin face and follow the seam to a bolt. Continue straight up and slightly right to an overhang. Then step right around the overhang, work up to a small ledge, and traverse left about 20 feet left to a belay at a tree at the base of a gully. (At the overhang, it is also possible to traverse left on good holds to the final bulge on Never Say Never.) Rappel. (100 feet)

A 150-foot rope is just long enough for the rappel.

FA 1959: Art Gran, Dave Craft, and Jim McCarthy
FFA 1964: Jim McCarthy and George Hurley

261. J'ACCUSE 5.10 R
Start: On the face 13 feet right of Never Never Land.

Pitch 1: Climb straight up past a vertical fracture, staying about 10 feet right of the Never Never Land bolt, and join Never Never Land on the right side of the overhang. Rappel. (100 feet)

FA 1971: Jim McCarthy and Patrick Cordier
FFA 1973: Scott Stewart and Rich Romano

262. WELCOME TO MY NIGHTMARE 5.10 X
Start: On the face just left of Absurdland.

Pitch 1: Diagonal up left past a broken right-facing flake to an angle piton. Continue up the face past a horizontal crack (bushes on either side) to a narrow ledge. Then traverse left to the Never Never Land belay tree and rappel.

FA 1986: Todd Swain and Randy Schenkel

263. ABSURDLAND 5.9 PG ★
Start: At a thin crack, 40 feet uphill to the right of Never Never Land.

Pitch 1: Climb the crack and steep face to a small ledge. Then, either traverse left about 40 feet (if you have one rope) to the Never Never Land belay tree and rappel, or continue straight up (if you have two ropes) and rappel from a higher tree.

FA 1960: Jim McCarthy and George Bloom

264. BLUNDERBUS 5.9 R
Start: On the face 10 feet right of Absurdland, just before the trail makes a sharp descent to the right.

Pitch 1: Climb up right past the left side of a long, narrow overhang and continue up past a bulge to a belay.

Pitch 2: Rappel or finish on a nearby climb.

Named after an incident involving a bus that went through the guardrail on the hairpin turn and was left dangling precariously.

FA 1981: Mike Sawicky and Gene Smith

265. WISECRACK 5.6 G
Start: At a bushy, flake-filled corner, below a crack in some overhangs and part way up a left-slanting gully, 30 feet right of Absurdland.

Pitch 1: Climb up past the crack to a ledge. (90 feet)   5.6   G

Pitch 2: Rappel or continue up to the GT Ledge. (70 feet)   5.5

Pitch 3: Move up and right past the obvious overhang, and finish up the face. (60 feet)   5.5

FA 1965: Art Gran and Pete Vlachos

265A. WISELAND 5.9+ PG–R
Start: Immediately right of Wisecrack at a cluster of 3 trees.

Pitch 1: Climb to the base of a short, broken, left-facing corner at the left side of an overhang. Climb the corner, move up and slightly right, then climb up the steep pebbly face (between Wisecrack and Wonderland). Continue up past the final overhang to easier rock and a ledge (some parties belay here). Walk right about 30 feet to a pine tree belay.

FA 1989: Dick Williams and Dave Craft

266. WONDERLAND 5.8 PG
Start: At a small grassy ledge beneath an overhang, just right of Wisecrack.

Pitch 1: Traverse to the right side of the overhang, move up right, and continue up past a bolt to another overhang. Climb left around this overhang, move back right, and continue up to a ledge. (It is also possible to climb straight up to the bolt from the ground—slightly harder.) (90 feet) 5.8 PG

Pitch 2: Walk right about 30 feet to a pine tree.

Pitch 3: Climb straight up easier rock to the highest of several ledges—the GT Ledge. (70 feet) 5.4

Pitch 4: Walk right about 10 feet and work up to a point just left of the break in the overhangs above. Then move right, climb past the break, and continue up and left to a white corner which leads to the top. (80 feet) 5.5

FA 1959: Art Gran and Eric Stern

267. FAITHFUL JOURNEY 5.8+ G
Start: Below a small, short left-facing corner that begins at a small overhang 8 feet above the ground, 5 feet left of Middle Earth.

Pitch 1: Climb past the overhang and corner to a thin crack and a left-facing corner that arches left. Work up this corner, and continue up and slightly right past another overhang and a tree to a belay at a pine tree. (120 feet) 5.7 PG

Pitch 2: Climb up and slightly left past a short right-facing corner to the GT Ledge. (50 feet) 5.3

Pitch 3: Climb up to the overhang 10 feet left of Bombs Away Dream Baby, clear this at a right-facing corner, and continue to the top. (80 feet) 5.8+ G

FA 1982: Paul Trapani, Joe Bridges, and Faith Aubin

268. MIDDLE EARTH   5.7 −   G   ★

Start: At a crack that is 25 feet to the right of a point directly below the Wonderland ledge. The trail rises to the left below this ledge.

Pitch 1: Follow the crack up the face to a ledge with a pine tree. (100 feet)   5.7 −   G

Pitch 2: From the pine tree, climb straight up past some dirty ledges to the GT Ledge. (80 feet)   5.0

Pitch 3: (V1)   Continue up a right-facing corner to an overhang, step left, and work up through more overhangs to a steep face. Climb the face and diagonal up right to a right-facing corner that leads to the top. (80 feet)   5.7 −   G

Variation 1:   Rhun   5.7   Climb the face 10 feet right of the corner to a large overhang. Traverse left about 15 feet out around the corner to a small ledge. Continue up and slightly right on the face, and then climb straight up to the top. (90 feet)

FA 1967: Joe Kelsey and Roman Laba

269. BOMBS AWAY DREAM BABY   5.8   G

Start: At a flaky ramp that diagonals up right to a ledge, 5 feet right of Middle Earth.

Pitch 1: Scramble up to the ledge and climb past an overhang to a vertical fault that leads to a crack and a pine tree. Then continue past the tree to a short, arching right-facing corner and a belay above. (90 feet)   5.6

Pitch 2: Climb up past a series of right-facing flakes and ledges to the GT Ledge. (80 feet)   5.4

Pitch 3: Walk left about 15 feet until below a small right-facing corner. Follow this through an overhang and past some right-facing flakes and a crack to the top. (80 feet)   5.8   G

FA 1980: Ray Dobkin and Stan Hayes

270. JOURNEY'S END   5.10 −   G

Start: On the face a few feet left of Red's Ruin.

Pitch 1: Climb the face past a bushy ledge to a right-facing corner capped by an overhang. Continue past the overhang, avoiding the bushes above, and then diagonal up right to a belay.

THE TRAPPS

Pitch 2: Climb up past a pine tree and some flakes to a ledge, and then diagonal up right to a belay on the GT Ledge.

Pitch 3: From a block, climb past an overhang to low-angle rock and belay under a roof.

Pitch 4: Traverse to the left side of the roof, step onto a big block, and go around left onto the face, which is then climbed to the top.

FA 1985: Ivan Rezucha and Annie O'Neill

271. RED'S RUIN   5.2   G

Start: At a short dirt-filled crack, 35 feet right of Middle Earth, or on the easy face 12 feet farther right.

Pitch 1: Using either start, climb up to some dirty ledges and scramble up to a large belay ledge. (90 feet)

Pitch 2: Climb up past more ledges and continue up the face to the GT Ledge at a point below a large left-facing corner. (100 feet)

Pitch 3: Follow the corner for 20 feet, diagonal up left for another 20 feet, and continue to the top. (40 feet)

272. SMEGMA GARDEN and PIGEON   4th Class

Start (Smegma Garden): On the face just around the outside corner to the left of Snowpatch.

Start (Pigeon): On the left wall of the Snowpatch corner.

Pitches 1–3: Both routes wander up and left past a series of ledges and easy steps to the top.

An easy way up and a convenient way down when climbing in this section of the Trapps.

FA (Smegma Garden) 1966: Gerd Thuestad and a large group of friends

FA (Pigeon) 1948: Hans Kraus and Roger Wolcott

273. SNOWPATCH   5.5   PG

Start: At a dirty right-facing corner, 95 feet right of Middle Earth and on the left side of the Senté face.

Pitch 1:   (V1)   Climb the corner to an overhang, traverse right, and work up past a tree to another right-facing corner.

Then continue up the face past white rock to the GT Ledge. (140 feet) 5.5−

Pitch 2: Walk left about 40 feet to a left-facing corner. (40 feet)

Pitch 3: Work up the corner and step right to a small ledge. Continue up the face to a large overhang, traverse to its left end, and climb to the top. (80 feet) 5.5 PG

Variation 1: Pigpen 5.6 Climb straight up past grass bogs to the tree on the regular route.

FA 1970: Art Gran and Dick Williams

274. SENTÉ 5.9− PG ★

Start: On the face 6 feet left of Thin Slabs.

Pitch 1: Climb the face past three bolts to a belay ledge.

Pitch 2: Finish on Thin Slabs, or traverse right and scramble back down to the ground.

FA 1960: Willie Crowther, after placing the bolts on rappel

275. YENTA 5.10 (Toprope)

Start: On the face midway between Senté and Thin Slabs.

Pitch 1: Climb the face between Senté and Thin Slabs.

276. THIN SLABS 5.7 PG−R ★

Start: At a thin crack that ends at a horizontal crack 7 feet above the ground, 33 feet right of Snowpatch.

Pitch 1: (V1) Follow the crack until it ends, step right, and continue up the face past a bolt to a ledge with a pine tree. (80 feet) 5.7 PG−R

Pitch 2: Climb up, go right around an overhang, and continue straight up to a large ledge. Walk left and then back up right to an easy face that leads to a corner, which is followed to the GT Ledge. (60 feet) 5.3

Pitch 3: (V2) Climb a chimney in a left-facing corner, traverse right to a ledge, and finish up a short face. (50 feet) 5.5

Variation 1: 5.7 G Start 10 feet farther right and climb the crack that diagonals up right to the regular route.

Variation 2: Thin Slabs Direct 5.7 Climb up right into a left-facing corner below the left edge of a huge blocky roof. Then

ART GRAN on THIN SLABS DIRECT

DICK WILLIAMS on First Ascent of ON ANY MONDAY

Joe Bridges

traverse out right and around onto the face, and continue to the top. (80 feet)
FA 1956: Art Gran, John Wharton, and Bob Chambers
FA (Variation 2) 1958: Art Gran and friend
FFA (Variation 2) 1958: John Turner

277. ON ANY MONDAY 5.11− PG ★

Start: At the right edge of a small overhang that is 7 feet above the ground, 20 feet right of Variation 1 of Thin Slabs.

Pitch 1: Climb past the overhang and bulge (at a short vertical seam), and follow a groove to a ledge. (40 feet) 5.11− PG

Pitch 2: Continue straight up the grey face to an overhang, staying to the left of some sharp flakes. Go around the left end of the overhang, move back right, and climb up to the GT Ledge. (110 feet)

Pitch 3: Follow Thin Slabs Direct to the top. (80 feet) 5.7

FA 1971: Dick Williams and Joe Bridges

278. SNAKE 5.6 PG

Start: At a small broken right-facing corner directly below a crack in some white rock, 17 feet right of On Any Monday. (If the corner is wet, start 10 feet farther right, below a small pine growing out of a crack.)

Pitch 1: Climb the corner and face above to a crack, and continue straight up to the GT Ledge. (150 feet) 5.6 PG

Pitch 2: Work up a grungy corner that ends in an often slimy crack, which is followed to the top. (80 feet) 5.6

If the second pitch corner is wet, climb the last pitch of Red Pillar instead.

FA 1944: Hans Kraus and Susanne Simon

279. TALUS OF POWDER 5.8 R−X

Start: On the face 5 feet right of Snake.

Pitch 1: Climb directly up the unprotected face (5.6) to a ledge below a small right-facing corner and laurel bush. Move up onto the face, step right, and continue up the face past a very old ring piton to the base of GT Ledge. (130 feet) 5.8 PG

Pitch 2: Scramble up past a huge block and belay. (20 feet)

Pitch 3: From the base of the huge right-facing corner above, diagonal up left on the face (no protection) to a horizontal band of shale. Then traverse left under an overhang and around the corner onto the face, and continue to the top. (60 feet) 5.7 R–X

FA 1981: Rich Perch and Russ Clune

280. STEEP HIKIN' 5.8+ PG

Start: Near the center of the pillar just left and around the corner from Red Pillar.

Pitch 1: Climb the face of the pillar (5.6, PG) to a ledge at its top (40 feet—some parties belay here to reduce rope drag). Then move right and continue up the face to the GT Ledge. (80 feet) 5.8+ PG

Pitch 2: Climb the face just right of Deep Lichen to the top. (100 feet) 5.6+ PG

FA 1985: Todd Swain and Andy and Randy Schenkel

281. RED PILLAR 5.5 G

Start: At a broken right-facing corner with trees in it that is formed by a pillar leaning against the face, at the high point in the trail, 70 feet right of Snake.

Pitch 1: Climb up left to the top of the pillar and continue directly up the face to the GT Ledge. (100 feet) 5.5 G

Pitch 2: Move right and climb to the top of a right-facing corner, past a well-worn bush. Then step left and finish up a crack through a bulge. (120 feet) 5.4

282. DEEP LICHEN 5.10 X

Start: Same as Red Pillar.

Pitch 1: Climb 15 feet up the right side of the pillar to a platform below the steep white face. Continue up the face past a series of small overhangs to a small right-facing corner. Then step left and work up to the GT Ledge. (90 feet) 5.10 X

Pitch 2: Scramble left about 20 feet to a huge boulder.

Pitch 3: Climb straight up the face above, past a small alcove, to the top. (100 feet) 5.8– PG

FA 1975: Dick Williams, Roy Kligfield, and Kevin Bein

283. HAWKEYE 5.9+ PG

Start: On the GT Ledge about midway between Red Pillar and Three Doves.

Pitch 1: Work up the face past a protruding grass ledge to the right side of a large, narrow block sitting on a higher ledge. Climb up right past an overhang to the optional Three Doves belay at the first pine tree. (40 feet) 5.6 PG

Pitch 2: Move up left to a small pine tree. Then climb straight up the steep face past a very short crack to a cleft in the overhang above, which leads to the top. (50 feet) 5.9+ PG

Sometimes referred to as Three Duds.

FA 1988: Dick Williams, Joe Bridges, and Dave Craft

284. THREE DOVES 5.8+ PG ★★

Start: On the right side of a large white, blocky-looking flake that leans against the cliff, 25 feet right of Red Pillar.

Pitch 1: Climb the right side of the flake past some grassy ledges to an overhang. Go past the overhang and continue up steep white rock to the GT Ledge and a belay at a large pine tree. (120 feet) 5.7 PG

Pitch 2: Move up past some broken rock and diagonal up left to a ledge with a pine tree (some parties belay here). Climb straight up the steep face above to a long overhang. Then traverse right about 12 feet to a small ledge and follow a diagonal crack up right to a belay ledge. (100 feet) 5.8+ PG

Pitch 3: Rappel or continue to the top. (20 feet)

FA 1968: Dave Ingalls, Al Rubin, and Richie Petrowich

285. ANNIE OH! 5.8 PG

Start: On the face 15 feet right of Three Doves.

Pitch 1: Climb up the face past a grassy ledge and a small overhang to a fault just below and to the right of some big blocks. Follow the fault to a tree and then diagonal up left to the GT Ledge. (100 feet) 5.8

Pitch 2: Climb straight up the obviously cleaned white rock above to a groove at the top of the cliff between Three Doves and Limelight. (100 feet) 5.8

FA 1980: Ivan Rezucha, Annie O'Neill, Rod Swartz, and Maury Jaffe

286. ROAD LESS TRAVELED   5.9−   PG

Start: Below a grassy ledge, 10 feet right of Annie Oh! and just left of a blocky, broken left-facing corner.

Pitch 1: Climb up to the ledge and follow a lightly colored green streak up past a bulge to a very short, blocky right-facing corner. Step left and continue up steep white rock to easier ground and a ledge. Then traverse left to a belay at a large pine tree. (90 feet) 5.9−   PG

Pitch 2: Rappel, or scramble 20 feet up to the GT Ledge and finish on a nearby climb.

Named after a Scott Peck book.

FA 1988: Dick Williams, Joe Bridges, and Dave Craft

287. LIMELIGHT   5.7   PG   ★★

Start: On a grassy ledge 15 feet above the ground, at a groove directly below some large right-facing flakes that are about 50 feet up, 10 feet right of Road Less Traveled.

Pitch 1: Climb the face and the right side of the flakes to the GT Ledge. (100 feet)   5.6−   PG

Pitch 2: (V1) Scramble up left past some boulders to a ledge.

Pitch 3: (V2) Climb up to a small overhang below a white groove with an overhang at its top. Pass the overhang and follow the groove to an obvious 15-foot traverse left to a crack that leads to the top. (70 feet)   5.7   PG

Variation 1: Climb the face past an overhang to a thin crack and continue up to rejoin the regular route.

Variation 2: Scimitar   5.7   PG   Climb the face between Limelight and Quiver to the top.

FA 1965: Dick Williams and Art Gran

288. ARROW   5.8   PG   ★★★

Start: Same as Easy Verschneidung.

Pitch 1: Climb straight up the face, past a bulge near the top of the pitch, to the GT Ledge. (100 feet)   5.6   PG

Pitch 2: Start to the left and angle up right to a notch in an

JAMES P. McCARTHY on ARROW

overhang. Go through the notch (5.7, G) (some parties belay just above the overhang) and climb straight up to a smooth, steep white face with a bolt. Then continue past the bolt and a second bolt to the top. (130 feet)   5.8   PG

Height-related—easier for taller climbers.

FA 1960: Willie Crowther and Gardiner Perry, after rappelling down to clean the face and place the bolts

289. QUIVER   5.9   PG

Start: Same as Easy Verschneidung.

Pitch 1: Climb the face between Arrow and Easy Verschneidung and angle up right to the Easy V corner below a bush. Work up the corner until it is possible to angle up left to the obvious overhang, near its center. Pass the overhang and then continue up to the GT Ledge. (100 feet)   5.8   PG

Pitch 2: Follow Arrow to a belay just above the overhang. (30 feet)   5.7   G

Pitch 3: Climb the face 5–10 feet left of Arrow to the top. (80 feet)   5.9   PG

FA 1984: Ivan Rezucha and Annie O'Neill

290. EASY VERSCHNEIDUNG   5.2   G   ★

Start: On a ledge that is 20 feet above the ground and 15 feet left of a broken, white left-facing corner, 35 feet right of Limelight.

Pitch 1: Climb up right to the corner and follow it to a large ledge. (130 feet)   5.2

Pitch 2: Walk right about 60 feet until below a chimney-groove which goes through an overhang.

Pitch 3: Climb up to the chimney-groove and follow it through the overhang. Then step right and continue up to the top. (100 feet)   5.2

FA 1944: Fritz Wiessner and Hans Kraus

291. COLD TURKEYS   5.9 −   G

Start: At the nose or arête to the right of Easy Verschneidung.

Pitch 1: Follow the arête past old pitons to orange rock and some overhangs. Then climb through the approximate center of the overhangs and continue up to the GT Ledge. (100 feet)

Pitch 2: Climb a short left-facing corner, go past the obvious ceiling, and diagonal up right to join Proctoscope, which is followed to the top. (80 feet) 5.9− G

FA 1980: Ivan Rezucha and Ewe Bischoff

292. NURSE'S AID 5.10 R ★★

Start: On the face 30 feet left of a short dirt- and rock-filled gully that leads up right to the start of Hans' Puss.

Pitch 1: Climb up the face past a large block sitting on a ledge. Continue up orange rock and a steep face with black streaks to a ceiling, step left, and clear the ceiling. Then move right into a left-facing corner and follow it to the GT Ledge. (130 feet) 5.10 PG−R

Pitch 2: Go right about 10 feet, climb the obvious blocky left-facing corner, and diagonal up left to a short chimney or alcove. Then hand traverse right around onto the white face and continue to the top. (100 feet) 5.10 R

Be careful of loose rock on the ledges.

FA 1977: Rich Romano and Russ Raffa

293. SUPPER'S READY 5.12− PG ★★

Start: At a tree just left of the gully that leads up right to Hans' Puss.

Pitch 1: Climb basically straight up to join Hans' Puss, which is followed until it traverses right. Continue up the overhanging corner above to its end. Then climb straight through the roof at a very short left-facing corner that meets the lip and continue up to the GT Ledge. (150 feet) 5.12− PG

Pitch 2: Scramble about 15 feet up to a ledge and climb up to a right-facing corner. Move left, go up and right through the overhangs above, and continue to the top. (50 feet) 5.12−

FA 1984: Jim Damon and Felix Modugno

294. HANS' PUSS 5.7 PG ★

Start: At the base of a huge, yellow, overhanging left-facing corner, 75 feet right of the Easy Verschneidung corner.

JIM DAMON on SUPPERS READY
Peter Bonsteel

Pitch 1: Diagonal up left to a short, thin crack, follow it to its top, and climb up right to the corner. Then traverse out right across the steep face to a small stance around the corner. (80 feet) 5.6

Pitch 2: Continue to traverse right and up for about 50 feet to a small ledge below a small overhang. Then work straight up past the overhang to a pine tree on the GT Ledge. (120 feet)   5.7   PG

Pitch 3: Climb the large broken corner above to the top. (80 feet)   5.5

FA 1951: Hans Kraus and Bonnie Prudden

295. THE FEAST OF FOOLS   5.10   PG   ★★

Start: Same as Hans' Puss.

Pitch 1: Climb straight up the yellow corner to a ceiling, which is passed at the overhang on the right. Move left and work up through a notch to a small overhanging open book. Climb this, continue past another overhang, and then step right to a small belay stance. (70 feet)   5.10   PG

Pitch 2: Diagonal up right to a small overhanging left-facing corner. Climb the corner, step right, and continue straight up to the GT Ledge. (70 feet)   5.10−   PG

Pitch 3: Climb a broken crack and diagonal up left until below an overhang. Then step right, go through the overhang at a shallow notch, and continue to the top. (50 feet)

Beware! The protection grade on the first pitch would be R–X if the fixed piton (which isn't a bomber) were to fail. A large Friend to back it up is advised.

FA 1977: Russ Raffa and Mark Robinson

296. TOO OLD TO KNOW BETTER   5.9   R

Start: At a crack and fault system in broken rock, between two trees with double trunks, 32 feet right of Hans' Puss and 18 feet left of Proctoscope.

Pitch 1: Climb the crack and fault system past a small bulging overhang to a ledge. (50 feet)   5.8+   PG

Pitch 2: Continue up black and orange rock at a vertical seam 10 feet right of the arête to the first belay for either Hans' Puss or Proctoscope. (70 feet)   5.9   R

Pitch 3: Go right and work up a groove to the right of the overhanging Feast of Fools corner. Then angle up right to the GT Ledge. (70 feet)   5.8   PG

Pitch 4: Finish on a nearby climb.

FA 1986: Jeff Lea and Al Rubin

297. PROCTOSCOPE   5.9+   PG

Start: At a 6-inch-wide crack in white rock, at the point where the trail begins to rise, 50 feet right of Hans' Puss.

Pitch 1: At the top of the crack, move left and go up a short chimney. Then step right, climb a thin fault-crack to an overhang, and diagonal up left to a belay at the higher of two stances. (120 feet)   5.9+   PG

Pitch 2: Continue up left past an overhang and a left-facing corner to the GT Ledge. (75 feet)   5.8

Pitch 3: Walk left to a huge left-facing corner and follow it to the top. (75 feet)   5.8

FA 1969: Richard Goldstone, Dick DuMais, and Raymond Schrag

298. SNAGGLEPUSS   5.8   PG

Start: At a broken right-facing corner, 14 feet right and uphill from Proctoscope.

Pitch 1: Climb past a cluster of trees to the narrow or pointed top of the corner, and diagonal up right to a vertical fracture. Work up the fracture and face to a small right-facing corner capped by an overhang. Then climb past this and continue up the face to join Hans' Puss. (140 feet)

FA 1982: Todd Swain and Val Risner

299. PROCTOR SILEX   5.9+   PG   ★

Start: At a short, shallow left-facing corner on top of the huge stacked blocks just right of Snagglepuss.

Pitch 1: Follow the corner to its top, step left, and climb straight up the face to a small right-facing corner beneath the widest part of a long overhang. Clear the overhang, move up and slightly right, and work straight up to an overhanging section of orange rock 10 feet left of the upper crack on Silhouette. Climb past a bulge and then continue up to the GT Ledge. (140 feet) 5.9+ PG

Pitch 2: Finish on a nearby climb.

FA 1987: Jason Kahn and Joe Bridges

300. SILHOUETTE 5.7+ PG–R ★

Start: At a short right-facing corner on the Andrew ledge, 30 feet above the ground.

Pitch 1: (V1) Climb the corner to a stance, move left, and work up the bulging face to a small right-facing corner below an overhang. (V2) Diagonal up right and go past the right side of the overhang. Then continue up and slightly left to a crack that leads to the GT Ledge. (130 feet) 5.7+ PG–R

Pitch 2: Scramble up to the next ledge on the left, past some loose blocks. (40 feet) 5.7

Pitch 3: Climb up to an overhang. Then traverse left about 15 feet, work up to a ledge, and finish up a short face. (80 feet) 5.7− PG

Variation 1: Start at a broken, cavelike left-facing corner behind some blocks, below and about 20 feet left of the regular start. Climb up to the bulging face on the regular route.

Variation 2: 5.8+ Climb directly over the overhang and rejoin the regular route.

FA 1965: Art Gran and Dick Williams

301. MAN'S QUEST FOR FLIGHT 5.8 PG

Start: Same as Andrew.

Pitch 1: Climb up left to the arête, and climb this and the face to the GT Ledge. (90 feet) 5.8 PG

Pitch 2: Finish on a nearby climb.

FA 1983: Jim Munson, Morris Hershoff, and Hardie Truesdale

302. TRAVERSE OF THE CLODS 5.8 PG

Start: On the GT Ledge at the top of the first pitch of Andrew. Walk up left, climb up a few feet, and walk over to the large right-facing corner on the right.

Pitch 1: Climb up and slightly right to the first overhang, move right, and work up through some small overhangs until below a ceiling. Move right and up to the ceiling (V1), and then make a very long traverse right to the hanging belay on Twilight Zone. (80 feet) 5.8 PG

Pitch 2: Climb over the ceiling above, and traverse right just above the lip and around a corner to a prominent 2-inch-wide crack, which is followed past a final overhang to the top. (50 feet)

Variation 1: **5.11−** **PG** Climb up through the ceilings and exit left to the top.

FA 1976: Ivan Rezucha and Paul Potters
FA (Variation 1) 1973: John Stannard and John Bragg

303. SKELETAL REMAINS 5.11+ X
Start: On the GT Ledge above the Andrew corner.

Pitch 1: Climb straight up the face past a tiny right-facing corner to the obvious ceiling. Traverse right about 20 feet to the base of an overhanging right-facing corner. Then climb up through the imposing roof above and step left to a belay stance. (80 feet) 5.11+ X

Pitch 2: Continue to the top.

FA 1984: Jeff Gruenberg

304. TWILIGHT ZONE 5.7 PG, A3
Start: On the GT Ledge about halfway along the second pitch of Andrew. (This point can also be reached by following Goldner's Grunge to the GT Ledge and walking left.)

Pitch 1: (V1) Scramble up onto the left side of a large ledge at a right-facing corner below two laurel bushes. Climb the corner to a ledge at the second laurel bush. (40 feet) 5.3

Pitch 2: (V2) Climb the chimney above to a horizontal crack on the left face of the corner, beneath the ominous roof. Follow the crack out left about 25 feet to a vertical crack, which is followed to the top of a small right-facing corner. Then diagonal up left to a hanging belay. 5.7 PG, A3

Pitch 3: (V3) Move left, climb a small corner to an overhang, step right, and continue up to the top. 5.6

Variation 1: **5.2** **G** Follow the third pitch and Variation 1 of Andrew until a traverse left on a ledge can be made to the second laurel bush on the regular route.

Variation 2: The Zone 5.13− PG Hand traverse left about 20 feet to a stance on the arête and climb up (5.11 X) to some fixed pitons at the first roof. Move out right to a bolt, work up past a small right-facing corner to another roof, and join the regular route. Follow the regular route left about 10 feet to a crack in the ceiling. Clear the ceiling and hand traverse left to the "victory" stance. Then continue on the regular route to its hanging belay. (Because the 5.11 X section is so serious, it is often toproped from the regular route.)

Variation 3: The French Connection 5.12+ PG Hand traverse right 10–15 feet along the tier in the main roof and join The Best Things in Life Aren't Free, which is followed to the top. (Also known as Jack Hammered.)

The regular route is still a classic aid problem, which can be done with nuts.

FA 1963: Art Gran and Phil Jacobus

FA (Variation 2) 1986: Jeff Gruenberg and Jack Mileski, after chiseling holds, placing protection on rappel, cleaning, toproping, and hangdogging

FA (Variation 3) 1986: Jack Mileski and Jeff Gruenberg, after chiseling holds, placing protection on rappel, cleaning, and hangdogging

305. THE BEST THINGS IN LIFE AREN'T FREE 5.12+ PG, A4

Start: At the belay ledge on Twilight Zone.

Pitch 1: Follow Twilight Zone up the chimney and traverse left with aid for about 15 feet to a very thin crack. Aid up the crack to the second and smaller of two right-facing corners, and continue with aid to the top of the corner. Then climb free past a flake that forms a tiered overhang to a black seam or fault, which is followed out past the lip of the roof to the top.

The free-climbing crux of this route was first freed as the crux of The French Connection.

FA 1984: Mike Sawicky and Chris Monz

306. ANDREW 5.4 PG ★★

Start: On a ledge 30 feet above the ground, below a huge right-facing corner, 40 feet right of Proctoscope.

Pitch 1: Climb the corner and the face on its right to the GT Ledge.

Pitch 2: Walk right about 50 feet to a tree below a flaky right-facing corner that begins 30 feet up.

Pitch 3: Climb up to the corner and go up it a few feet. (V1) Then traverse up and right on small ledges to a flaky left-facing corner. Follow the corner to its top, move left, and work up to a stance at some flakes and a short left-facing corner. Then continue climbing up and right, following the path of least resistance, to the top. (110 feet)   5.4   PG

Variation 1:   5.4   G   Continue up the corner (loose flakes) to its top. (V1a) Then, at the overhang, traverse right about 12 feet to a groove and join the regular route.

Variation 1a: Moby Dick   5.8   PG   Traverse left and work up into a small flaring chimney. At the overhang above, exit left and continue to the top.

FA 1947: Hans Kraus, Fritz Wiessner, and Bonnie Prudden
FA (Variation 1a) 1955: Hans Kraus and John Rupley
FFA (Variation 1a): Unknown.

307. GOLDNER'S GRUNGE   4th Class

Start: At a steep, dirty, broken gully, 35 feet right of Andrew.

Pitch 1: Follow the gully and much broken rock past numerous trees and bushes to the GT Ledge. (150 feet)   4th Class

Pitch 2: Finish on a nearby climb.

FA 1960: Bill Goldner, Sonja and Lotte Jensen, and Al DeMaria

308. ANDROID   5.10 −   PG

Start: On the thin-looking face about 10 feet left of Three Vultures.

Pitch 1: Climb the face past a broken fault to the GT Ledge, staying to the right of some broken rock on the way. (110 feet) 5.10 −

Pitch 2: Walk left and climb some right-facing flakes to the left-facing flakes under the ceiling above. Traverse right, clear the ceiling, and then diagonal up right to a belay below another ceiling. (50 feet)   5.8 −

Pitch 3:   (V1)   Traverse left about 15 feet to a short right-facing corner, climb this, and diagonal up right past two small ledges to a ceiling (some parties belay here). (V2) Climb past the right side of the ceiling to a left-facing groove and then continue to the top. (70 feet) 5.10−

Variation 1: Amber Waves of Pain 5.9 G Climb up and slightly right past some right-facing corners and through a notch in the overhang. Then continue up the face and go through another notch in the final overhangs to the top.

Variation 2: Traverse left and join Andrew.

FA 1980: Ivan Rezucha and Annie O'Neill

FA (Variation 1) 1987: Stephen Lewanik and Mark Goldman

309. THREE VULTURES 5.9 PG ★

Start: Below a short, thin crack that starts 7 feet above the ground, at the left edge of a small overhang that arches right, 50 feet right of Goldner's Grunge.

Pitch 1: Follow the crack up the broken face, step right, and work up past a bulge. Then continue up the face to the GT Ledge. (110 feet) 5.9

Pitch 2: Scramble to the top of a pedestal, which is below a flaring crack. (20 feet)

Pitch 3: Climb the crack to the ceiling above, traverse right (some parties belay here), and continue up a corner to the top. (110 feet) 5.9

FA 1961: Willie Crowther, Bill Homeyer, and Mike Levin

310. FACE TO FACE 5.9 PG

Start: In a shallow scoop about 20 feet above the ground, 40 feet right of Three Vultures.

Pitch 1: Climb up past the scoop and diagonal up left to a bulge. Traverse right and move up to a small, short right-facing corner. Work up past the left side of the corner, angle up right to whitish rock, and then continue up to the GT Ledge. (150 feet) 5.7

Pitch 2: Walk left and climb to the top of some blocks. Traverse diagonally up and right to a ceiling at a left-facing corner. Move up into the corner, hand traverse right to the nose, and then continue straight up to join Three Vultures (V1), which is followed to the top. (60 feet)   5.9   PG

Variation 1:   **5.10**   **PG**   Traverse left and climb up past a short, thin crack to another crack that is 3–4 inches wide. Follow this until it ends at a ceiling and traverse left to better handholds. Then move up and left to easier rock, and continue to the top. (40 feet)

FA 1977: Alan Long, Roy Kligfield, John Kingston, and Al Rubin

311. NO GLOW   5.9   PG   ★

Start: On the face just right of a 7-foot-high groove containing a small vertical fracture that continues above it, 15 feet right of Face to Face.

Pitch 1: Climb up and right past a slab to a belay ledge. (40 feet)

Pitch 2: Climb up past a bulge at the right edge of the overhangs above and continue up a corner. Then move out left past an overhang to the GT Ledge. (110 feet)

Pitch 3: Just to the left is a left-facing corner. Climb out onto its right face, continue up through an overhang at a small notch, and head straight up to the top. (120 feet)   5.9   PG

Height-related—easier if taller.

FA 1954: Jim McCarthy and Tim Mutch

FFA 1965: Art Gran and Lito Tejada-Flores

312. SHELL SHOCK   5.10+   PG

Start: At the second of two ramp systems that lead up right, 40 feet right of Face to Face and 20 feet left of a mungy, grass-filled vertical fault that contains a tree and is below a grassy ledge.

Pitch 1: Go up the ramp system and some cracks to low-angle rock that leads to a steep face. Then continue up to a blocky right-facing corner, which is followed to the GT Ledge. (150 feet)   5.6 or 5.7

Pitch 2: Climb up to the ceiling above and clear it at a short right-facing corner. Then move out right around the corner and continue up the face to a large triangular block and some ledges. (60 feet)   5.10+   PG

Pitch 3: Traverse right about 20 feet and finish up the last 30 feet of Keep on Struttin'. (50 feet)
FA 1982: Russ Clune and Dan McMillan

313. WOP STOP   5.11 –   PG
Start: On the face midway between two grassy, mungy vertical faults, each with a tree part way up, 30 feet left of Keep on Struttin'.
Pitch 1: Climb up the face to a short right-facing corner capped by a small triangular overhang. Go up left to a ledge to the left of the trees. Then continue up past a shallow right-facing corner to the GT Ledge. (150 feet)   5.6
Pitch 2: Climb the roof overhead and continue to the top. (100 feet)   5.11 –   PG
FA 1982: Russ Raffa and Rich Romano

314. KEEP ON STRUTTIN'   5.9   PG–R   ★
Start: On a grey face directly below a pine tree, 30 feet left of Moonlight.
Pitch 1: Climb straight up the face past the pine tree to the GT Ledge. (160 feet)   5.8   PG
Pitch 2: Walk right about 30 feet to a thin crack on a steep face and belay.
Pitch 3: Follow the crack past an overhang and move left about 5 feet. Climb up and left to a bolt, and continue straight up to a horizontal crack. Then traverse left about 8 feet to a notch in the overhang, clear the overhang, and climb up to a right-facing corner. (50 feet)   5.9   PG–R
Pitch 4:   (V1)   Traverse left along some horizontal cracks for about 30 feet until below two large stacked flakes. Climb past these on their left and step right. Then, either continue up past a thin crack in a shallow right-facing corner to the top or finish up right on easier rock. (60 feet)   5.7   G
Variation 1:   **PG**   Continue up the corner, traverse left about 20 feet, and work up to a large flake capped by an overhang. (V2) Clear the overhang and then climb to the top.
Variation 2:   **5.9+**   **PG**   Climb the thin vertical seam just

right of the flake and then diagonal up right past an overhang to the top.

Named in memory of fellow climber Joe Strutt.

FA 1973: Dave Loeks and Walter Bauman

FA (Variation 2) 1984: Ivan Rezucha, Don Lauber, and Annie O'Neill

315. STEP LIVELY 5.9+ PG

Start: On the slab just left of Moonlight.

Pitch 1: Climb the slab past bulging rock to the GT Ledge. (110 feet)

Pitch 2: Follow Moonlight to the beginning of its traverse. Then climb up left past an overhang to a second corner, and continue right and up past a crack to the top. (100 feet) 5.9+ PG

FA 1984: Ivan Rezucha and Annie O'Neill

316. MOONLIGHT 5.6 PG ★

Start: On some slabs below a flaky left-facing corner, just right of Step Lively. There are left-facing flakes at the top of the slabs.

Pitch 1: Climb up to the corner, and follow it and the face on its left to the GT Ledge. (130 feet) 5.6

Pitch 2: Walk right about 40 feet and belay.

Pitch 3: Climb up left to a right-facing corner below a large ceiling. Then traverse out left around the corner and continue up the face past a pine tree to the top. (100 feet) 5.6

FA 1960: Bill Ryan and Willie Crowther

317. POINT-BLANK 5.12 R

Start: Same as Moonlight.

Pitch 1: From the right side of the grassy ledge, diagonal up right, following some right-facing flakes, to a ledge with blocks. Then follow a short, broken left-facing corner until it ends, move right, and continue up to the GT Ledge. (110 feet) 5.8 PG

Pitch 2: Follow Moonlight for about 15 feet until it goes up left. Then continue up the face to a notch in an overhang that leads to another overhang. (V1) Traverse out right, following a crack-fault onto the face, and continue up right to an arête. Then move right and climb up to join Crack'n-Up, which is followed to the top. (100 feet)   5.12   R

Variation 1:   Vanishing Point   5.11   R   Before the crux of Point-Blank, climb the overhang on the left side. Then work up a scooped-out face, go past the ceilings above, and follow a shallow corner to the top.

The first pitch is height-related—if you're over 6 feet tall, it's 5.6 and if you're under 5 feet 9 inches, it's harder than 5.8.

FA 1981: Russ Raffa

FA (Variation 1) 1983: Jeff Gruenberg, Russ Clune, Hugh Herr, Mike Freeman, and Jack Mileski

318. ERECT DIRECTION   5.10   PG   ★★★

Start: At the prominent crack system on the left face of the Updraft corner.

Pitch 1:   (V1)   Climb the crack system and face to the GT Ledge. (110 feet)   5.8   PG

Pitch 2: Follow Moonlight for about 40 feet to a ledge. Climb up to the overhang with the short off-width crack on the left and work up past this to a second overhang. Then traverse right to a right-facing corner and continue up to a hanging belay below a roof. (80 feet)   5.10   PG

Pitch 3: Climb up to the roof and traverse left until the holds run out. Reach over the lip and traverse right to a small, short right-facing corner, which is followed to a ceiling. Then traverse out left onto the face and continue up to the top. (60 feet)   5.10   PG

Variation 1:   5.6   PG   Walk down left to an overhang below the arête. Climb the overhang and follow the arête to the regular route.

A terrific climb, but when will the original aid line go free?

FA 1966: Bill Goldner and Dennis Mehmet

FFA 1973: John Stannard and John Bragg

319. CRACK'N-UP   5.11+   PG–R   ★★

Start: On the GT Ledge, at the top of the first pitch of Updraft.

Pitch 1: Follow the second pitch of Updraft until it is possible to traverse left to a small crack on the left face of the Updraft corner.

Follow the crack up and slightly right until below an overhang beneath the obvious sentry-box corner. Climb up into the sentry box, exit out its top, and continue up the face above to a large horizontal crack. Then traverse out left to the arête and follow it to the top. (90 feet)

FA 1978: John Bragg, Mark Robinson, and Bob Murray

320. UPDRAFT 5.5 G ★

Start: At the base of a large right-facing corner, 60 feet right of Moonlight and directly below a prominent chimney in the large roof at the top of the cliff.

Pitch 1: Follow the corner and face on the right to the GT Ledge. (110 feet) 5.3

Pitch 2: Continue up the corner and face on the right to the chimney, which then leads to the top. (120 feet) 5.5 G

Watch out for loose rock on the first pitch.

FA 1944: Fritz Wiessner and Hans Kraus

321. CASCADING CRYSTAL KALEIDOSCOPE
5.8 PG ★★★

Start: At the left edge of a bulge that forms a short left-facing corner, 17 feet right of Updraft.

Pitch 1: Climb up around the bulge and move right to a left-facing corner. Go left around the bulges above to an overhang, which is split by a crack. Then continue past the overhang and crack to the GT Ledge. (120 feet) 5.5

Pitch 2: (V1) Walk right to a short left-facing corner. Climb this to a small platform, step right, and work up past a bulge. Traverse left, move up (V2), and then continue left to a belay near the Updraft corner. (50 feet) 5.7

Pitch 3: Traverse right to a left-facing flake-crack and follow it to the obvious overhang. (V3) Then traverse right again and continue up to the top. (60 feet) 5.8 PG

Variation 1: 5.7 or 5.8 R Climb straight up through the overhang above and rejoin the regular route.

Variation 2: 5.9 PG–R Climb straight up to the left-facing flake-crack on the regular route.

DICK WILLIAMS on First Ascent of CASCADING CRYSTAL KALEIDOSCOPE
Dick DuMais

Variation 3: **5.9** **PG** Continue up and left through the overhang to the top.
FA 1968: Dick Williams and Dick DuMais

322. DIANA 5.8 – PG

Start: At a shallow, grassy open book with a crack that is just below and left of some large boulders on a grassy ledge, 55 feet right of the Updraft corner, where the trail descends steeply.

Pitch 1: Go up past the boulders to a higher grassy ledge and then climb basically straight up to the GT Ledge. (150 feet) 5.6 R

Pitch 2: (V1) Walk right about 40 feet and belay.

Pitch 3: Climb past an overhang and diagonal up left 20–25 feet to another overhang, which is climbed on the right. Work left, go up through a notch in a third overhang, and continue up to a belay. (90 feet) 5.8 – PG

Pitch 4: Continue to the top. (40 feet)

Variation 1: **Wicked Diana** **5.9 R** Climb straight up the face through an overhang and rejoin the regular route.

FA 1964: Art Gran and Pete Vlachos
FA (Variation 1) 1973: Jim Kolocotronis and Lincoln Stoller

323. KEN'S BLIND HOLE 5.6 PG

Start: At a point on the face between two thin parallel cracks that are 10 feet high, 30 feet right of Diana, where the trail stops descending and levels off.

Pitch 1: Climb up the face to a belay at a large boulder on the GT Ledge. (140 feet) 5.5

Pitch 2: Walk right about 40 feet and belay directly below the left side of a left-facing corner where it meets an overhang 30 feet up.

Pitch 3: Climb the face to the top of a very short right-facing corner. Step up, traverse left, and diagonal up left to a point level with the overhang to the right. Move up right across the overhang to easier, broken rock, which leads up and left to a block under a roof. (V1, V2) Then exit up right to the top. (70 feet) 5.6 PG

Variation 1: 5.4 G Climb up the left side of the block and exit right to the top.

Variation 2: Old Dogs, New Tricks 5.11 G Climb up the left side of the block and traverse left to a loose flake in a corner. Then continue left to the nose and follow a crack on the face to the top.

FA 1948: Ken Prestrud and Hans Kraus
FFA 1961: Jim McCarthy
FA (Variation 1) 1985: Todd Swain and David Levenstein
FA (Variation 2) 1988: Dick Williams and Joe Bridges, after placing some of the protection on rappel

324. UNHOLY WICK 5.8 G
Start: Below a small overhang that is 10 feet above the ground and directly below a right-facing corner capped by an overhang, 40 feet right of Ken's Blind Hole.

Pitch 1: Climb to the top of the corner and move up past some pointed flakes to some blocks on the left. Then traverse right and continue up to a ledge. (50 feet) 5.7 PG

Pitch 2: Step right and continue up and slightly right, past an overhang on the right, to the GT Ledge. (100 feet)

Pitch 3: Follow Ken's Blind Hole to the top of a short right-facing corner. Step left and climb up the face (5.6 R; a chopped bolt of unknown origin is in this section) to the obvious overhang (this point can also be reached via the corner on the right). Clear the overhang and continue up to a small overhang at the top of a shallow open book. Move left and climb up through a notch formed by a huge block to a ledge. (V1) Walk left to a corner and follow it to an overhang. Then exit left and continue to the top. (90 feet) 5.8 G

Variation 1: Bow-Tie Ceiling 5.9 PG Climb through the middle of a bow-tie-shaped ceiling directly above the block and continue to the top.

FA 1965: Dick Williams and Bill Goldner
FA (Variation 1) 1979: Hardie Truesdale and Beau Haworth

325. LOST AND FOUND 5.7 PG
Start: Below a vertical seam that begins about 15 feet up, 9 feet left of The Last Will Be First.

Pitch 1: Climb the face to a narrow, grassy ledge and the seam, and continue up to the right side of the long overhang above. Move right and diagonal up right for several feet. Then step left and continue up the face past the center of an overhang to some left-facing corners that lead to the GT Ledge. (160 feet) 5.7 PG

Pitch 2: Finish on a nearby climb.

When Ivan Rezucha climbed this in 1984, he found some old pitons that suggested it had already been done, perhaps in the late 1950s.

326. THE LAST WILL BE FIRST 5.6 PG

Start: At a 10-foot-high groove below a grassy ledge that is 15 feet above the ground, 70 feet right of Unholy Wick.

Pitch 1: Climb up past a tree and follow some cracks on the left to a left-facing corner. At the top of the corner, step around right onto the face and continue up to a ledge. (110 feet) 5.6

Pitch 2: Climb up to the GT Ledge. (60 feet) 5.6

Pitch 3: Climb up and left past the left edge of an overhang to meet Ken's Blind Hole. Then continue up and right to the top. (60 feet) 5.6

FA 1965: Ants Leemets and Elmer Skahan

327. STROLLING ON JUPITER 5.10+ PG–R

Start: At a very thin broken crack on the low-angle face 15 feet right of The Last Will Be First.

Pitch 1: Climb up the face past grassy ledges to a small left-facing corner and oak tree. Continue up to the overhang above at a 2-foot-high right-facing corner. Clear the overhang, traverse right about 10 feet, and continue up to a small stance. (V1) Then diagonal up right to a belay stance next to some loose flakes. (100 feet) 5.10+ PG–R

Pitch 2: Climb up to the overhang above, move left a few feet, and continue past the overhang to the GT Ledge. (50 feet) 5.9

Pitch 3: Climb the face about 15 feet left of Jim's Gem and work up past a large detached blocklike flake to a ceiling. Then move left, diagonal up right, and continue to the top. (60 feet) 5.10

Variation 1: 5.6 PG Step left, climb up to some loose rock, step left again, and continue up to the GT Ledge.

FA 1982: Sam Slater, Bruce Thompson, Rich Strang, and Mark Bourque

328. EXIT STAGE LEFT   5.9   PG

Start: At an obvious right-facing corner, 20 feet right of Strolling on Jupiter and 32 feet left of Jim's Gem.

Pitch 1: Climb about 40 feet up the corner. Then continue up a thin crack, angle up right, and work up to a large flake under an overhang. (90 feet)   5.8

Pitch 2: Move up and slightly right through the overhang, and continue up to the GT Ledge. (80 feet)   5.8

Pitch 3:   (V1)   Follow Modern Times to a crack in the ceiling, follow the crack past the ceiling, traverse left, and continue to the top. (50 feet)   5.9   PG

Variation 1:   Gem's Gym   5.9   R   Walk left and climb the face past an overhang. Then continue up 2 feet right of the first ceiling to the next ceiling, traverse left onto the face, and continue to the top. (Also known as Slime and Punishment.)

FA 1979: Hardie Truesdale, Morris Hershoff, and Dave Feinberg

FA (Variation 1) 1981: Rich Romano and Rod Swartz

329. JIM'S GEM   5.8   PG

Start: At a short, black open book that is below an orange ceiling 30 feet above the ground, 32 feet right of Exit Stage Left and 30 feet left of Modern Times.

Pitch 1: Climb the open book and fault system past a small overhang, and follow a crack up and slightly left to a big orange flake under the orange ceiling. Exit right and go up a ramplike fault and groove system to a ledge under an overhang (some parties belay here). More left and work up past the right side of another overhang. Then diagonal up left and continue up to the GT Ledge. (150 feet)

Pitch 2: Walk left about 20 feet to the base of a yellow corner.

Pitch 3: Diagonal up right past an overhang to a small alcove (or reach the alcove by climbing the corner and traversing right). Then step out right and continue to the top. (80 feet)   5.8   PG

FA 1954: Jim McCarthy and Stan Gross

FFA 1960s: Art Gran

330. MODERN TIMES 5.8+ PG ★★

Start: At a short face below a grassy open book, 30 feet right of Jim's Gem and 30 feet left of High Exposure.

Pitch 1: Climb the face and open book, and continue to a triangular overhang. Traverse left about 15 feet to a small ledge at the base of a right-facing corner (75 feet—some parties belay here). Step right and climb up and back left until above the ledge. Then diagonal up left for 10 feet before heading straight up past a small overhang to the GT Ledge. (150 feet) 5.7 PG

Pitch 2: Walk left about 20 feet and climb a right-facing corner. Diagonal up right to a very large flake, which is climbed to its top. Move up to a notch in the ceiling above, and exit up and out right. Continue up and right through more overhangs past another notch to a steep white face. Then traverse right about 15 feet to a ledge with a tree. (100 feet) 5.8+ PG

Pitch 3: Continue to the top.

FA 1964: Dick Williams, Dave Craft, and Brian Carey

331. PSYCHEDELIC 5.8+ PG

Start: Same as High Exposure.

Pitch 1: Climb the first pitch of High Exposure. (50 feet) 5.4

Pitch 2: Continue up the corner to the GT Ledge. (60 feet) 5.6

Pitch 3: Walk right to a chimney and follow it to a small ledge. Then move up left past the obvious overhang to a belay stance. (50 feet) 5.8 G

Pitch 4: Climb up a few feet, and then traverse down and right about 40 feet to a spot about 10 feet below the level of the third-pitch belay stance. Then continue up the face and back left to a belay, which is positioned to help protect the second. (80 feet) 5.8+ PG

Pitch 5: Scramble to the top.

FA 1965: Yvon Chouinard and Dick Williams

332. HIGH EXPOSURE 5.6+ G–PG ★★★

Start: At a large left-facing corner to the left of a prominent nose, 30 feet right of Modern Times.

YVON CHOUINARD and DICK WILLIAMS on MODERN TIMES
Art Gran

HANS KRAUS on HIGH EXPOSURE
Dick Williams

Pitch 1: Follow the corner past a small overhang formed by broken rock to a belay stance in the corner. (50 feet) 5.4

Pitch 2: Continue up the corner to some ledges that lead out right onto the face. Go out the ledges and climb up the approximate center of the face to a superb triangular ledge. (90 feet) 5.4

Pitch 3: Starting on the left, diagonal up right to a roof. Move right and reach up and around to a horizontal crack on the steep face above. Then move left and continue up to a crack that leads to the top, or traverse left to the nose and follow it to the top. (70 feet) 5.6+ G–PG

Probably the most sought-after classic in the Gunks.

FA 1941: Hans Kraus and Fritz Wiessner

333. BEYOND GOOD AND EVIL 5.11− PG

Start: Same as High Exposure.

Pitch 1: Climb up about 20 feet and belay on a grassy ledge to the left.

Pitch 2: Traverse right along an obvious horizontal crack to the nose. Climb up past an overhang, step left, and work up through more overhangs (some parties belay here). Then continue up the face to the triangular High Exposure belay ledge. (150 feet) 5.10 R

Pitch 3: Walk left to a tree and belay.

Pitch 4: Climb up the face to a diagonal crack splitting the overhangs above. Follow the crack until it ends, and continue up left (crossing Psychedelic) and then up right to the top. (70 feet) 5.11− PG

FA (Pitch 4) 1978: Henry Barber
FA 1982: Dan McMillan, Russ Clune, Hugh Herr, and Morris Hershoff

334. DIRECTISSIMA 5.9 G ★★★

Start: On top of a block just right of High Exposure.

Pitch 1: (V1) Follow a slanting groove up right (V2) and around the corner, and continue up to a small ledge. (50 feet) 5.8 PG

Pitch 2: Hand traverse left to a thin crack and climb up to a stance. (30 feet) 5.9 G

DICK WILLIAMS on DIRECTISSIMA
Dick DuMais

Pitch 3: Diagonal up right to the arête and follow it to the triangular High Exposure belay ledge. (80 feet) 5.6 R

Pitch 4: Finish on the last pitch of High Exposure.

Variation 1: 5.11 (Toprope) Climb the arête between Enduro Man's Longest Hangout and Directissima directly up to the first belay ledge on the regular route.

Variation 2: Wagissima 5.12 R Climb straight up over a bulging nose and step left to a stance. Continue up past a small flake and a thin crack on the right to an overhang. Move left and follow a seam up left to some large overhangs. Then work up to a belay on the regular route. (Usually toproped.)

FA 1956: Hans Kraus and Stan Gross

FFA 1963: Jim McCarthy

FA (Variation 2) 1983: Sam Slater, Harry Brielman, Bruce Thompson, and Tony Trocchi

335. ENDURO MAN'S LONGEST HANGOUT 5.11 R ★★★

Start: On an orange face with a vertical seam, 20 feet right of Directissima and 10 feet left of the Directissima Variation 1 arête.

Pitch 1: Climb the face to the top of the seam, move up right to a stance, and continue up to the first Directissima belay ledge. (50 feet) 5.11 R

Pitch 2: Climb straight up the overhanging face (V1), following some faults, to the triangular High Exposure belay ledge. (70 feet) 5.10+ PG

Pitch 3: Follow the third pitch of High Exposure for a few feet, and then diagonal out and up left through the overhangs (V2) to join Psychedelic, which is followed to the top. (70 feet) 5.11 PG

Variation 1: Tripleissima 5.11− R Move right at the earliest opportunity and follow some parallel faults to the triangular High Exposure belay ledge.

Variation 2: Ignorance 5.11 G Climb out right to the nose and continue to the top.

The second pitch is known as Ridicullissima.

FA 1980: John Bragg and Doug Strickholm

FA (Pitch 2) 1975: John Stannard and John Bragg

FA (Pitch 3) 1978: John Bragg, Mark Robinson, and Bob Murray

FA (Variation 1) 1984: Jeff Gruenberg and Russ Clune
FA (Variation 2) 1985: Collin Lantz and friend

336. DIRECTISSISSIMA 5.10 PG ★★★

Start: At some left-facing flakes and cracks, 37 feet right of High Exposure and 10 feet left of First Trapps Chimney; or on the face at a fault system 5 feet left of First Trapps Chimney.

Pitch 1: Climb up to the Directississima ledge and belay on its left end. (50 feet) 5.8

Pitch 2: Move back right and work up the steep, bulging face to a short, very thin crack. Follow the crack and then diagonal up right to an overhang. Pass the overhang and continue up easier rock to the GT Ledge. (70 feet) 5.10 PG

Pitch 3: Step left and climb a crack and the face to the top. (40 feet) 5.8

The stability of your brain on this one is directly proportional to the strength in your arms.

FA 1957: Jim McCarthy, Hans Kraus, and John Rupley
FFA 1967: John Stannard and Howie Davis

337. LAKATAKISSIMA 5.10 R–X

Start: Same as First Trapps Chimney.

Pitch 1: Climb the chimney to a ledge with a tree.

Pitch 2: Follow some thin cracks past an overhang and up a steep face to a ledge. (120 feet) 5.10 R–X

Pitch 3: Climb up through the break in the overhang above and continue to the top. (80 feet)

Be careful of loose rock on the second pitch.

FA 1978: Jack Mileski and Todd Ritter

338. FIRST TRAPPS CHIMNEY 5.3 G

Start: At the first dirty, broken chimney to the right of High Exposure.

Pitch 1: (V1) Climb the broken face just right of the chimney to the second ledge. (140 feet)

Pitch 2: Climb up a short chimney to a left-facing corner (V2), which is followed to the top. (50 feet)

Variation 1: Start at a flaring crack that leads to a right-facing

THE TRAPPS

corner to the right of the chimney. Follow the crack and corner to a ledge, and then continue up and left to join the regular route.

Variation 2: 5.6 PG Step left to a prominent jagged crack and climb it to the top.

If the variations are used, this is a worthwhile climb.

339. SECOND TRAPPS CHIMNEY 5.4 G

Start: At a dirty, broken, 8-foot-wide chimney system, 40 feet right of First Trapps Chimney.

Pitches 1–2: Follow the chimney system to the top.

340. BUCKETS ABOVE 5.9+ G

Start: At a wide right-facing corner capped by a ceiling, 20 feet downhill to the right of Second Trapps Chimney.

Pitch 1: Scramble up to a ledge and walk to the back of the corner. Climb up to the ceiling, traverse left, and work up some cracks in a corner system to the broken face above. Then continue up to a large ledge. (60 feet) 5.9+ G

Pitch 2: Continue up a loose crack past loose blocks to a ledge. (60 feet)

Pitch 3: Climb the corner above to a ceiling, exit right, and continue up the face to the top. (50 feet)

Be careful of loose rock.

FA 1980: Rick Cronk and Peter Behme

341. THIRD TRAPPS CHIMNEY 5.3 G

Start: At the third major chimney system to the right of High Exposure. (Don't confuse it with the chimney in the orange corner to its left.)

Pitches 1–2: Follow the chimney system to the top.

342. OBSTACLE DELUSION 5.10− PG

Start: On the left face of the large flake just right of Third Trapps Chimney and 3 feet left of Insuhlation.

Pitch 1: Climb directly up the face to a grassy ledge. Then continue up past orange rock to a stance below a double overhang. (60 feet)

Pitch 2: Climb directly over the double overhang and traverse a few feet right until below a short left-facing corner. Follow the corner to an overhang, move left onto a steep face, and continue up and left along a short groove to a triangular ledge. Then move up and right, following a corner to the GT Ledge. (90 feet) 5.10− PG

Pitch 3: (V1) Scramble to the top.

Variation 1: **5.10 G** Climb the obvious thin crack in the ceiling above and continue to the top.

FA 1973: Dave Loeks and Claude Suhl
FA (Variation 1): John Stannard

343. INSUHLATION 5.9 PG

Start: At the large flake 10 feet right of Third Trapps Chimney.

Pitch 1: Climb the flake and step right onto the main face. Then continue up and right past two ledges to a third ledge below an overhang. (80 feet) 5.8

Pitch 2: Climb directly past the overhang and enter a small groove. Continue up the groove past some flakes and follow a thin crack through some overhangs to the GT Ledge. (130 feet) 5.9 PG

Pitch 3: Scramble to the top.

FA 1973: Dave Loeks and Claude Suhl

344. ALPINE DIVERSIONS 5.8 G

Start: On the face just left of some jutting rocks in a broken chimney-corner, 5 feet right of Insuhlation.

Pitch 1: Move up the face to an irregular crack, which is followed to a large pine tree. Then continue up and right to the base of an open book capped by an overhang. (90 feet) 5.8

Pitch 2: Climb the open book, go past an overhang to another open book, and continue up past another overhang to a ledge with a tree. (100 feet) 5.8

Pitch 3: Finish on a nearby climb.

Originally known as Alpine Deviates.

FA 1982: Todd Swain and John Thackery

THE TRAPPS

345. MISSING, BUT NOT LOST 5.4 G
Start: Same as Alpine Diversions.
Pitch 1: Climb the broken chimney-corner to a large ledge. (75 feet) 5.4 G
Pitch 2: Continue up a chimney to the top, staying to the right. (75 feet) 5.2
FA 1984: Todd Swain

346. 50–50 5.5 G
Start: At a thin crack that begins at the left edge of a large overhang which juts out right at ground level, 30 feet downhill to the right of Insuhlation.
Pitch 1: Climb the crack, following a corner and the face on the right. Then diagonal up left and work back up the face on the right to a dirty ledge with a pine tree. (80 feet) 5.5 G
Pitch 2: Continue up past a chimney and corner system to the top. (100 feet)
FA 1949: Hans Kraus and Bonnie Prudden

347. 60–40 5.7 PG
Start: On the right side of a roof that is formed by a bottomless arête, 15 feet downhill to the right of 50–50.
Pitch 1: Scramble up to a horizontal crack in a right-facing corner. Traverse out left to the arête and continue up the left face to a dirty ledge with a pine tree, staying as closely as possible to the arête. (80 feet) 5.7 PG
Pitch 2: Rappel or follow a dirty gully to the top.
FA 1984: Todd Swain and Andy Schenkel

348. LICHEN 40 WINKS 5.7 PG
Start: At a horizontal crack that begins on the ground and goes out right to the Sleepwalk arête, 12 feet right of 60–40.
Pitch 1: Climb the center of the face past three small overhangs to a belay at a pine tree that hangs down from a ledge. (90 feet) 5.7 PG
Pitch 2: Move right about 5 feet, climb white rock up past an

overhang, and continue to the top, passing to the left of a small tree. (80 feet) 5.7− PG

FA 1988: Dick Williams, Joe Bridges, and Dave Craft

349. SLEEPWALK   5.7   PG
Start: Below a small pointed right-facing flake, 15 feet left of Ants' Line and just left of the Ent Line tree.
Pitch 1: (V1) Climb up past the flake to a horizontal crack, traverse left to the arête, and continue up the face near the arête to the Ants' Line belay ledge. (80 feet) 5.7 PG
Pitch 2: (V2) Follow Ants' Line to the top. (90 feet) 5.4 PG–R
Variation 1: 5.8 PG Start on the right side of the low triangular roof formed by the bottomless arête, to the left of the regular route. Climb up to the first horizontal crack, traverse left to the arête, and move up to join the regular route.
Variation 2: Cool Hand Dukes   5.8   PG Diagonal up right and climb a vertical fault in the 10-foot-wide columnlike face to the top.

Something to do on one of those daze.

FA 1970: John Waterman and Al Rubin
FA (Variation 1) 1988: Joe Bridges, Dave Craft, and Dick Williams

350. ANTS' LINE   5.9   G   ★★
Start: At the large right-facing corner 15 feet to the right of Sleepwalk.
Pitch 1: (V1) Follow the corner past an overhang to a small belay ledge. (110 feet) 5.9 G
Pitch 2: Rappel from a spot 15 feet higher up or continue up some cracks past a large pine tree to the top. (90 feet) 5.4 PG–R
Variation 1: Ent Line   5.10+   PG–R Start on the left side of the large oak ("ent") tree to the left of the regular route. Climb up left to a crack-fault system, and work up past a ledge and some blocks. Then move right to a thin crack or seam, continue up to the right side of an overhang (V1a), and step right to join the regular route.

RICHARD GOLDSTONE on ANT'S LINE
Dick Williams

Variation 1a: 5.11 (Toprope) Climb past the overhang and continue up to the small belay ledge on the regular route.

A great corner to climb, its variations have become quite popular as toprope problems.

FA 1960s: Ants Leemets and an acquaintance
FFA 1968: Dave and Jim Erickson
FA (Variation 1) 1979: John Bragg, Bob Murray, and Mark Robinson
FA (Variation 1a: Toprope) 1987: Kevin Bein

351. CONDEMNED MAN 5.12− R
Start: On top of the block just left of Bonnie's Roof.
Pitch 1: Climb up to a triangular ceiling and go past it, following a thin crack out right onto the face. Continue up and left to the arête above, and then diagonal up left to a vertical fault and a belay stance. (60 feet) 5.12− R
Pitch 2: Climb up a short, shallow right-facing corner, and diagonal up left to an open book and some tiered ceilings. Then follow a major fault through the ceilings and up the face to join Ants' Line. (50 feet) 5.12− R
FA 1981: Hugh Herr and Jack Mileski

352. THE THRONE 5.12− PG ★
Start: At some cracks on the left face of the Bonnie's Roof open book.
Pitch 1: Follow the cracks up the face to a stance in the Bonnie's Roof open book. Then climb up and left around the arête to a belay ledge. (90 feet) 5.12− PG
Pitch 2: Continue up the arête to the top. (60 feet) 5.7
The most difficult part of the first pitch is often toproped.
FA 1963: Art Gran and Ants Leemets
FFA 1973: John Stannard and Steve Wunsch

353. BONNIE'S ROOF 5.9 G-PG ★★★
Start: At the base of a large yellow open book capped by a ceiling, below the left edge of a ledge that is 20 feet above the ground, 25 feet right of Ants' Line.
Pitch 1: Scramble up to the ledge and climb the open book

HUGH HERR on First Ascent of CONDEMNED MAN
Russ Clune

(often wet) past an overhang to a stance (some parties belay here). Then continue up the left face and the open book to a belay ledge below the roof. (130 feet) 5.9 G-PG

Pitch 2: (V1) Traverse left to the nose and continue up to the top. (50 feet) 5.8 PG

Variation 1: **5.10−** **G** Walk right, climb up to a crack, clear the overhang, and move up to another overhang. Then step left and follow a crack to the top.

A golden climb—one of the best. The second pitch was first climbed as an aid variation. The original route traversed out right around the corner onto the face and continued to the top.

FA 1952: Bonnie Prudden and Hans Kraus
FA (Pitch 2) 1958: Hans Kraus
FFA 1961: Dick Williams and Jim McCarthy
FA (Variation 1) 1975: Ivan Rezucha and Jeff Pofit

354. KNOCKOUT DROPS 5.11 R

Start: On the face 10 feet right of Bonnie's Roof.

Pitch 1: Climb up the face, following an ill-defined system of cracks and flakes, to a small left-facing corner that leads to an overhang. Climb past the overhang to a ceiling, traverse right, and then move up left to the optional belay stance on Bonnie's Roof. (70 feet) 5.11 R

Pitch 2: Diagonal up right, weave up through the large overhangs above, and continue past a narrow right-facing corner to the Bonnie's Roof belay ledge. (60 feet) 5.10

Pitch 3: Finish on Bonnie's Roof or its variation.

FA 1978: Mark Robinson, Bob Murray, and John Bragg

355. URSULA 5.5 PG

Start: At a small right-facing corner beneath the right end of a ledge that is 20 feet above the ground, 25 feet right of Bonnie's Roof.

Pitch 1: Climb up the corner and a groove on the right, and then diagonal up right to a ledge. (80 feet) 5.5

Pitch 2: Step left and continue up the steep but easy face to the top. (100 feet) 5.5

FA 1958: John Wharton, F. and B. Adams, and Al Alvarez

356. NOSE DROPS 5.9+ PG

Start: At a short right-facing corner that contains a series of small overhangs, 10 feet right of Ursula.

Pitch 1: Climb the left face of the corner and continue up a crack to a sentry box. Step right and work up the face to some overhangs. Pass the overhangs on the right and then diagonal up left to a belay. (70 feet) 5.9+ PG

Pitch 2: Move up left and continue straight up the face to the top. (80 feet) 5.6

FA 1982: Russ Clune, Rich Gottlieb, and Bill Ravitch

357. GROOVY 5.9− G

Start: At an open book capped by an overhang, 25 feet right of Ursula and just left of a low, blocky pinnacle.

Pitch 1: Follow the open book to the overhang, move left around the overhang, and continue up to the Ursula belay ledge. (70 feet) 5.9− G

Pitch 2: Finish on Ursula.

FA 1963: Jim McCarthy and Bob and Jane Culp

358. SPACE INVADERS 5.10+ PG

Start: At the blocky nose just right of Groovy.

Pitch 1: Follow the nose to an overhang, step right, and climb up to a crack system that diagonals up right. Follow the crack to its top, traverse left about 10 feet, and then continue up to the Ursula belay ledge. (70 feet) 5.10+ PG

Pitch 2: Finish on Ursula.

FA 1981: Felix Modugno, Rich Strang, and John Goobic

359. IN THE GROOVE 5.6 G

Start: At a low-angle, ramplike left-facing corner that begins at the right edge of a blocky pinnacle, 30 feet right and uphill from Groovy.

Pitch 1: (V1) Follow the corner to a small ledge, then continue up the main corner past some left-facing flakes to a belay ledge. (80 feet) 5.6 G

Pitch 2: Continue following the overhanging flaky corner to lower-angle rock. Then diagonal up left and move up to the top. (60 feet)   5.4

   Variation 1: Climb the face immediately to the right, or climb the left-facing corner farther to the right (usually wet).
   Why not get out of a rut and into this groove?
   FA 1963: Art Gran, Al DeMaria, and Jim Mays

360. IN THE SILLY   5.3   G
   Start: Same as In the Groove.
   Pitch 1: Follow the grassy, ramplike left-facing corner to a small ledge. Step up and move right to a ledge and belay. (50 feet)
   Pitch 2: Climb to the top of the chimney, move right onto the face, and continue straight up to the top. (100 feet)
   FA 1972: Art Reidel and Greg Lee

361. SLIPPING INTO INCIPIENCY   5.10   R
   Start: On the face of the left-facing corner immediately to the right of In the Groove.
   Pitch 1: Climb the face to an overhang, step right around the overhang, and continue up to a ledge. (30 feet)   5.10   PG
   Pitch 2: Climb the orange face above, following a very thin or incipient crack, to an overhang. Pass the overhang and then continue to the top, staying left of In the Silly. (70 feet)   5.10   R
   FA 1987: Jason Stern and Alex Gordon

362. SILLY GROOVE   5.9   PG
   Start: At a crack that leads to a pebbly horizontal band, 25 feet right of In the Groove and 12 feet left of Silly Chimney.
   Pitch 1: Climb the crack to the pebbly band, and continue up past some left-facing flakes and a short left-facing corner to a wide horizontal crack. Then continue up the broken face above to the top, staying to the right of a nose.
   FA: circa 1970

363. SILLY CHIMNEY   5.1   G
   Start: At the base of a large broken chimney, 40 feet right of Groovy and on the left side of an overhanging yellow face.

Pitches 1–2: Follow the chimney to the top, staying on the left for the first half and on the right for the second half. (150 feet)

Often used as a descent route.

FA 1941: Hans Kraus

364. NO MAN'S LAND 5.11 PG ★★

Start: In a groovelike open book in the middle of some broken rock, 30 feet right of Silly Chimney.

Pitch 1: Climb the groovy open book past a tree to an overhang, step left. Continue up to a large ledge. (60 feet) 5.8

Pitch 2: Climb a short, blocky right-facing corner through the tiered overhangs above, and move up and right to a semihanging belay stance in a short, orange open book. (60 feet) 5.11 PG

Pitch 3: Diagonal up right to a conspicuous flake that juts out left, hand traverse right, and continue up to a ledge. (75 feet) 5.8

Pitch 4: Skirt the ceiling above by going right and continue up to the top. (30 feet)

FA 1964: Dick Williams and Art Gran

FFA 1973: John Stannard and Ajax Greene

365. TIERS OF FEAR 5.12 PG ★★

Start: At a wide, broken open book with a tree, 24 feet right of No Man's Land and 23 feet left of a crack that is formed by the Yellow Wall boulder pile. The crack also has a tree in it.

Pitch 1: Follow the open book system to an overhang. Move right and then back up left to a short, wide right-facing corner. Climb up to a ceiling and exit left. Continue left a few more feet, move up, and then traverse back right. Then climb up through the point of the ceilings above, step right, and belay. (90 feet) 5.12 PG

Pitch 2: Continue up the steep face above to join No Man's Land. (50 feet) 5.10 R

FA 1983: Russ Raffa and Russ Clune

366. THE YELLOW WALL 5.11 PG–R ★★★

Start: On top of a boulder pile, 75 feet right of Silly Chimney.

Pitch 1: Climb about halfway up the inside corner on the right,

JOHN BRAGG on First Free Ascent of THE YELLOW WALL

Russ Raffa

step left around the outside corner onto the face, and continue up to a small belay stance. (60 feet) 5.8

Pitch 2: Step right and diagonal up left until above the belay stance. Continue straight up steep rock to a bolt and traverse right about 20 feet to another bolt. Then climb up past a ceiling, and move left and up to an awkward belay stance under another ceiling. (80 feet) 5.11 PG

Pitch 3: (V1) Climb through the notch directly overhead, and diagonal up and right about 30 feet to some overhangs. Then step right and continue up to the top. (80 feet) 5.10+ PG–R

Variation 1: 5.10 R Traverse left and join Tiers of Fear.
FA 1966: Dick Williams and Ants Leemets
FFA (Pitch 2) 1973: Steve Wunsch
FFA 1977: John Bragg and Russ Raffa
FA (Variation 1) 1973: Steve Wunsch and John Bragg

367. SCARY AREA 5.12 G ★

Start: Below a shallow open book with an incipient crack that diagonals up right, 12 feet right of The Yellow Wall. Two bolts about 20 feet up mark the line of the route.

Pitch 1: Starting a few feet right, climb up the face to the bolts. Diagonal up right to some horizontal holds and an overhang. Then step left, continue up an open book, and move left to a belay stance. (90 feet) 5.11 R

Pitch 2: Traverse back right about 30 feet to a right-facing corner and then move down a bit to a left-facing flake. From the top of the flake, move right to the base of a shallow groove. Climb the groove and move slightly left to an obvious notch. Hand traverse right 12 feet (5.10 R) to a stance under a large overhang. Move right, climb past the overhang into a notch, and then hand traverse right around the corner to a belay. (100 feet) 5.12 G

Pitch 3: Continue to the top. (50 feet)
Height-related—harder for shorter climbers.
FA P1 1977: John Bragg
FA P2 1979: Mark Robinson

368. SCARY AREA DIRECT 5.12− (Toprope)

Start: On a block 3 feet left of Airy Aria.

Pitch 1: Climb the steep, bulging face and weave up through the overhangs above to some obvious belay hardware.

369. AIRY ARIA 5.8 G ★★

Start: At the base of a long orange open book, at the right edge of the Yellow Wall boulder pile.

Pitch 1: Climb the open book to a ledge on the left. (60 feet) 5.8 G

Pitch 2: Traverse right to some right-facing corners that lead to a notch in an overhang. Climb through the notch then step right around the corner (some parties belay here) and move up to the GT Ledge. (100 feet) 5.6

Pitch 3: Climb the easy face above to the top. (30 feet) 5.4

FA 1956: Hans Kraus and Ken Prestrud
FFA 1960: Jim McCarthy

370. CARBS AND CAFFEINE 5.11− R ★

Start: In a short, shallow right-facing corner directly behind a cluster of trees, 10 feet downhill to the right of Airy Aria.

Pitch 1: Climb up the corner past a horizontal break to a right-facing flake. Then continue up past a thin crack to the first Airy Aria belay ledge. (80 feet) 5.9−

Pitch 2: Follow the corner above up right past an overhang to some red rock on the right face. Traverse left and work up to a bolt. Continue left until it is possible to move up the face. Then go back right to a second bolt, move up right to the roof, and belay on the right. (50 feet) 5.10

Pitch 3: Go back left and climb through a notch to another roof. Then traverse out right onto the face and continue up to the top. (70 feet) 5.11− R

Originally known as Ordeal by Flyer. The bolts were placed by a previous party on an old aid line.

FA 1979: Mark Robinson and Kevin Bein

371. LOTS OF MALARKEY 5.7 PG

Start: At a nose below a crack, 20 feet right of Airy Aria.

Pitch 1: Climb the nose and follow the crack for about 25 feet to the second horizontal crack system. Then traverse about 20 feet right to a ledge and continue up the nose past a crack to a belay. (80 feet) 5.7 PG

Pitch 2: Climb up about 10 feet and traverse right to the outside corner. Then continue up the face to the optional Airy Aria belay ledge. (60 feet)

Pitch 3: Follow Airy Aria for about 20 feet, traverse diagonally up and left for about 50 feet to some small vertical fractures, and then continue up to the top. (80 feet)

FA 1973: Dick Williams and Roy Kligfield

372. WASP STOP   5.11+   G

Start: At an arching right-facing corner with a thin crack, 50 feet downhill and around the corner from Airy Aria.

Pitch 1: Follow the arching corner to a pointed ledge and climb a crack to an overhang. Step right and work up a shallow left-facing corner to a stance. Continue up past another overhang and overhanging corner to a block stuck under the ceiling above, and then exit up left to a belay. (80 feet)   5.11+   G

Pitch 2: Rappel, or climb up and right onto the face, and continue up to the GT Ledge. (100 feet)

Pitch 3: Continue through the ceilings above to the top. (30 feet)

Height-related—easier for shorter climbers.

FA 1968: Dave Ingalls and Roy Kligfield
FFA 1975: John Stannard

373. THE STING   5.11+   PG   ★★

Start: On top of a 4-foot-high block, 12 feet left of Lisa.

Pitch 1: Step across to a thin horizontal crack and move up to a large horizontal crack. Continue up past an overhang to a small ledge. Diagonal up left to the Wasp Stop corner and block, climb up a few feet, and then traverse out right under a roof to a belay on the face beyond. (90 feet)   5.11+   PG

Pitch 2: Continue up the face to the GT Ledge. (100 feet)   5.5

Pitch 3: Walk off or finish on a nearby climb.

The first part of the climb is often toproped from the small ledge, which can be reached via Lisa. Also, most climbers who lead this section traverse off right to Lisa and rappel.

FA 1983: Russ Clune, Dan McMillan, and Russ Raffa

374. LISA 5.9 G

Start: On the left side of a large 15-foot-wide boulder, below parallel cracks on opposite sides of a nose, 12 feet right of The Sting.

Pitch 1: (V1, V2) Step over to the main face and work up to a stance below a thin crack in the small left-facing corner. Climb the crack and go up right to an overhang. Then move right and continue up to a belay. (60 feet) 5.9 G

Pitch 2: Rappel, or climb some cracks and a corner on the left side of an overhang to a ledge. Then continue up the face to the GT Ledge. (110 feet) 5.4

Pitch 3: Step right and climb a right-facing corner until near its top. Then move left and continue to the top. (60 feet) 5.5

Variation 1: Asil 5.9 Start at a right-facing corner immediately to the right of the regular route. Follow the corner past an overhang to join the regular route.

Variation 2: Mona 5.9 G Start on the face just right of the boulder. Climb up the face past a short chimney to an open book capped by a roof. Then diagonal up left to join the regular route.

The first pitch is height-related—easier if taller.

FA 1963: Ants Leemets and Jim Andress
FFA 1964: Ants Leemets
FA (Variation 1) 1983: Russ Raffa, Dan McMillan, and Mike Freeman
FA (Variation 2) 1982: Russ Raffa and Laura Chaiten

375. FULL FACE 5.8 PG

Start: On a grassy ledge below a crescent-shaped left-facing corner that is pink in color, 50 feet right of the Lisa boulder.

Pitch 1: Climb past the pink spot, and follow some small grooves and cracks to a grassy ledge. Then step right and continue up a groove and the face above to the GT Ledge. (120 feet) 5.8 PG

Pitch 2: Climb up to a right-facing corner in the overhang above, swing out left onto the face, and continue to the top. (70 feet) 5.7

FA 1962: Art Gran and Ants Leemets

THE TRAPPS

376. LONG DISTANCE OF THE LONELY RUNNER 5.10 G
Start: At a small left-facing corner that contains a wide crack, 12 feet right of Full Face.

Pitch 1: Climb the corner to a small ledge and continue up a right-facing corner and a crack to another corner on the left. (60 feet)

Pitch 2: Step right and climb a groove and the face on its right to the GT Ledge. (60 feet)

Pitch 3: (V1) Climb up a left-facing corner capped by a very large overhang, traverse around right onto the face, and continue up to the top. (60 feet) 5.10 G

Variation 1: Foops Trapp 5.11+ G Step left and climb the steep face past a crack in the overhang to the top.

FA 1968: Dick Williams and Dick DuMais
FFA 1973: Henry Barber and John Stannard
FA (Variation 1) 1974: Henry Barber and John Stannard

377. 48 5.2 G
Start: At the right edge of the chimney that is just right of Long Distance of the Lonely Runner.

Pitch 1: Climb the outside corner and the face on the right past some blocks to a ledge. (50 feet)

Pitch 2: Continue up a dirty chimney to the bush-covered GT Ledge. (70 feet)

Pitch 3: Follow a corner past several ledges to the top. (50 feet)

FA 1948: Hans Kraus and Bonnie Prudden

378. VADER 5.10 R
Start: At a short chimney below a roof and behind a block, 40 feet right of 48 and 20 feet left of Ventre de Boeuf.

Pitch 1: Follow the chimney to the top of the block, step across to the main face, and climb a corner system to the roof. Then traverse left and continue up the face to a ledge. (50 feet) 5.10 G

Pitch 2: Walk left to a block leaning against the face. Step across from the block and climb up the face past some overhangs to a ceiling. Clear the ceiling and then continue up to the dirty GT Ledge. (70 feet) 5.10 R

Pitch 3: Scramble to the top.

May the Force be with you—especially if you're short.

FA 1980: Joe Rommel and Darcy Smith

379. VENTRE DE BOEUF   5.9   PG

Start: At a crack immediately right of a chimney in a flaring, overhanging right-facing corner, 60 feet right of 48 and just right of some huge blocks leaning against the cliff.

Pitch 1: Follow the crack to a small triangular overhang. Climb up and left to an off-width crack and a green face. Then continue up past an overhang into a flaring bombay chimney and belay on the ledge above. (80 feet)   5.9   PG

Pitch 2: Rappel or finish on 48.

You'll either love this one or hate it.

FA 1958: Jim McCarthy, Claude Lavallee, and Jim Andress
FFA 1968: Gary Brown and John Stannard

380. UPHILL ALL THE WAY   5.12 −   PG   ★

Start: At a crack that diagonals up right to a right-arching overhang, 3 feet right of Ventre de Boeuf.

Pitch 1: Follow the crack to the overhang, move right, and climb up 10–15 feet. Move left around the outside corner and work up the face to the ceiling (50 feet). Then, either rappel or traverse right about 20 feet to a notch and continue up to a belay. (80 feet)   5.12 −   PG

Pitch 2: Climb straight up about 15 feet and diagonal up left past the left side of some overhangs. Then diagonal up right to a nose and continue up to the GT Ledge. (150 feet)   5.9

Pitch 3: Continue to the top. (50 feet)

Unfortunately, this route was incorrectly named and credited in the 1980 guidebook, and many climbers know it as The Man Who Fell to Earth.

FA 1965: Dennis Mehmet and Bill Goldner
FFA 1981: Hugh Herr

381. WHERE FOOLS RUSH IN   5.11 −   R

Start: Same as Double Crack.

Pitch 1: Climb up a few feet to the first horizontal crack and traverse left to the nose. Work up past some flakes to a shallow open book and then continue up past an overhang to a belay. (50 feet) 5.11− R

Pitch 2: Continue following the nose and some cracks on the right to the GT Ledge. (120 feet) 5.10

Pitch 3: Continue to the top. (50 feet)

FA 1978: John Bragg and Bob D'Antonio

382. DOUBLE CRACK 5.8 G ★★

Start: At a steep crack that begins at the right edge of an overhang which juts out from the ground, 60 feet right of Ventre de Boeuf.

Pitch 1: Climb up the crack to the overhang, step left to an alcove, and diagonal up right to a ledge. (70 feet) 5.8 G

Pitch 2: Diagonal up left past a short right-facing corner to an off-width crack or narrow chimney, and follow this to a small overhang. Then climb up right to a fault system that leads to the top. (80 feet) 5.7

Pitch 3: Continue to the top. (50 feet)

FA 1955: Jim McCarthy and Hans Kraus

FFA 1958: Jim Geiser and Jim McCarthy

383. LITO AND THE SWAN 5.9 R

Start: At some greenish right-facing flakes, just left of Broken Hammer.

Pitch 1: Climb up the flakes and a crack to a projecting flake, and continue up to a boulder and a ledge. (50 feet) 5.9 R

Pitch 2: Climb the right-facing corner above, continue up the face past some overhangs to the GT Ledge, and belay on a ledge higher up. (90 feet) 5.7+

Pitch 3: Continue up the face to the top. (40 feet) 5.6

McCarthy's flight pattern on this climb was more bomblike than swanlike. Watch out for loose rock on the first pitch.

FA 1965: Jim McCarthy and Lito Tejada-Flores

384. IVAN AND THE SAUM 5.9 PG

Start: Same as Broken Hammer.

Pitch 1: Climb up to a ledge on the left with a tree. Continue

BURT ANGRIST on DOUBLE CRACK
Dick Williams

up a broken crack-fault system to a stance, step left, and work up and right through some overhangs to the face above. Then continue up to the GT Ledge, staying about 10 feet right of some red rock. (120 feet)

Pitch 2: Follow an obvious crack past a ledge and continue to the top. (60 feet)

FA 1976: Ivan Rezucha and Dick Saum

385. HIGH JINX 5.9+ G

Start: Same as Broken Hammer.

Pitch 1: Follow Ivan and the Saum to the ledge on the left with the tree. Step right and work up to a crack in an overhang. Climb the overhang on the left, go past the next overhang, and then follow some cracks up the face to the Broken Hammer belay on the GT Ledge. (130 feet) 5.9+ G

Pitch 2: Rappel or finish on a nearby climb.

FA 1985: Ivan Rezucha and Annie O'Neill

386. BROKEN HAMMER 5.3 PG

Start: In the large corner with the broken chimney 45 feet right of Double Crack.

Pitch 1: Climb up the corner to a ledge. (80 feet)

Pitch 2: Continue up a mossy chimney to the GT Ledge. (50 feet)

Pitch 3: Follow the corner above to the top. (40 feet)

In winter, this sometimes offers steep ice climbing; in summer, it offers plenty of vegetation for a botanist.

FA 1952: Hans Kraus and Ruth Tallan

387. THE ZIGZAG FACE 5.7− R

Start: Same as Broken Hammer.

Pitch 1: Traverse right along a pebbly ramp to a crack. Climb the face just left of the crack to a ledge at the base of a short left-facing corner. Move around the corner to the face on the right and then continue up past a notch in an overhang to a ledge. (80 feet) 5.7− R

Pitch 2: Climb up to the overhangs above, move left around them, and continue up to the GT Ledge. (80 feet) 5.4

Pitch 3: Continue to the top. (60 feet)   5.2
FA 1970: Art Gran and Dick Williams

388. 49   5.2   G
Start: At a large left-facing flake that forms a small chimney, 20 feet right of The Zigzag Face.
Pitch 1: Climb the chimney and corner, and diagonal up and right to a belay ledge. (130 feet)   5.2
Pitch 2: Climb up and left to the top, following the path of least resistance. (90 feet)   5.2
FA 1949: Hans Kraus and Bonnie Prudden

389. FORCES OF NATURE   5.11   PG
Start: Below a small overhang, under which is a 12-inch-high left-facing corner on the right, where a very thin crack begins, 24 feet downhill to the right of 49.
Pitch 1: Step onto the face, move right and continue up past the overhang and crack to a belay ledge. (50 feet)   5.11   PG
Pitch 2: Climb up past some grass and weeds to a left-facing corner and some overhangs in a roof. Climb through the roof at its weakest point and then continue up to the GT Ledge. (80 feet) 5.11 –
Pitch 3: Continue to the top.
FA 1983: Mike Robin and Mike Law

390. QUIÉN SABE   5.10 –   PG–R
Start: At an open book, 20 feet downhill to the right of Forces of Nature and 24 feet left of The Nose.
Pitch 1:   (V1)   Follow the open book to an overhang, move right, and climb up past a horizontal crack to a small ledge. Then traverse out left onto the face and continue up to join The Nose.
Variation 1:   Lord Knows   5.11   G   Start 8 feet right of the regular route. Climb up past a bulge, move right, and work up to a horizontal crack or fault. Then traverse out left to the nose and continue up the face to join the regular route.
FA: circa 1979
FA (Variation 1) 1985: Al Diamond, Scott Franklin, and Jordan Mills

THE TRAPPS

391. THE NOSE 5.7 PG–R
Start: At a crack in an open book capped by a ceiling 25 feet above the ground, 24 feet right of Quién Sabe.

Pitch 1: Climb the crack and open book to the ceiling, traverse right, and continue up a low-angle open book to a horizontal crack. Follow the crack out left to the nose and then work up to a belay ledge. (120 feet) 5.7 PG–R

Pitch 2: Follow 49 to the top. (90 feet) 5.2

FA 1969: Charlie Porter and Roy Kligfield

FFA 1969: Gary Brown and John Stannard

392. LADY'S LAMENT 5.10 – G
Start: On the fairly nondescript face left of Fillipina.

Pitch 1: Climb up to a horizontal crack, where a broken vertical fracture begins. Continue up the fracture (crossing Fillipina) and the face to a belay below some overhangs under a roof. (70 feet)

Pitch 2: Climb up past an overhang, traverse out left onto the face, and continue up to join Fillipina.

FA 1981: Ivan Rezucha and Don Lauber

393. FILLIPINA 5.9 – G
Start: At a slightly overhanging right-facing corner which contains some cracks that lead up and slightly right, 25 feet right of The Nose.

Pitch 1: Follow the corner to a stance at the base of an open book. Traverse left to a right-facing corner, climb this, and move left again to another corner that leads to an overhang. Then step out left to a belay below the overhang. (70 feet) 5.8

Pitch 2: Go back right, climb past the overhang at two parallel cracks, and work up to a ledge. Then diagonal up right and continue up to the GT Ledge. (70 feet) 5.9 – G

Pitch 3: Continue to the top. (40 feet)

FA 1954: Jim McCarthy and Stan Gross

FFA 1968: Howie Davis and Pat Crowther

394. BOULDER-VILLE 5.10 PG
Start: Same as Bold-Ville.

Pitch 1: Follow Bold-Ville for about 20 feet, step left to the obvious fault, and continue up the face to a belay. (70 feet) 5.10− R

Pitch 2: Climb up and slightly right for about 10 feet, move left, and work up through some large overhangs. Then continue up the face above to the GT Ledge. (90 feet)   5.10   PG

Pitch 3: Continue to the top. (40 feet)

FA 1978: John Bragg and Russ Raffa

395. BOLD-VILLE   5.8   G   ★

Start: At a crack and corner that lead up right past an overhang which is about 20 feet above the ground, 20 feet right of Fillipina.

Pitch 1: Climb the crack and corner to the overhang, traverse left around the overhang, and continue up to a ledge. (70 feet) 5.8   G

Pitch 2: Traverse left about 30 feet along a small ledge to a comfortable belay.

Pitch 3: Climb up to a right-facing corner with a whitish, overhanging left face. Traverse left across the face and then continue up to the GT Ledge. (50 feet)

Pitch 4: Continue basically straight up to the top. (100 feet)

FA 1959: Art Gran and Rittner Walling

396. WINTERLUDE   5.10   PG

Start: On the face 5 feet right of Bold-Ville.

Pitch 1: Climb up to an overhang and pass it at its weakest point. Then continue up the face to the first Bold-Ville belay ledge, staying left of an outside corner or nose.

Pitch 2: Finish on a nearby climb.

FA 1984: Ivan Rezucha

397. THE WINTER   5.10+   PG   ★

Start: At a short, flaring open book, 23 feet right of Bold-Ville and 30 feet left of The Spring.

Pitch 1: Climb up past an overhang to some blocks that stick out and form a double-tiered overhang. Work up and right to a right-facing corner (V1), follow the corner to its top, and continue up to the first Bold-Ville belay ledge. (70 feet)   5.10+   PG

Pitch 2: Traverse right (joining The Spring and reversing its traverse) to a left-facing corner above the beginning of the Spring traverse. Climb the corner system through the overhangs above and continue up to the face to join Shit Creek, which is followed to its second-pitch belay.   5.10−

Pitch 3: Finish on a nearby climb.

Variation 1:   5.10−   **R**   Move right and climb up the face to the first Bold-Ville belay ledge.

FA 1974: John Bragg, Steve Wunsch, and Rich Perch

398. THE FALL   5.11−   R   ★
Start: Below a flake, 10 feet left of The Spring.

Pitch 1: Climb past the flake to an overhang. Step right and work up a crack in a right-facing flake. Then diagonal up left to a vertical fault and follow this to an overhang. Exit right and move up to a belay. (80 feet)   5.11−   R

Pitch 2: Rappel, or climb through some overhangs and a ceiling (at a notch), and belay on the face above. (70 feet)

Pitch 3: Follow Shit Creek to the top. (150 feet)

FA 1974: Henry Barber and Rick Hatch

399. THE SUMMER   5.11+   (Toprope)
Start: On the face between The Fall and The Spring.

Pitch 1: Climb the face between The Fall and The Spring.

400. THE SPRING   5.10   PG−R   ★★
Start: At a large left-facing corner, 55 feet right of Bold-Ville.

Pitch 1:   (V1)   Climb the corner to its top, step right, and diagonal up left to a belay in an alcovelike recess. (60 feet)   5.9 PG

Pitch 2: Move up to a ledge, traverse left about 10 feet, and diagonal up left to a small right-facing corner. Continue up to a roof formed by a multitude of ceilings and overhangs that abut another right-facing corner. Then work up past the roof at the corner and belay on the face above. (70 feet)   5.10   PG−R

Pitch 3: Continue straight up to the top. (100 feet)

Variation 1:   Manly, Yes, But I Like It Too   5.10   **X**   Climb the arête and its right face to join the regular route.

FA 1962: Bill Ryan, Willie Crowther, and Phil Nelson

FFA 1964: John Reppy and Sam Streibert
FA (Variation 1) 1985: Scott Franklin and Jordan Mills

401. OBLIQUE TWIQUE 5.8 G
Start: At a groove that becomes a chimney, 15 feet right of The Spring. There is a block at the top of the chimney.
Pitch 1: Climb the chimney, step left, and work up a short open book. Then follow a series of corners and overhangs diagonally up right to a belay anywhere on the long ledge above. (120 feet) 5.8 G
Pitch 2: Traverse right and up around a corner, and then continue along a narrow ledge to a wider one. Belay below a small right-facing corner. (130 feet) 5.4
Pitch 3: Climb the corner and the face on the right past an overhang to a ledge with boulders. Then walk right to a belay behind a huge flake. (120 feet) 5.4
Pitch 4: Climb the obvious corner and the left-hand of two cracks to the top. (50 feet) 5.4
FA 1949: Ken Prestrud, Hans Kraus, Bonnie Prudden, and Lucien Warner
FFA 1957: Jim McCarthy

402. SHIT CREEK 5.7 PG
Start: At the left edge of some large boulders, 35 feet right of Oblique Twique.
Pitch 1: Diagonal up left and follow a groove to an overhang. Then step around right and continue up to a ledge below some overhangs. (60 feet) 5.7 PG
Pitch 2: Climb past the overhangs and angle up left to a block (some parties end the first pitch here and do the whole climb in two long leads). Traverse left out around a corner and then continue up to a belay in some broken rock on the GT Ledge. (100 feet) 5.4
Pitch 3: Climb up to an obvious crack that leads to the top. (40 feet) 5.5
What do you suppose happened on the first ascent?
FA 1961: Bill Goldner and Bill Yates

THE TRAPPS

403. UNSLUNG HEROES 5.10− PG−R
Start: On top of the large boulder pile just right of Shit Creek and 27 feet left of Blistered Toe.

Pitch 1: Climb the face and a vertical seam past some small overhangs to a ledge. (50 feet) 5.10−

Pitch 2: Climb up orange rock and a corner to the ceilings, which are passed on the right, and continue up to the GT Ledge. (80 feet) 5.10−

Pitch 3: Finish on a nearby climb.

FA 1979: Mark Robinson, Bob D'Antonio, Bill Ravitch, and Sandy Stewart

404. LOS TRES CABRONES 5.9 PG
Start: On the face 7 feet left of Blistered Toe.

Pitch 1: Climb about 25 feet up the face to a vertical seam and follow this past some weeds to a ledge. (50 feet) 5.9

Pitch 2: Climb up the obvious corner until below an overhang. Move left and work up a broken right-facing corner and the face to a large overhang, which is climbed by staying to the right. Then continue up to the GT Ledge. (70 feet) 5.8

Pitch 3: Diagonal up right to the right edge of the ceiling above, climb through the obvious notch, and continue up the face to the top. (60 feet) 5.9

FA (Pitch 1) 1983: Ivan Rezucha and Annie O'Neill

FA 1963: Dick Williams, Jim McCarthy, José Anglada

405. BLISTERED TOE 5.8− PG
Start: At some flakes on the face, 40 feet right of Shit Creek and about 10 feet left of a short right-facing corner and a crack.

Pitch 1: (V1) Climb the face, move up right to the crack mentioned in the start, and follow the crack to its top. Then traverse left to a ledge. (70 feet) 5.8− PG

Pitch 2: Diagonal up right to a left-facing corner and climb up until near a large overhang. Then diagonal up left and continue up to the GT Ledge. (60 feet) 5.6

Pitch 3: Climb up left on easier rock to the top.

Variation 1: **5.9+** Climb the short right-facing corner mentioned in the start and join the regular route.

FA 1958: Jim McCarthy and John Wharton

406. TORTURE GARDEN 5.8 PG
Start: Same as Blistered Toe.

Pitch 1: Follow Blistered Toe or its variation for about 30 feet to a long horizontal crack. Traverse right about 40 feet along the crack to a tree and a thin vertical crack. (60 feet) 5.5 PG

Pitch 2: Then follow the thin cracks and face past some small ledges and final headwall to the GT Ledge and berry tree. (120 feet) 5.8 PG

Pitch 3: From the right side of the tree, climb up past an overhang and continue up the face past some right-facing flakes to the top. (50 feet)

FA 1968: Howie Davis and Pat Crowther

407. LAST FRONTIER 5.10 G
Start: At a right-facing corner capped by an overhang, 45 feet right of Blistered Toe. There is a bombay chimney above on the right.

Pitch 1: (V1) Climb the corner and chimney, move out right, and continue up to a ledge. (40 feet) 5.10 G

Pitch 2: Continue up the corner to another ledge. (50 feet)

Pitch 3: Follow a groove up a short but steep face and past an overhang to the GT Ledge. (70 feet) 5.8 PG

Pitch 4: Climb up to the overhangs above and go around them on the right. Then continue up and right to the top. (80 feet) 5.8 PG

Variation 1: Climb and Punishment 5.11 G Start 30 feet farther right, at a crack that diagonals up left to a small ledge and alcove. Climb the crack past the alcove and continue up a right-facing corner to the face above. Then follow another crack and a small left-facing corner to a ledge, traverse left, and either rappel or finish on the regular route.

FA 1963: Dick Williams, John Hudson, and Jim McCarthy
FFA 1964: Rick Horn
FA (Variation 1) 1970s: John Stannard

408. THE YELLOW CRACK   5.12   R–X

Start: At a right-facing corner below a crack in yellowish rock, 45 feet right of Last Frontier.

Pitch 1: Climb the corner and crack to a left-facing corner (V1), which is followed to its top. Diagonal up right to a short right-facing corner, continue up to the overhang above, then climb up right to a belay at a pine tree. (70 feet)   5.12   R–X

Pitch 2: Rappel or climb a crack to the highest of two ledges. Step up and right, and continue up the face to an overhang. Move up right past a left-facing corner in the overhang to a tree. Then continue up and left on the steep face above to the GT Ledge. (80 feet)

Pitch 3: Climb a chimneylike crack to a ledge and continue to the top, passing some overhangs on the right. (70 feet)

Variation 1:   **5.11**   **R**   Traverse right 6–8 feet under an overhang, continue up the steep face past the next overhang, and diagonal up left to the short right-facing corner on the regular route.

FA 1963: Art Gran and Jorge Pons

FFA 1984: Lynn Hill and Russ Raffa

FA (Variation 1) 1973: Henry Barber, John Bragg, John Stannard, and Paul Rezucha

409. THE BRAGG-HATCH ROUTE   5.10+   PG

Start: On top of some blocks that are below a left-facing corner, 24 feet right of The Yellow Crack.

Pitch 1: Climb the corner to an overhang, move 4 feet right, and follow a vertical fault to a horizontal crack. (V1) Traverse right about 8 feet to another vertical fault and follow this to a left-facing corner. Continue up the corner past a flake to a ceiling, step left, and climb over the ceiling to the face above. Then traverse left and either rappel or join The Yellow Crack. (70 feet)

Variation 1: Continue up the right-facing corner above, past an overhang, to a pine tree. Then, either rappel or join The Yellow Crack.

FA 1975: John Bragg and Rick Hatch

410. KLIGFIELD'S FOLLIES 5.11+ PG ★★★
Start: At a ramp on the right side of a block, below and a few feet right of The Bragg-Hatch Route. (The original aid line started on the face directly below the right-arching crack.)
  Pitch 1: Scramble up the ramp and climb up the face to a ledge. Walk right and work up a thin crack to a small overhang. Move left a few feet and continue up blackish rock to a big horizontal crack. Then traverse right, follow the arching crack up and right to an overhang, and climb past the overhang to a ledge. (90 feet) 5.11+ PG
  Pitch 2: Continue up and left to the left end of some stacked blocks. Climb past the overhang above at a tiny left-facing corner and diagonal crack, and then continue straight up about 20 feet to a small belay ledge. (60 feet)
  Pitch 3: Climb up the face, heading toward an outside corner on the right. Then step right around the corner and continue up to the GT Ledge. (120 feet)
  Pitch 4: Continue to the top. (90 feet)
  FA 1971: Roy Kligfield and Robert Krumme
  FFA 1973: John Stannard

411. CLUNEY'S JOLLIES 5.12 R
Start: On the face below a shallow, scooped-out right-facing corner, 25 feet right of Kligfield's Follies and below and to the left of the Simple Suff corner.
  Pitch 1: Climb to the top of the corner and continue up the steep face to a left-facing flake. Traverse right to a stance below a small overhang, move up left, and work up to a second small overhang. Continue up a left-facing flake and the face above to the first Kligfield's Follies belay ledge. (70 feet) 5.12 R
  Pitch 2: Rappel or finish on Kligfield's.
  FA (Toprope) 1984: Russ Clune
  FA (Lead) 1984: Russ Clune

412. SIMPLE SUFF 5.10− G ★★
Start: At a large yellow right-facing corner that begins on a ledge 15 feet above the ground, 43 feet right of Kligfield's Follies.
  Pitch 1: (V1) Climb directly up to the corner or walk out left

THE TRAPPS

to it from the top of the boulder pile to the right. Follow the corner past a bulge and some overhangs to a ceiling. Then, either rappel or traverse left around the ceiling and continue up to a belay. (100 feet) 5.10− G

Pitch 2: Climb straight up the easier face above to the GT Ledge. (70 feet)

Pitch 3: Continue up to join Kligfield's Follies, which is followed to the top.

Variation 1: Simple Suff Direct 5.10 PG-R Use the same start as Cluney's Jollies. Diagonal up the face, following a sickle-shaped crack that goes out right, and continue up to the ledge on the regular route.

One of the most atypical routes in the area.

FA 1962: Ants Leemets and Olaf Sõõt
FFA 1972: Bob Anderson and Henry Barber

413. TECHO-STUFF 5.12− (Toprope)
Start: At an arching crack 5 feet right of Simple Suff.
Pitch 1: Climb the crack and the face 5 feet right of Simple Suff.
FA (Toprope) 1985: Russ Clune

414. THE BLUE STINK 5.3 PG
Start: On top of some blocks that are directly below a large, broken right-facing corner, 25 feet right of Simple Suff.

Pitch 1: Diagonal up right to a tree and left-facing corner. Climb the corner, traverse left below an overhang to the large right-facing corner, and continue up this corner to a ledge on the left. (90 feet) 5.3

Pitch 2: Go right around the corner and walk along a ledge to a belay below an easy face. (40 feet) 5.3

Pitch 3: Continue up and slightly right to the large, vegetated GT Ledge. (50 feet) 5.2

Pitch 4: (V1) Walk right to an easy white face that leads to the top. (100 feet)

Variation 1: 5.5 Follow a flake straight up from some blocks, diagonal up right to a short groove, and continue to the top.

FA 1947: Hans Kraus, Bonnie Prudden, and Ken Prestrud

415. HOOKY 5.6− PG

Start: At a short right-facing corner, just right of a right-facing corner formed by a pedestal and 50 feet right of The Blue Stink.

Pitch 1: Climb the face to the top of the pedestal (V1) and belay about 15 feet to the left, beneath a short right-facing corner. (50 feet)

Pitch 2: Climb into the corner and exit left about halfway up. Step up and make a long traverse right along the lip of an overhang to a belay just beyond a white face. (60 feet)

Pitch 3: Diagonal up right on a grey low-angle slab and then continue straight up the steep face above to a belay on the tree-covered GT Ledge. (80 feet)

Pitch 4: Continue to the top.

Variation 1: Hooky Direct 5.9 PG Continue up the face, moving slightly right, and then diagonal up right to a short left-facing corner at the top of some overhangs, where Yesterday is joined. Follow Yesterday up the corner and a few feet up the face to the traverse on the regular route.

FA 1971: Nick Pott and Steve Jervis
FA (Variation 1) 1984: Ivan Rezucha and Don Lauber

416. YESTERDAY 5.10− PG

Start: On the face a few feet right of Hooky.

Pitch 1: Climb the face and a corner, and continue up and right to an orange overhang in a ceiling marked by a short left-facing corner. Climb the overhang at the corner, step up, and traverse left under the next overhang to another short left-facing corner. Continue up this corner and face above (crossing Hooky) to the tree-covered GT Ledge. (150 feet)   5.10−   PG

Pitch 2: Rappel or continue to the top.

FA 1982: Russ Clune and Hugh Herr

417. TOMORROW AND TOMORROW AND TOMORROW 5.11 R

Start: On a smooth face below the right edge of a small overhang that is 15 feet above the ground, 75 feet downhill to the right of The Blue Stink.

Pitch 1: Climb up to the right edge of the overhang, traverse left to a vertical seam, and continue up the seam to a grassy ledge. (50 feet) 5.11 R

Pitch 2: Continue up the face, clear the ceiling above, and belay on a stance at the lip. (60 feet) 5.9

Pitch 3: Continue up the face to the tree-covered GT Ledge. (50 feet)

Pitch 4: Continue to the top. (70 feet)

FA 1966: Dick Williams and Jim McCarthy

FFA 1973: John Stannard and John Bragg

418. FALLED ON ACCOUNT OF STRAIN 5.10− PG−R ★

Start: At a very thin crack, 14 feet right of Tomorrow and Tomorrow and Tomorrow.

Pitch 1: Climb the face just left of the crack (the original route climbed the crack) to a horizontal crack. Move right and work up to a stance (most climbers traverse right about 20 feet to a rappel station). Then follow a corner to a ledge below the ceiling above. (60 feet) 5.10−

Pitch 2: Diagonal up right through the ceiling at a small right-facing corner and continue up the face to the tree-covered GT Ledge. (60 feet) 5.10−

Pitch 3: Continue to the top. (70 feet)

FA 1977: Russ Raffa and Eliot Williams

419. WET DREAM 5.12− R

Start: At a vertical seam that starts 5 feet above the ground and is S-shaped about halfway up, 14 feet right of Falled on Account of Strain and 14 feet left of April Showers.

Pitch 1: Follow the seam to a stance below the steep face above. Continue up the face past a bulging overhang to a very short right-facing corner under an overhang. Pass the overhang and continue up to a belay. (60 feet) 5.12− R

Pitch 2: Climb up through the ceiling above (just left of its widest point), continue up to a belay, and rappel. (60 feet) 5.10+

FA 1982: Russ Clune, Jeff Gruenberg, Mike Freeman, Dan McMillan, and Russ Raffa

420. APRIL SHOWERS   5.11   PG   ★

Start: At a tree below the center of a small overhang that is 20 feet above the ground, 28 feet right of Falled on Account of Strain.

Pitch 1: (V1, V2)   Climb up to the overhang and traverse to its left edge. Then continue up the face and a shallow left-facing corner, and step right to a small ledge. (60 feet)   5.10   R

Pitch 2: Climb the face to the left of the corner to the obvious ceiling (V3), which is climbed at its widest point, and continue up to a belay. (This was the original aid pitch.) (60 feet)   5.11   PG

Pitch 3: Continue up the face past trees and large ledges to the top. (130 feet)

Variation 1:   **5.11+**   Step to the right of the tree and boulder up to join the regular route below the overhang (V1a).

Variation 1a: **5.11+**   **R**   Continue past the overhang and up the thin face, staying about 10 feet left of Golden Showers, and join the regular route at its first belay ledge.

Variation 2:   Spring Piss   5.11+   (Toprope)   Start on the face 5 feet farther left. Climb up to join the regular route at the left side of the overhang.

Variation 3:   **5.11**   Climb out right through the ceiling and continue up to the second belay on the regular route.

The bolt just above the first-pitch overhang was NOT placed by the first ascent party.

FA 1966: Ants Leemets, Dick Williams, and Jim McCarthy
FFA 1978: Rich Romano and Fred Yakulic
FA (Variation 1a) 1988: Dave Karl and Dave Luhan
FA (Variation 2: Toprope) 1986: Russ Clune
FA (Variation 3) 1973: John Stannard and John Bragg

421. GOLDEN SHOWERS   5.11   G-PG   ★

Start: At a vertical seam beginning at a 2-inch-deep overhang 5 feet above the ground, 12 feet right of April Showers.

Pitch 1: Climb up past the overhang, step left, and follow the seam and fault system to a short, shallow left-facing corner. Then continue up and left to the first April Showers belay ledge. (60 feet)   5.11   G–PG

Pitch 2: Move back right, continue up the face, and diagonal up right to a ceiling. Then climb through the ceiling and belay on the face above. (70 feet) 5.10 R

Pitch 3: Continue to the top.

FA 1982: Russ Raffa and Eliot Williams

422. CALLED ON ACCOUNT OF RAIN 5.11+ R

Start: On the face just right of a 7-foot-high left-facing corner, 40 feet right of April Showers.

Pitch 1: Climb the face past a thin crack to a grassy ledge. Then continue up the steep face above to a belay in an alcove at a left-facing corner or on a ledge just above. (40 feet) 5.11+ R

Pitch 2: Climb up to a crack, follow it straight through the ceiling above, and continue up to a ledge. (70 feet)

Pitch 3: Continue up to the tree-covered GT Ledge.

Pitch 4: Continue to the top. (70 feet)

Originally rated 5.10 until a crucial hold broke in 1985.

FA 1963: Ants Leemets and Elmer Skahan

FFA 1973: John Stannard and John Bragg

423. COMEDY IN THREE ACTS 5.11 PG ★

Start: On the face directly below a flaring crack that begins 25 feet above the ground, 25 feet right of Called on Account of Rain. There is a triangular block at the base of the crack.

Pitch 1: Climb the face past an overhang to a small ledge below the crack. Then continue up the crack to a small ledge and short left-facing corner (most parties rappel from here). (40 feet) 5.11− PG

Pitch 2: Continue up the corner, traverse right about 10 feet, and work up the face to a left-facing corner under an overhang. Climb past the overhang and work up the face to a ceiling. Then go through the ceiling and continue up the face to the GT Ledge. (80 feet) 5.11 PG

Pitch 3: Climb easier rock to the top. (70 feet)

FA 1963: Dick Williams, Jim McCarthy, and Ants Leemets

FFA 1968: John Stannard and Gary Brown

424. DROP ZONE   5.12 –   R
Start: Below a bulging face that has a short seam 15–20 feet above the ground, 15 feet right of Comedy in Three Acts.
Pitch 1: Climb the face past the seam and some grass hummocks to a short, shallow left-facing corner. Move up and slightly right, and then continue up to a ledge below a left-facing corner. (40 feet)   5.12 –   R
Pitch 2: Rappel, or step right and climb the face to the GT Ledge. (120 feet)   5.9
Pitch 3: Rappel or finish on a nearby climb.
FA 1982: Russ Clune and Russ Raffa

425. PRESSURE DROP   5.11+   R
Start: At an oak tree, 15 feet right of Drop Zone.
Pitch 1: Climb the face to a detached flake and continue straight up to a seam in an overhang (V1). Then step right to a short left-facing corner, work up the corner, and traverse right to Frustration Syndrome. (40 feet)   5.11+   R
Pitch 2: Rappel or finish on Frustration Syndrome.
Variation 1:   5.11+   R   Climb straight up.
Harder for climbers less than 6 feet tall.
FA 1980: John Bragg and Don Hamilton

426. FRUSTRATION SYNDROME   5.10   G   ★★
Start: On a smooth face below and 20 feet left of a left-facing corner that begins about 25 feet above the ground, 45 feet right of Comedy in Three Acts.
Pitch 1: Climb up the face about 15 feet, traverse right about 10 feet, and diagonal up right to the corner. Then follow the corner past an overhang to a belay. (60 feet)   5.10   G
Pitch 2: Rappel or continue up to GT Ledge. (70 feet)
Pitch 3: Continue to the top. (70 feet)
FA 1964: Dick Williams, Jim McCarthy, and John Reppy

427. THE STAND   5.11 –   PG   ★
Start: At a low, flaky right-pointing rock, 15 feet right of the Frustration Syndrome corner.
Pitch 1: Climb up about 10 feet to a small overhang, traverse

left, and continue up a very thin crack system to a short left-facing corner capped by an overhang. At the overhang, step right 2–3 feet and move up to a stance. Step back left until just above the overhang and continue up to some horizontal cracks. Then traverse left to the Frustration Syndrome belay (most parties rappel from here). (70 feet) 5.11− PG

Pitch 2: Traverse back right and continue up the face past an overhang to the GT Ledge. (90 feet)

Pitch 3: Rappel or finish on a nearby climb.

FA 1981: Russ Raffa and Rich Goldstone

428. COPROPHAGIA 5.10− PG

Start: Directly below a small, short, arching right-facing corner that leads up to a small overhang 15 feet above the ground, 7 feet right of The Stand. (There is a diagonal seam in the overhang 2 feet right of the corner. This was the original aid line and, as of this writing, it has not gone free.)

Pitch 1: Climb up to the overhang, traverse left, and work up to a stance below a scoop. Continue up past a white spot to an overhang and traverse right 15–20 feet to a very thin crack that leads up right. Then, either continue up the crack to a rappel spot or diagonal up right to join W.A.S.P., which is followed to the GT Ledge. (150 feet) 5.10− PG

Pitch 2: Finish on a nearby climb.

FA 1969: Dick DuMais and Rick Wheeler
FFA 1973: John Stannard and Henry Barber

429. W.A.S.P. 5.9 PG ★★

Start: On a ledge at a small, short, shallow left-facing corner below a crack, 30 feet right of Coprophagia.

Pitch 1: Climb the corner and crack to an overhang. Then move left and continue up easier rock to the GT Ledge. (160 feet) 5.9 PG

Pitch 2: Climb a right-facing corner on the left and then diagonal up right through some overhangs to the top. (90 feet) 5.5

FA 1961: Jim Andress, John Hudson, Dave Craft, and Pete Geiser

430. J.A.P.   5.10   PG

Start: On the steep polished face, 5 feet right of the W.A.S.P. corner.

Pitch 1: Climb the face to the right side of a 12-inch-deep, four-foot-wide overhang. Work straight up past bulging rock to the right side of another overhang and then continue up the face to the GT Ledge. (160 feet)   5.10   PG

Pitch 2: Follow W.A.S.P. until it is possible to diagonal up right to a ceiling. Then traverse right a few feet, climb through a notch at a short left-facing corner, and continue to the top. (60 feet) 5.8+ or 5.9   G

Originally known as Up Your W.A.S.P.

FA 1985: Dick Williams, Burt Angrist, and Rosie Andrews

431. EXPEDITION TO NOWHERE   5.10−   R

Start: At a narrow, flaky, 11-foot-high left-facing corner, 15 feet left of the huge Sticky Gate boulder pile.

Pitch 1: Climb up to a vertical seam, continue up past a horizontal crack, and work up the steepening face to a small tree below and to the left of a small, short, broken left-facing corner. Then traverse right to the top of the boulder pile. (70 feet)

FA 1983: Russ Clune and Bill Ravitch

432. STICKY GATE   5.3   PG

Start: On top of a huge boulder pile, on the face just left of a small right-facing corner. The top of the boulder pile is best reached from its right side.

Pitch 1: Climb the face past a small left-facing corner to a right-facing corner, which is followed a short distance to the GT Ledge. (100 feet)   5.3

Pitch 2: Walk left about 70 feet past a right-facing corner to a low-angle face.

Pitch 3: Diagonal up left on the face and go right around the overhang above to an easy scramble to the top. (150 feet)   5.3

FA 1949: Hans Kraus and Dick Hirschland

THE TRAPPS

433. MUD, SWEAT, AND TEARS 5.10− PG

Start: At a small 10-foot-high right-facing corner at the right edge of the Sticky Gate boulder pile.

Pitch 1: Climb the corner and face to another right-facing corner above and to the left. Follow this corner to the GT Ledge (loose rock). (120 feet) 5.6 or 5.7

Pitch 2: Climb past a notch in the overhang above and continue up to the next overhang. Then traverse right (V1) about 40 feet to a belay beneath the right edge of an overhanging corner system. (60 feet) 5.10− PG

Pitch 3: Diagonal up right and around onto the face. (V2) Traverse right and then continue up the face past a large pine tree to the top. (150 feet) 5.6

Variation 1: Traverse 15–20 feet diagonally right and up, and climb up the face past an overhang. Then diagonal up left under some large overhangs until it is possible to climb straight up easier rock to the top. (80 feet)

Variation 2: Climb straight up the face and go left until near the lip of the overhangs. Climb up and slightly left, and then continue straight up to the top. (80 feet)

To make a long story short, the indirect line of this route is directly related to the thawing and freezing that occurred when it was first climbed on a short winter day.

FA 1964: Dick Williams and Jim McCarthy
FFA 1973: Henry Barber and John Stannard

434. WITHERING HEIGHTS 5.11 PG–R

Start: Below the middle of three blocky right-facing corners that begin above the ground, approximately 125 feet uphill to the right of Mud, Sweat, and Tears.

Pitch 1: Climb up to the middle corner, go about halfway up it, and step around left. Then continue up the face past three hollow flakes to an overhang and belay on the ledge below the ceiling above. (70 feet)

Pitch 2: Walk right about 8 feet and climb the ceiling. Move up left a few feet and follow a horizontal crack back right for about 10 feet. Then climb through the next ceiling, and continue up and slightly right on the face for about 30 feet to an alcove. (130 feet) 5.11 PG–R

Pitch 3: From the left side of the alcove, climb to the top. (50 feet)

Beware of loose rock.

FA 1978: Ivan and Paul Rezucha
FFA 1979: Ed Webster and Russ Raffa

435. MOONDANCE 5.6 G–PG

Start: At a blocky arête formed by a large left-facing corner, 20 feet left of Sundance.

Pitch 1: Climb the arête and face to a large ledge, and walk right about 15 feet to a belay below a blocky left-facing corner. (40 feet) 5.1

Pitch 2: Follow the corner to an overhang, step right, and move up the face a few feet. (V1) Diagonal up left to a short right-facing corner capped by an overhang. Step left and climb up past a short left-facing corner in the overhang. Then step right, work up the face past a 3-foot-high wedged block to the final headwall (V2); continue to the top. (100 feet) 5.6 G–PG

Variation 1: 5.3 PG   Continue straight up to the right side of an overhang, move up a few feet, and traverse left about 10 feet to join the regular route.

Variation 2: 5.6– G   Step left and climb up to the top.

FA 1982: Todd Swain

436. SUNDANCE 5.6 PG ★

Start: Below some grey streaks in a lichen-covered face, just before the ground drops sharply to the right.

Pitch 1: Climb up the easy face to a ledge (40 feet—some parties belay here to reduce rope drag). Diagonal up right to a grassy ledge below a crack that slants up right. Follow the crack to an arching right-facing corner, move left around the corner, and continue up to the top. (120 feet)

FA 1954: Jim McCarthy and John Rupley

THE TRAPPS

437. GHOSTDANCE 5.7 PG–R
Start: Below the center of an overhang, 8 feet right of a short, broken right-facing corner with a tree, just left of Raindance.

Pitch 1: Climb the unprotected overhang (or start to the left of the corner and tree, climb up a few feet, and traverse right to join the regular route). Continue up the face to a large ledge (some parties belay here). Go past another overhang (poor protection) and work up the face until below a small overhang. Then, either climb straight up to the top (harder), or traverse left about 15 feet and continue up to a pine tree, where Sundance is joined and followed to the top. (130 feet)

FA 1984: Mike Steele

438. RAINDANCE 5.5 G
Start: At a huge blocklike left-facing corner with a pine tree on top near its left side, 45 feet right of Sundance. Scramble 20 feet up right to the base of the corner from the Ghostdance start.

Pitch 1: Avoiding the grungy corner, climb up and left on the face to a ledge at the same height as the top of the corner. Then walk up right to a belay. (60 feet)

Pitch 2: Continue up the face past two small overhangs to the top. (60 feet) 5.5 G

FA 1982: Todd Swain

439. CONTRADANCE 5.6 – PG
Start: Below a white face about two thirds of the way up Roger's Escape Hatch, 25 feet right and generally uphill from the top of the Raindance corner.

Pitch 1: Climb up the white face to the top. (60 feet)

You might consider doing this climb if you are on your way DOWN Roger's Escape Hatch!

FA 1982: Todd Swain

440. ROGER'S ESCAPE HATCH 3rd Class
Start: At a prominent tree-filled gully, about 50 feet below and 100 feet to the right of Sundance.

Pitches 1–2: Follow the gully up right to a short headwall. Climb easily up the headwall, diagonal up left a bit, and then continue up right to the top, which is marked by a cairn.

Generally used as a descent route in this section of the cliff. The next climb, Casa Emilio, begins several hundred feet farther right. From the bottom of the Roger's Escape Hatch gully, follow the trail down along the base of the cliff. When it stops descending, continue along the face past a broken open book for about 100 feet. The trail descends again, goes around an overhanging white face, and rises to the top of a boulder field. About 100 feet beyond is a gully that leads up left. Scramble up the gully behind an 80-foot-high blocklike pinnacle to Casa Emilio.

441. CASA EMILIO   5.2   PG   ★

Start: On a ledge next to a large pine tree, on the top left side of the 80-foot-high pinnacle. There is a huge, very prominent right-facing corner immediately to the right.

Pitch 1: (V1) Climb up and right to a large ledge with a pine tree on the right. (80 feet)   5.0   G

Pitch 2: Climb basically straight up the clean face above to the top. (70 feet)   5.2   G

Variation 1:   5.5   PG   Climb the face just right of the huge right-facing corner and join the regular route.

FA 1953: Bonnie Prudden and Norton Smithe

442. CREAKY JOINTS AND TRIGGER POINTS   5.10   PG

Start: On a large boulder leaning against the face, near the middle of the 80-foot-high pinnacle.

Pitch 1: Step across to a crack and work up to a flaring alcove. Diagonal up right along a thin crack and climb up to a short, shallow left-facing corner. Continue up past a right-facing corner to a cleft in an overhang. Step right, clear the overhang, and climb to the top of the pinnacle. Then walk left to the large pine tree at the base of Casa Emilio. (80 feet)   5.10   PG

Pitch 2: Climb the first pitch of Casa Emilio. (80 feet)   5.0   G

Pitch 3: Diagonal up to the right about 20 feet, and climb the face between Casa Emilio and Casablanca to the top. (130 feet)   5.5   PG

FA 1988: Dick Williams and Joe Bridges

443. THE DEVIL MADE ME DO IT 5.9 R

Start: At a crack that rises above a ledge, 8 feet left of the right side of the 80-foot-high pinnacle. The ledge goes left 32 feet from the right side of the pinnacle to Creaky Joints and Trigger Points.

Pitch 1: Step up to the point where the crack begins to zigzag right. Then diagonal up left 5 feet and climb up the bulging face to a 3-foot-high right-facing corner capped by an overhang. Pass the overhang, move up a few feet, and then diagonal up right past a small pine tree to a large pine tree just below the top right side of the pinnacle. Rappel. (60 feet)

Placing protection on rappel, that is! But only because of not being as tall as Rich Gottlieb.

FA 1988: Dick Williams and Joe Bridges

444. ALMOST PURE AND SIMPLE 5.8 G

Start: Same as The Devil Made Me Do It.

Pitch 1: Follow the zigzag crack to the obvious overhang. Climb past the overhang and continue past the right side of an even larger overhang to a ledge. Then traverse left under a ceiling and out onto the face, and climb up to the large pine tree on The Devil Made Me Do It. Rappel. (60 feet)

FA 1988: Joe Bridges and Dick Williams

445. STRINGS ATTACHED 5.12 (Toprope)

Start: At the center of the left face of the huge corner mentioned in Casa Emilio, 30 feet left of Casablanca.

Pitch 1: Climb the center of the face.

FA (Toprope) 1987: Jeff Morris

446. CASABLANCA 5.8 PG ★

Start: On the face 30 feet right of the huge corner mentioned in Casa Emilio.

Pitch 1: Climb the face to a slight bulge, step right, and diagonal up left to a small right-facing corner and ledge. Continue up the orange face to a ledge with loose rock. Move right to an obvious flake in an overhang, climb the overhang, and move up and left to a belay at a pine tree. (90 feet) 5.8 PG

Pitch 2: Continue up an obvious fault and past a crack to a large block. Move left, climb up a few feet, and move back right. Then follow the outside edge of a left-facing corner capped by an overhang to the top. (120 feet) 5.5

FA 1973: Dick Williams and Roy Kligfield

447. EMILIO 5.7+ PG

Start: Directly below a large flake that is 20 feet above the ground, 40 feet right of the huge corner mentioned in Casa Emilio. There is a small grassy ledge a few feet above the ground.

Pitch 1: Climb up past the flake to the right side of an overhang. Then continue up past a scooped-out area on the face to a ledge below a large overhang, at a point just above and to the right of a left-facing flake. (80 feet) 5.6 R

Pitch 2: Climb straight up over the overhang and diagonal up right to a corner, which is followed to its top. Then traverse right to a left-facing corner and continue up this to a belay ledge. (120 feet) 5.7+ PG

Pitch 3: Climb the corner on the right past a ledge to the top. (60 feet) 5.4

The first aid climb (a shoulder stand) in the Trapps.

FA 1941: Hans Kraus and Fritz Wiessner
FFA 1955: John Turner

448. CASANOVA 5.8 PG–R

Start: At two blocky formations on the face about 15 feet right of a 12-foot-high right-facing corner, 75 feet right of Emilio and 15 feet left of Independent Hangover.

Pitch 1: Climb the face (no protection for the first 30 feet) until just below the right side of some bulging white rock. Then traverse right 5–10 feet and continue up the face to a small belay ledge. (80 feet) 5.7 PG

Pitch 2: Continue up past some loose rock to the obvious overhang. (V1) Traverse left about 10 feet, clear the overhang, and enter a left-facing corner. Then diagonal up left about 20 feet (crossing Emilio) and traverse left another 20 feet to a belay at a pine tree. (70 feet) 5.8 PG–R

Pitch 3: Continue straight up 30 feet to a very large pine tree. Then, either rappel or traverse left to join Casablanca. 5.1 PG

Variation 1: 5.9 − PG Climb past the overhang to a ceiling and hand traverse left on sandy holds to the left-facing corner on the regular route.

The third pitch probably has an independent finish, but the original line is unknown.

FA 1985: Mike and John Steele

449. INDEPENDENT HANGOVER 5.10+ PG–R

Start: At a groove on a nondescript face, below a short scoop that is 15 feet above the ground, 15 feet right of Casanova and just right of a ramplike left-facing corner.

Pitch 1: Follow the groove past a bulge to a ledge. Continue straight up past another bulge, step right, and then climb up the face to a belay on an orange block beneath a ceiling. (100 feet) 5.5

Pitch 2: Work up left through the ceiling to a small left-facing corner at the lip. Then continue up the face to a belay. (50 feet) 5.10+ PG–R

Pitch 3: Step right and continue up the face to join Casa Emilio near the overhang near the top. (120 feet)

FA 1965: Dick Williams and Ants Leemets
FFA 1973: Henry Barber and John Bragg

450. YO MAMA 5.10 PG

Start: Same as Independent Hangover.

Pitch 1: Climb up to a grassy ledge and walk right until below a white face capped by an overhang. Continue up the left side of the white face to a long block below the ceiling. (80 feet)

Pitch 2: Climb the flake that goes out left to the lip of the ceiling and continue up to a belay. (30 feet) 5.10 PG

Pitch 3: Continue up the face to the top. (80 feet)

FA 1985: Ivan Rezucha and Chris Monz

451. WORP FACTOR 1 5.11+ R–X

Start: At the left edge of a boulder pile, directly below two small pine trees that are about 20 feet above the ground, 55 feet right of Independent Hangover.

Pitch 1: Climb up past some flakes and the pine trees to a right-facing corner. Continue up the face to a ramp system below some flakes on the left. Then diagonal up right past an overhang and work up to a ledge beneath the obvious ceiling. (140 feet)   5.5

Pitch 2: Climb straight out past a bolt to the lip of the ceiling, and then move a few feet left and up to a belay spot. (40 feet)   5.11+   R–X

Pitch 3: Continue up the face past a small overhang, and follow a crack and the face above to the top. (70 feet)

Beware of the bolt which is poorly placed. If it comes out—it probably will someday—the landing below will be very bad.

FA 1968: Dick Williams and Dick DuMais
FFA 1973: John Stannard and Henry Barber

452. INTERSTELLAR OVERDRIVE   5.8   PG

Start: Below some very large left-facing flakes that are 20 feet right of some boulders, 60 feet right of Worp Factor 1 and 50 feet left of Emilietta.

Pitch 1: Climb to the top of the second flake and walk right to a belay.   5.6

Pitch 2: Climb up past an overhang at a notch (to the left of a ceiling) and work up past another overhang. Diagonal up left, continue straight up the face, and then move back right to a ledge.   5.8   PG

Pitch 3: Traverse and walk right to Emilietta, which is followed for 10–15 feet until it is reasonable to clear the overhang. Then traverse left and diagonal up left to the top.   5.4

FA 1981: Todd Swain, Corky Woodring, and Mike Steele

453. EMILIETTA   5.3   G

Start: At the base of a large, flaky, broken left-facing corner, 50 feet right of Interstellar Overdrive.

Pitch 1: Follow the corner to a large overhang and then diagonal up right to a ledge. (80 feet)

Pitch 2: Climb up right to a right-facing corner which leads to the top. (90 feet)

FA 1952: Hans Kraus and Bonnie Prudden

# THE TRAPPS

454. COUNTERSTRIKE 5.9 PG
Start: At a small left-facing corner on the right side of the Emilietta corner.

Pitch 1: Climb up the corner and the weaknesses above to a belay at a left-facing corner with a flake. (40 feet) 5.5 R

Pitch 2: Move up left several feet and continue up past some overhangs to a large horizontal crack under a ceiling. Then traverse right 5–10 feet and climb a left-facing corner to a belay ledge. (80 feet) 5.9 PG

Pitch 3: Rappel or continue up the face to the top. (80 feet) 5.4

FA 1981: Todd Swain and Corky Woodring

455. SUDDEN DEATH 5.8+ X
Start: At a short left-facing corner above the ground, 10 feet right of the Emilietta corner.

Pitch 1: Climb up right past the corner to a ledge. Then continue up past some steep flakes to a belay at a small left-facing corner. (50 feet) 5.7 X

Pitch 2: Traverse left about 10 feet and climb up to a bulge. Then work up and right to an arête, and continue up to a ledge. (60 feet) 5.8+ X

Pitch 3: Rappel or finish on Emilietta.

FA 1981: Todd Swain, Corky Woodring, and Derek Price

456. TRIGGER POINT 5.6 G
Start: Below some large left-facing flakes, 40 feet downhill to the right of Emilietta.

Pitch 1: Climb to the top of the flakes and walk right to a short, thin crack. (V1, V2) Then continue up past the crack to a belay ledge under a roof and a right-facing flake.

Pitch 2: Rappel, or traverse either right (5.3) to the large dirty ledge at the top of Krazy Krack, or left (5.4) to the Counterstrike-Sudden Death belay ledge and follow one of these routes to the top.

Variation 1: 5.7 Climb the face to the left of the crack and rejoin the regular route at the belay ledge.

Variation 2: 5.7 Climb through the V-notch on the right and rejoin the regular route at the belay ledge.

FA 1981: Todd Swain, Derek Price, and Corky Woodring

457. CRACK OF DESPONDENCY   5.4   G
Start: At the base of a broken crack system, 50 feet right of Trigger Point and 20 feet left of Pfui Teufel.
Pitch 1: (V1) Climb the main crack system to a large dirty ledge. (90 feet)   5.4   G
Pitch 2: From the blocks on the ledge, diagonal up right past an overhang to another large ledge. (70 feet)   5.2
Pitch 3: Continue up a short face to the top.
Variation 1: Krazy Krack   5.6   G Climb the crack, going up left to the right side of the ceilings. Move up, traverse left to a squeeze chimney, and continue up this to the dirty ledge.

FA 1972: Dick DuMais, Steve Scofield, and Keith LaBudde
FA (Variation 1) 1981: Todd Swain and Corky Woodring

458. PFUI TEUFEL   5.3   G
Start: At a long, grungy open book that leads to some large overhangs, 20 feet right of Crack of Despondency.
Pitch 1: Follow the open book to the overhangs, step left, and climb up to a ledge below some large ceilings. (90 feet)   5.3   G
Pitch 2: Go around the right end of the ceilings, move back left, and continue up to the top. (50 feet)

FA 1958: Marguerite Baumann and Bill Kemsley

459. FOUR-FOOT FACE   5.3   G
Start: Same as Pfui Teufel.
Pitch 1: Climb the right face of the open book and belay on a large ledge out on the right. (50 feet)   5.3   G
Pitch 2: Go up right around the corner and continue straight to the top. (90 feet)   5.2

FA 1953: George Evans and John Rupley

460. THOM'S THUMB, LEFT HAND   5.4   PG
Start: At the left side of a huge block or pinnacle, 30 feet downhill to the right of Pfui Teufel.

Pitch 1: Climb up some cracks, diagonal up right to an arête, and continue up to a ledge. (40 feet)   5.4

Pitch 2: Scramble up a vertical fault past a ledge to a second ledge and join Four-Foot Face, which is followed to the top. (60 feet)   5.4

FA 1981: Derek Price and Todd Swain

461. FUTURE SHOCK   5.12−   R

Start: On the left side of a pointed block, 55 feet downhill to the right of Thom's Thumb, Left Hand and 27 feet left of Art's Route.

Pitch 1: Step across onto the face and climb up past a bolt to a short right-facing corner. Diagonal up left to a short, shallow right-facing corner that overhangs and work up left around the corner to a stance. Then follow a crack up right to the top of the pinnacle and rappel. (60 feet)

FA 1986: Darrow Kirkpatrick, after toproping, cleaning, and placing protection on rappel

BOULDERING
On the trail from the S-turn on the carriage road to Future Shock is a huge boulder with an overhanging east face that is 50 feet wide and 30 feet tall at its highest point.

462. MEAT BY-PRODUCTS   5.10+   R

Start: At some right-facing flakes, 12 feet left of Art's Route.

Pitch 1: Follow the flakes up left to a blocky ledge and continue up to a short right-facing corner in an overhang. Clear the overhang, work up the face to the top of the pinnacle, and rappel. (60 feet)

FA 1987: Kevin Bein, Frank Minunni, and Ken Driese

463. THE NUMBERS RACKET   5.12   (Toprope)

Start: On the overhanging orange face 5 feet left of Art's Route.
Pitch 1: Climb the face 5 feet left of Art's Route.
FA (Toprope) 1987: Frank Minunni

464. ART'S ROUTE 5.9 G
Start: At a crack system in a large open book that goes up right to a blocky ceiling, 27 feet right of Future Shock.
Pitch 1: Follow the crack and open book through the ceiling to a rappel spot. (60 feet)
FA 1960s: Art Gran

465. RENAISSANCE 5.12 PG
Start: Directly below a thin crack in a ceiling that is 25 feet above the ground, just to the right of a corner or prow and down to the right of Art's Route.
Pitch 1: Climb up to a horizontal crack below a vertical seam. Work up and right a few feet, and then either continue straight up (5.11+) to the ceiling or diagonal up right (5.10+ R) to a short, shallow left-facing corner under the ceiling. Then traverse left to the crack in the ceiling, climb past the ceiling, and continue to the top of the pinnacle. Rappel. (60 feet)
FA 1986: Darrow Kirkpatrick and Frank Minunni, using aid to place protection on the lead

466. MODERN LOVE 5.13 (Toprope)
Start: At the top of the large triangular boulder immediately to the right of Renaissance.
Pitch 1: Step across to a short, thin crack and move up to a small ledge. Move left and work up the face (to the left of a thin crack) to the short, shallow left-facing corner of Renaissance that is capped by a ceiling. Climb the ceiling at a seam and then continue to the top of the pinnacle.
FA (Toprope) 1988: Dave Lanman

467. THOM'S THUMB, RIGHT HAND 5.10− PG
Start: Behind the right (north) side of the pinnacle.
Pitch 1: Climb the obvious fault to the top of the pinnacle. (35 feet) 5.10− PG
Pitch 2: Rappel or finish on a nearby climb.
FA 1984: Todd Swain and Tad Welch

468. RANGER'S REVENGE 5.5 PG

Start: Behind the right (north) side of the pinnacle.

Pitch 1: Scramble and climb up the backside of the pinnacle to two blocks that are wedged between the pinnacle and the main face. (30 feet) 5.4

Pitch 2: From the left block, climb up the main face past a short, bulging left-facing corner to an overhang. Step right, work up past the next overhang, and continue straight up the face to the top. (70 feet) 5.5

FA 1981: Todd Swain and Thom Scheuer

469. TRUE BRIT 5.7 G

Start: Same as Ranger's Revenge.

Pitch 1: Climb the first pitch of Ranger's Revenge. (30 feet) 5.4

Pitch 2: From the right block, climb up the main face past a bulge and go through the notch above to the top. (80 feet) 5.7 G

FA 1981: Todd Swain and Rick Ayres

470. THE CIRCUMCISOR 5.12 R

Start: On the right side of some boulders, just right of the pinnacle and gully and 22 feet left of Bone Hard.

Pitch 1: Diagonal up right on some left-facing flakes past a small overhang to a vertical seam or fault. Climb the fault and continue up the steep face above to a small overhang. Then step left to a ramp system that leads up right to a rappel spot. (60 feet)

FA 1986: Al Diamond and Russ Clune, after cleaning, placing protection on rappel, and toproping part of the route

471. BONE HARD 5.12 PG

Start: On a boulder pile, 22 feet right of The Circumcisor and 17 feet left of the Dick's Prick pinnacle.

Pitch 1: Step across to the face and climb a short left-facing corner-flake. Move left to the second thin vertical crack or fault, and work up past a short, shallow right-facing corner and an overhanging face to an overhang. Then move right and continue up to a rappel spot. (60 feet)

FA 1986: Al Diamond, Russ Clune, and Kevin Bein, after toproping, hangdogging, and placing protection on rappel

472. DEATH'S HEAD MASK 5.12+ R
Start: Same as Bone Hard.
Pitch 1: Follow Bone Hard to the top of the left-facing corner-flake, step right, and climb up past a short, thin, pocketed crack to an overhang. Move left, clear the overhang, and work up the face, intersecting a small, flaky right-facing corner at its top. Then continue up to the blocky right-facing corner above and move left to the Bone Hard rappel spot. (60 feet)
FA (Toprope) 1987: Lynn Hill
FA (Lead) 1987: Jason Stern, after toproping and hangdogging

473. PENAL COLONY 5.7 R
Start: Same as Circumcision.
Pitch 1: Climb straight up the face to lower-angle rock and the top of the pinnacle, and rappel. (40 feet)
FA 1982: Todd Swain and John Thackray

474. CIRCUMCISION 5.7 PG
Start: At the left (southeast) edge of the Dick's Prick pinnacle.
Pitch 1: Climb up and right to the top of the pinnacle, and rappel. (40 feet)
You should get some tips before trying this one.
FA 1963: Dave Ingalls and Sean Hayes
FFA 1963: Art Gran

475. PROPHYLACTIC 5.11 R
Start: On a flat rock that points to the main (east) face of Dick's Prick pinnacle, immediately to the right of a pine tree.
Pitch 1: Diagonal up right to a short, shallow left-facing corner that leads to a noselike overhang (fixed piton). Move left and then work back up right until forced to move right. Then continue straight up to the top of the pinnacle and rappel. (50 feet)
FA (Toprope) 1977: Don Hamilton
FA (Lead) 1987: Todd Swain, after toproping

476. FOREIGN LESION 5.10− (Toprope)
Start: At a couple of horizontal cracks that lead out left, just below the start of Dick's Prick.
Pitch 1: Traverse left about 9 feet and then climb up the face past a groove to the top of the pinnacle.
FA (Toprope) 1985: Todd Swain

477. DICK'S PRICK 5.6 PG
Start: On the right side of the right (northeast) edge of the prominent blocklike pinnacle, 200 feet right of Pfui Teufel.
Pitch 1: Climb up the right edge of the corner for about 15 feet, move left, and continue up the face to the top. Rappel. (40 feet)
FA 1954: Hans Kraus, Dick Hirschland, and Bonnie Prudden

478. PENIS COLADA 5.8+ X
Start: On the right (north) backside of the Dick's Prick pinnacle. The best approach is to go around behind the pinnacle from the right.
Pitch 1: Climb up the steep face past a horizontal crack, diagonal up left past a small pine tree to the top of the pinnacle, and rappel. (40 feet)
Height-related—harder if shorter.
FA 1981: Todd Swain

479. V.D. 5.10 PG
Start: At the low point of the crevice behind the Dick's Prick pinnacle. The best approach is to go around behind the pinnacle from the left.
Pitch 1: Diagonal up left to a crack that leads to the top of the pinnacle and rappel. (40 feet)
FA 1963: Sean Hayes, Joe Kelsey, and Dave Ingalls
FFA 1965: Layton Kor

480. GIRLS JUST WANT TO HAVE FUN 5.12+ PG–R
Start: On the main face of the cliff opposite V.D. The best approach is around behind the pinnacle from the left.
Pitch 1: Climb up the face past right-facing flakes and corners

to a blocky ledge. Then work up to a large bulging overhang, move left, and continue up to the top.

Don't get nervous if this is virgin territory, and remember, it's got to be hard to be good.

FA (Toprope) 1987: Lynn Hill

FA (Lead) 1987: Lynn Hill, using protection placed by another climber on rappel

481. 10,000 RESTLESS VIRGINS 5.10+ PG

Start: At the base of a flaky left-facing corner behind the Dick's Prick pinnacle.

Pitch 1: Climb up the corner and continue past a pointed block and the obvious ceiling to a stance. Work up to the overhangs above, and then either rappel from the fixed protection there or climb through the overhangs and past a roof, and continue up the face to the top. (75 feet)

FA 1982: Sam Slater and Mike Freeman

482. THE LONE RANGER 5.3 G

Start: On the face midway between the gully up behind the right edge of the Dick's Prick pinnacle and After the Prick.

Pitch 1: Climb up the face to the top and rappel. (100 feet)

FA 1981: Todd Swain

483. AFTER THE PRICK 5.4 PG

Start: About 15 feet below the base of a large white left-facing corner, 55 feet right of the Dick's Prick pinnacle.

Pitch 1: Move up the right side of the chimney in the back of the corner for about 15 feet and step right around the outside corner (or climb straight up to this point—5.6). Then diagonal up right across the face and around another corner to a ledge. (90 feet)

Pitch 2: Climb straight up to a large ledge and walk off left to easy scrambling that leads to the top. (80 feet)

FA 1967: Bill Goldner, Wally Schamest, Dick DuMais

484. SHUT UP AND EAT YOUR GREENS 5.12 (Toprope)

Start: On the face 20 feet left of Wegetables I've Never Seen Before.

Pitch 1: Climb up to the ceiling and clear it at a shallow left-facing corner that begins at the lip.

FA (Toprope) 1987: Colin Lantz

485. WEGETABLES I'VE NEVER SEEN BEFORE
5.10+ PG ★

Start: Below a triple-tiered overhang split by a crack, 40 feet downhill to the right of After the Prick.

Pitch 1: Climb up the face, follow the crack through the overhang, and continue up to a belay ledge. (50 feet) 5.10− PG

Pitch 2: (V1) Walk off left (as some parties do) or traverse right about 20 feet to a birch tree.

Pitch 3: (V2, V3) Rappel (as some parties do, often setting up a toprope for Tennish, Anyone? in the process), or climb up under the roof above and move right to a large pointed flake. Traverse out right and move up to a birch tree (most climbers rappel or get lowered from here). Then work up and left, passing an overhang on the left, and continue to the top. (80 feet) 5.10+ G

Variation 1: 5.9 PG Climb up and left around a roof to a left-facing corner, which is followed until it ends, and then continue up the face to the top. (70 feet)

Variation 2: 5.9 PG Climb up to a right-facing corner, follow it until it ends, and continue up the face to the top. (50 feet)

Variation 3: 5.11+ PG Traverse right about 20 more feet and climb up to a 15-foot-long crack that breaks the prominent roof. Follow the crack out to the lip and then continue up to a rappel spot.

FA 1974: Steve Wunsch and Kevin Bein
FA (Variation 1) 1980: Rich Romano and John Bragg
FA (Variation 2) 1980: Rich Romano and John Bragg
FA (Variation 3) 1980: John Bragg and Rich Romano

New routes beyond this point are not permitted, but the existing routes may still be climbed. This restriction has been imposed to protect the delicate environment and to preserve the area in its natural state as much as

BRUCE SLAVINSKI on WEGETABLES I'VE NEVER SEEN BEFORE
Norman Kirk

possible so that it can be compared to some of the more heavily used areas to assess climber impact. Please cooperate.

486. TENNISH, ANYONE? 5.10 PG
Start: Below a crack system that is just right of a tree, 15 feet right of Wegetables I've Never Seen Before.
Pitch 1: Follow the crack system through the first overhang, and work up past a horn and another overhang. Continue up and then traverse right to a small ramp that diagonals up left. (60 feet) 5.10 PG
Pitch 2: Continue up ramp and finish on Wegetables.
FA 1981: Ivan Rezucha and Don Lauber

487. HAWAII FIVE-TEN 5.10 R
Start: At a thin crack that leads to a right-facing flake about 15 feet up, 10 feet right of Tennish, Anyone?
Pitch 1: Climb up to the flake and move up a few feet. Angle up right past some bulges and the right side of an overhang. Then continue up past a wide crack to a belay. (60 feet)
Pitch 2: Rappel or finish on a nearby climb.
FA 1986: Todd Swain, Brad White, Andy Schenkel, Dave and Marie Saball, and Dick Peterson

488. FOOTLOOSE 5.8 PG
Start: At a crack-fault system, 25 feet left of Fancy Free.
Pitch 1: Climb the crack system and then move right to a huge corner. Traverse right around the arête and then continue up the face to a pine tree. (80 feet) 5.8 PG
Pitch 2: Rappel or continue to the top.
FA 1981: Ivan Rezucha, Don Lauber, and Annie O'Neill

489. THE BORON DESTROYER 5.10 PG
Start: At a short incipient crack that leads to a piton in a horizontal crack 15 feet up, 8 feet left of Fancy Free, on the left side of the large block.
Pitch 1: Climb up past the piton and follow the obvious crack and broken left-facing corner to a belay at some laurel bushes in the very large left-facing corner above.

Pitch 2: Rappel or finish on a nearby climb.
FA (Toprope) 1986: Todd Swain
FA (Lead) 1986: Todd Swain and Andy Schenkel

490. FANCY FREE 5.8+ PG
Start: On top of a block that drops off 15 feet on its right side.
Pitch 1: Step across to a crack and a corner, and follow them past an overhang on the left to a roof. (V1) Traverse right at a thin horizontal seam, go around a nose, and then diagonal up right to some blocks. (60 feet) 5.8+ PG
Pitch 2: (V2) Climb up and left to a pine tree, and rappel. 5.5
Variation 1: 5.6 Diagonal up left to a large corner. Then, at the bushes in the corner (some parties belay here), traverse all the way right to the blocks at the end of the first pitch.
Variation 2: 5.3 Climb the obvious chimney and then traverse left to the pine tree.
FA 1981: Ivan Rezucha and Annie O'Neill

491. HEADLESS HORSEMAN 5.10 G
Start: On top of a huge block with a pine tree, opposite a thin crack and 15 feet right of Fancy Free.
Pitch 1: Step across and climb the crack to a small ledge. Continue up the crack and face to the highest overhang, and then angle right and up to a rappel tree. (50 feet)
FA 1988: Mike Steele and Bill Ravitch

492. CRUSTACEAN SYNDROME 5.8 PG
Start: At a shallow right-facing corner, 25 feet right of a huge jutting block and 22 feet left of Slime World.
Pitch 1: From a block, climb up past the corner (or the crack to its right) to a stance. Diagonal up left to a roof, and traverse left and around into a left-facing corner. Follow the corner and then traverse right to a belay. (80 feet) 5.8 PG
Pitch 2: Continue up the face, pass an overhang by moving right, and continue to the top. (90 feet)
FA 1981: Ivan Rezucha and Annie O'Neill

493. SLIME WORLD 5.12− PG
Start: At a short nose with a double crack on its left side, below a double-tiered 15-foot roof and 50 feet right of the huge jutting block.

Pitch 1: Climb the double crack and move right to some cracks that split the roof. Surmount the roof and belay on a stance just above the lip. (30 feet) 5.12− PG

Pitch 2: Rappel or continue to the top.

FA 1978: Mark Robinson, Sandy Stewart, and John Bragg

494. SWAMP GAS 5.10+ PG
Start: On a ledge 15 feet above the ground which has two trees on its right end, 75 feet right of Slime world.

Pitch 1: From the right end of the ledge, climb up past a nose to a small overhang, step around left into a large but short left-facing corner, and continue up to a roof. Then traverse left about 40 feet, climb through a break, and diagonal up right to a belay. (120 feet) 5.10+ PG

Pitch 2: Follow some cracks up right to a tree and then continue straight up to the top. (70 feet)

FA 1978: Mark Robinson and Sandy Stewart

495. A LONG WALK FOR MAN, A SHORT CLIMB FOR MANKIND 5.4 G
Start: At a huge broken left-facing corner that arches left near its top, 150 feet uphill to the right of Swamp Gas.

Pitch 1: Climb the corner until about halfway to the overhangs. Then traverse left about 15 feet and continue up the face to the top, passing a corner and ceiling on the left.

FA 1973: Robert Fenichel and Ken Marts

Route Photographs

Photographs by Dick Williams unless otherwise indicated.

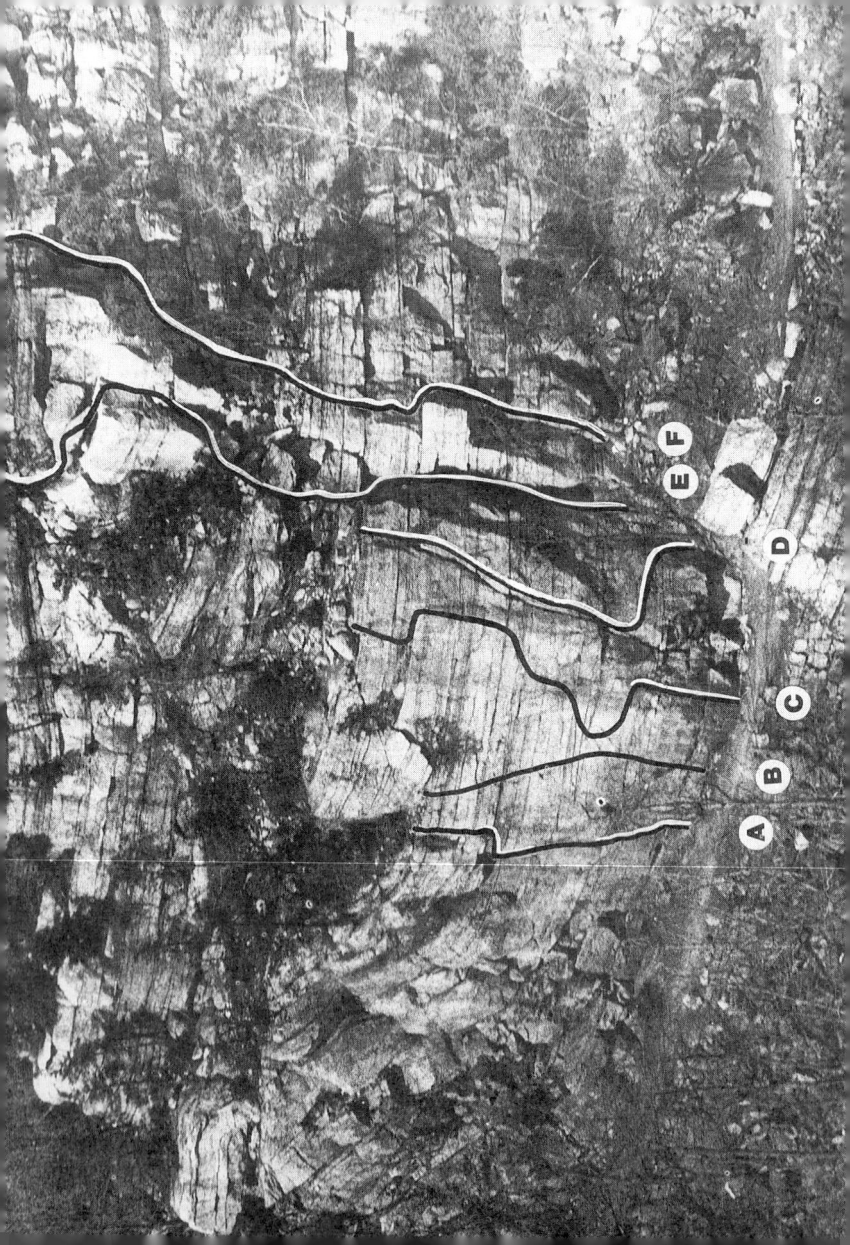

- A 4. KEYHOLE 5.7 G
- B 5. KATZENJAMMER 5.7 PG *
- C 6. THE BRAT 5.6 PG *
- D 7. HANDY ANDY 5.7 G–PG
- E 8. EASY KEYHOLE 5.2 G
- F 9. BLACK FLY 5.5 G

1-3 not shown

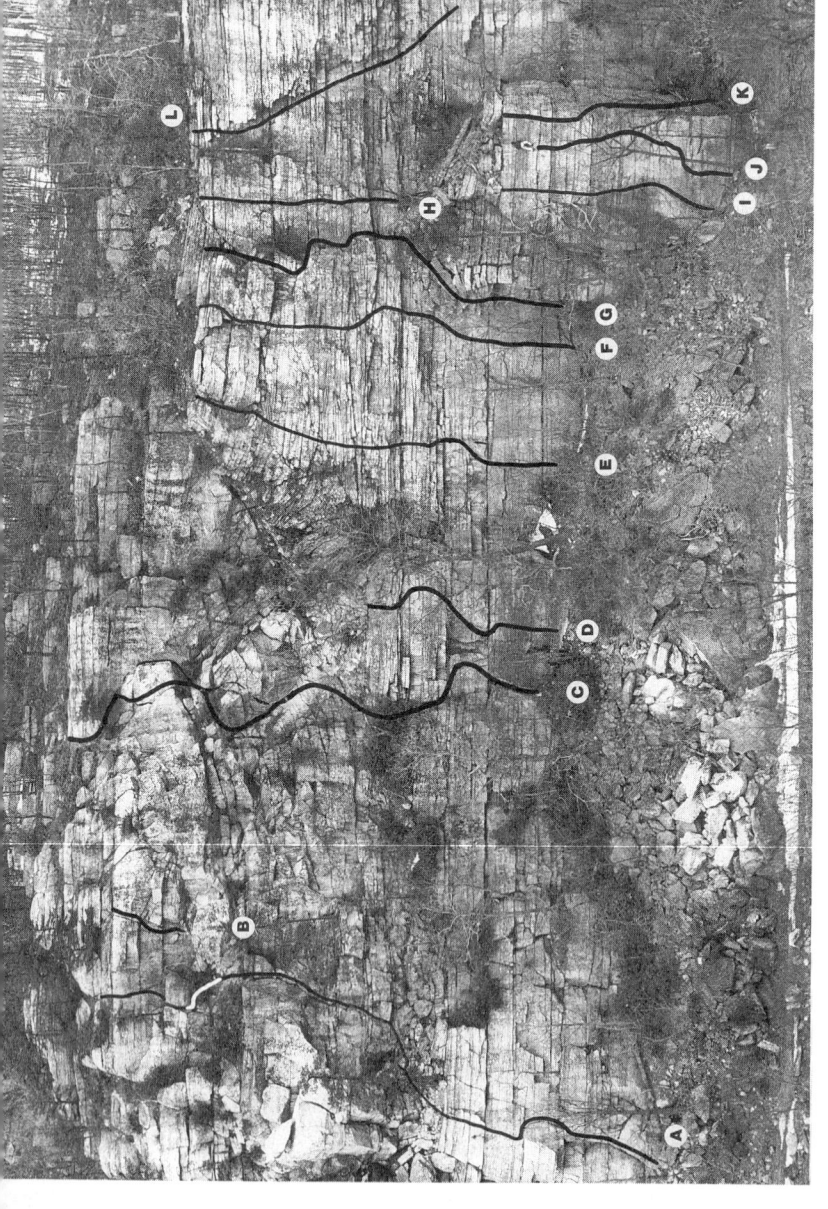

Photograph by Steven C. Faludi

- A 9. BLACK FLY 5.5 G
- B 10. ASTRO TRAVELER 5.10+ PG
- C 11. SHORT JOB 5.4 G
- D 12. 69 5.3 G
- E 13. NO PICNIC 5.4 G
- F 14. SHIT OR GO BLIND 5.8 G–PG
- G 15. SUDORIFEROUS 5.2 G
- H 16. HEEL HOOK AND HACK-IT 5.10– R-X
- I 17. HERDIE GERDIE 5.8 PG
- J 18. DIRTY GERDIE 5.9– PG *
- K 19. RED CABBAGE 5.9– G
- L 22. FANCY IDIOT 5.6 PG

20-21 not shown

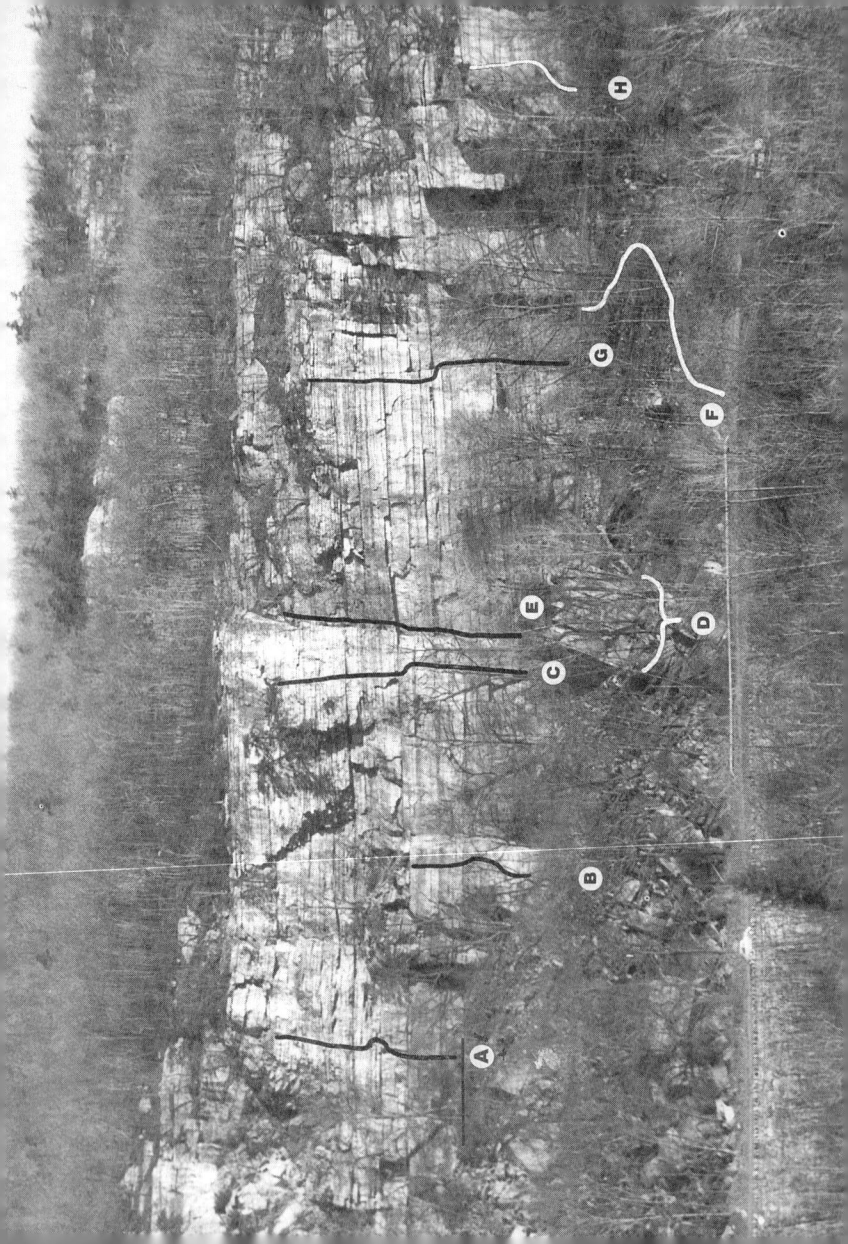

THE TRAPPS

- A 13. NO PICNIC 5.4 G
- B 18. DIRTY GERDIE 5.9– PG *
- C 26. NOSEDIVE 5.10 G **
- D THE MENTAL BLOCK
- E 27. DOUBLE CHIN 5.5 G *
- F TRAIL TO CARRIAGE ROAD
- G 35. HORSEMAN 5.5 G ***
- H 49. SQUIGGLES 5.4 G–PG *

14-17, 19-25, 28-34, 36-48 not shown

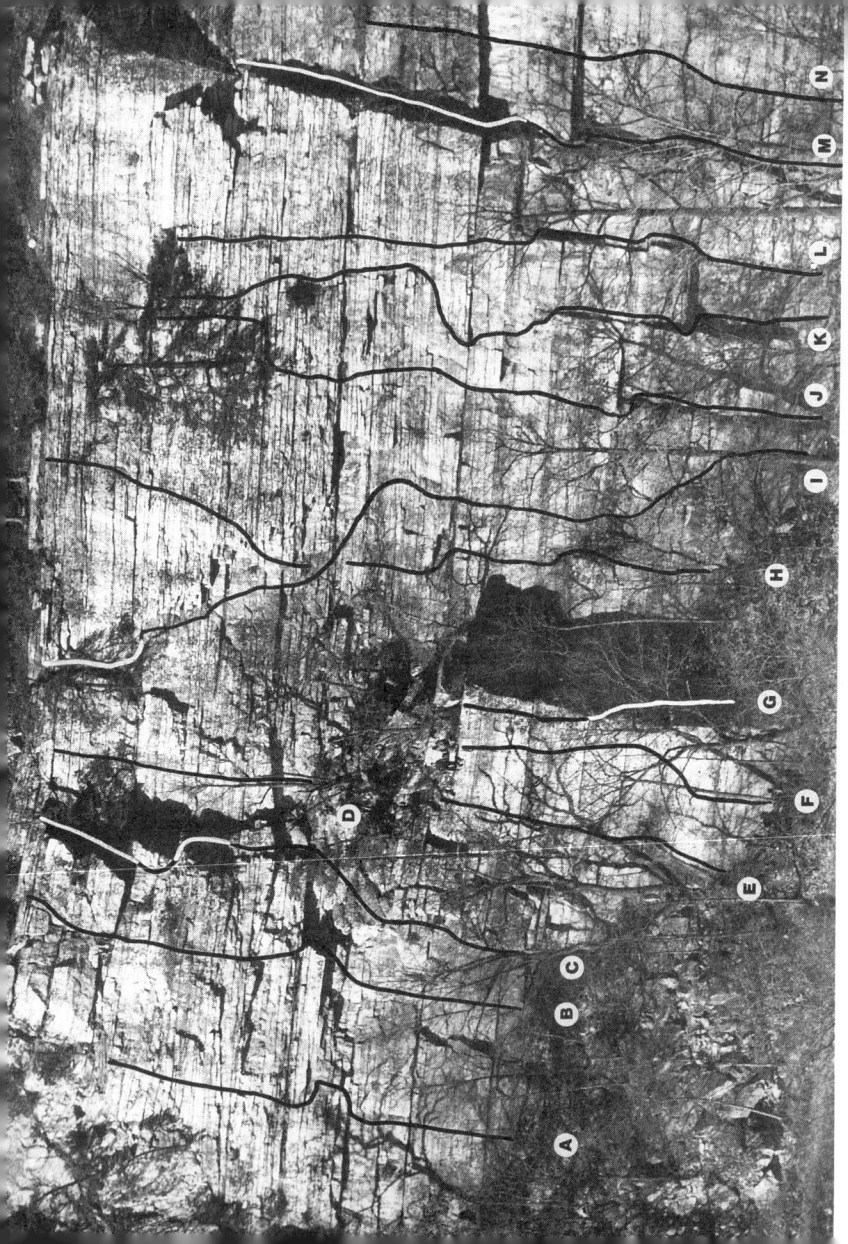

Photograph by Steven C. Faludi

- A 13. NO PICNIC 5.4 G
- B 14. SHIT OR GO BLIND 5.8 G–PG
- C 15. SUDORIFEROUS 5.2 G
- D 16. HEEL HOOK AND HACK-IT 5.10– R-X
- E 17. HERDIE GERDIE 5.8 PG
- F 18. DIRTY GERDIE 5.9– PG *
- G 19. RED CABBAGE 5.9– G
- H 21. FRIDAY THE 13TH 5.8 R
- I 22. FANCY IDIOT 5.6 PG
- J 23. BUNNY 5.4 G *
- K 24. RETRIBUTION 5.10 G **
- L
- M 26. NOSEDIVE 5.10 G **
- N 27. DOUBLE CHIN 5.5 G *
- 28. SOMETHING SCARY 5.10 PG–R

20, 25 not shown

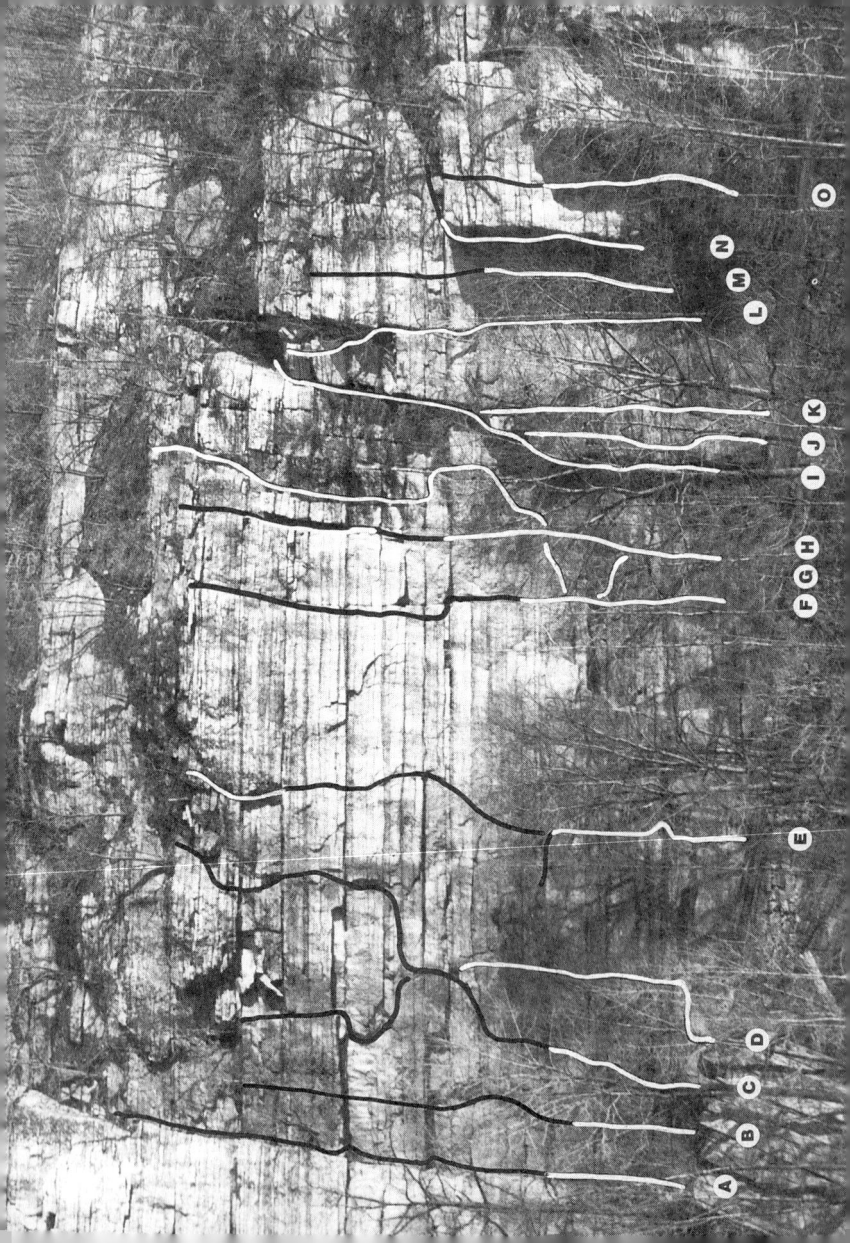

THE TRAPPS

- A 27. DOUBLE CHIN 5.5 G *
- B 28. SOMETHING SCARY 5.10 PG-R
- C 29. EYEBROW 5.6 PG
- D 30. DOUBLE CLUTCH 5.9+ G *
- E 33. DOUG'S ROOF 5.11+ G
- F 35. HORSEMAN 5.5 G ***
- G 36. PONY EXPRESS 5.6- PG
- H 37. APOPLEXY 5.9 PG **
- I 39. DIRTY CHIMNEY 5.0 G
- J 40. JUNIOR 5.9+ R
- K 41. LAUREL 5.7 G *
- L 43. RHODODENDRON 5.6- G *
- M 44. BIRCH 5.10+ PG-R
- N 45. DAS WIGGLES 5.3 PG
- O 47. WALTER MITTY 5.8 PG

31-32, 34, 38, 42, 46, 48 not shown

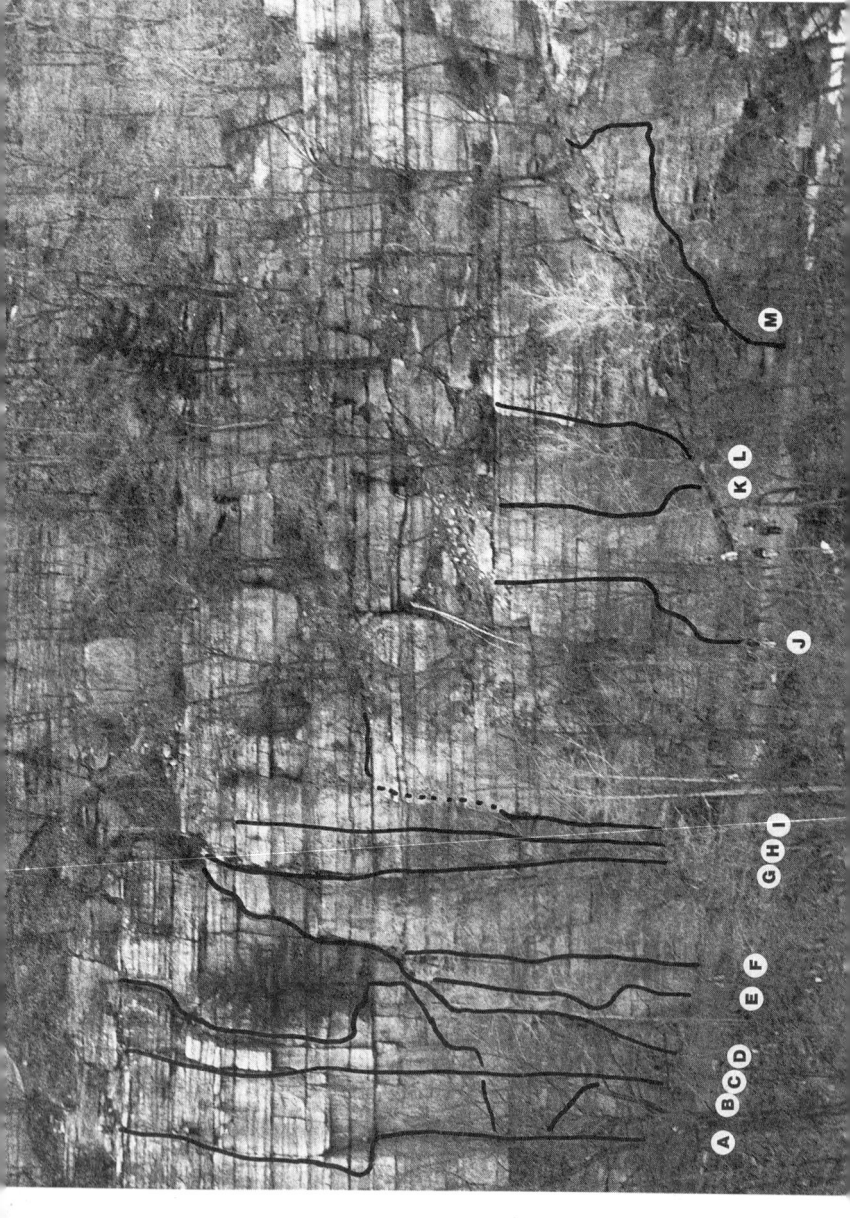

THE TRAPPS

- **A** 35. HORSEMAN 5.5 G ***
- **B** 36. PONY EXPRESS 5.6– PG
- **C** 37. APOPLEXY 5.9 PG **
- **D** 39. DIRTY CHIMNEY 5.0 G
- **E** 40. JUNIOR 5.9+ R
- **F** 41. LAUREL 5.7 G *
- **G** 43. RHODODENDRON 5.6– G *
- **H** 44. BIRCH 5.10+ PG-R
- **I** 45. DAS WIGGLES 5.3 PG
- **J** 49. SQUIGGLES 5.4 G-PG
- **K** 53. JACOB'S LADDER 5.10 X
- **L** 54. CROWBERRY RIDGE 5.6 PG
- **M** DESCENT ROUTE Class 3
- 38, 42, 46-48, 50-52 not shown

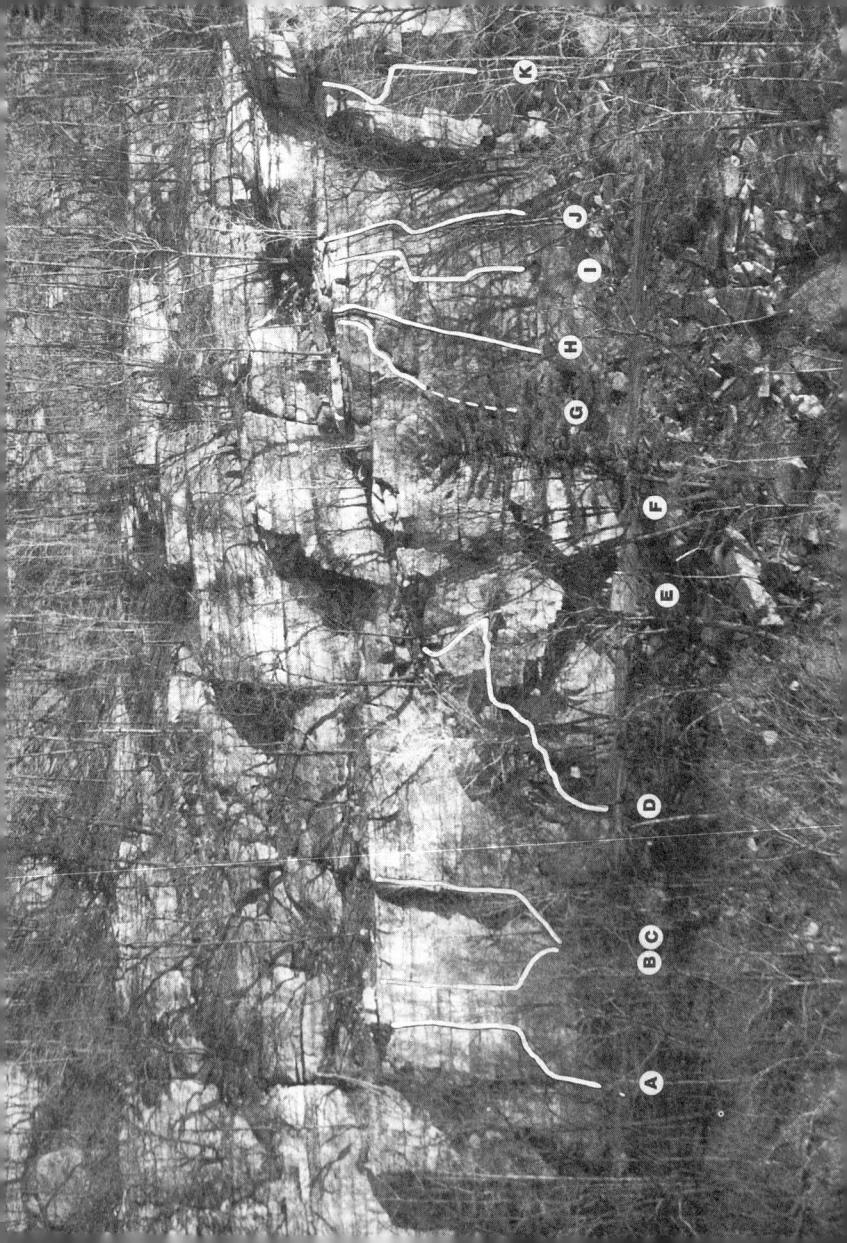

- A 49. SQUIGGLES 5.4 G-PG *
- B 53. JACOB'S LADDER 5.10 X
- C 54. CROWBERRY RIDGE 5.6 PG
- D DESCENT ROUTE Class 3
- E ÜBERFALL
- F 56. SUSIE A 5.10+ R-X
- G 57. THE FLAKE 5.1 PG
- H 58. KEN'S CRACK 5.7 G **
- I 59. PHOEBE 5.10 R-X
- J 60. BOSTON 5.5 PG
- K 65. C.C ROUTE 5.7- PG
  50-52, 55, 61-64, 66 not shown

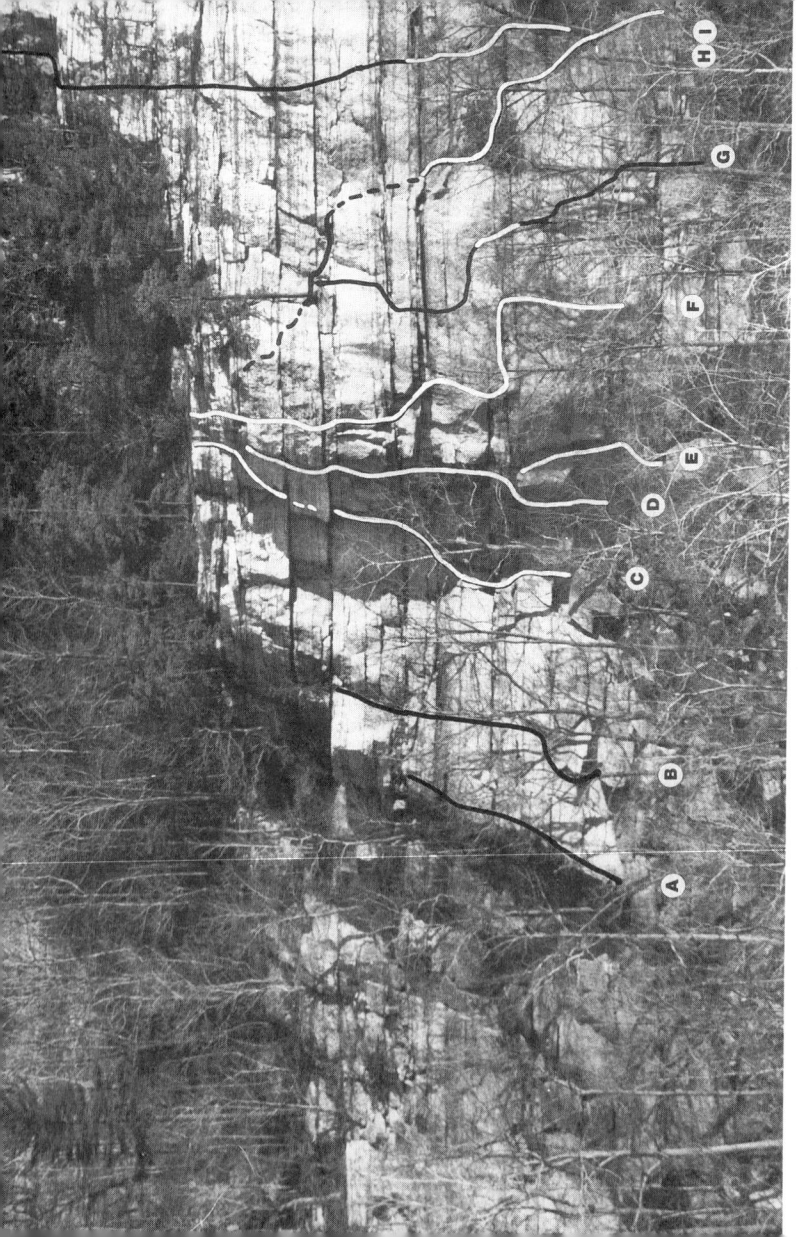

69, 74 not shown

- A 67. CRIMSON CORNER 5.0 G
- B 68. YALE 5.3 PG
- C 70. HARVARD 5.2 G
- D 71. TRAPPED LIKE A RAT 5.7 G
- E 72. CILLEY DICKEN' 5.12– PG *
- F 73. STIRRUP TROUBLE 5.10 PG ***
- G 75. P38 5.10 G **
- H 76. RADCLIFFE 4th Class
- I 77. BADCLIFF 5.10– PG

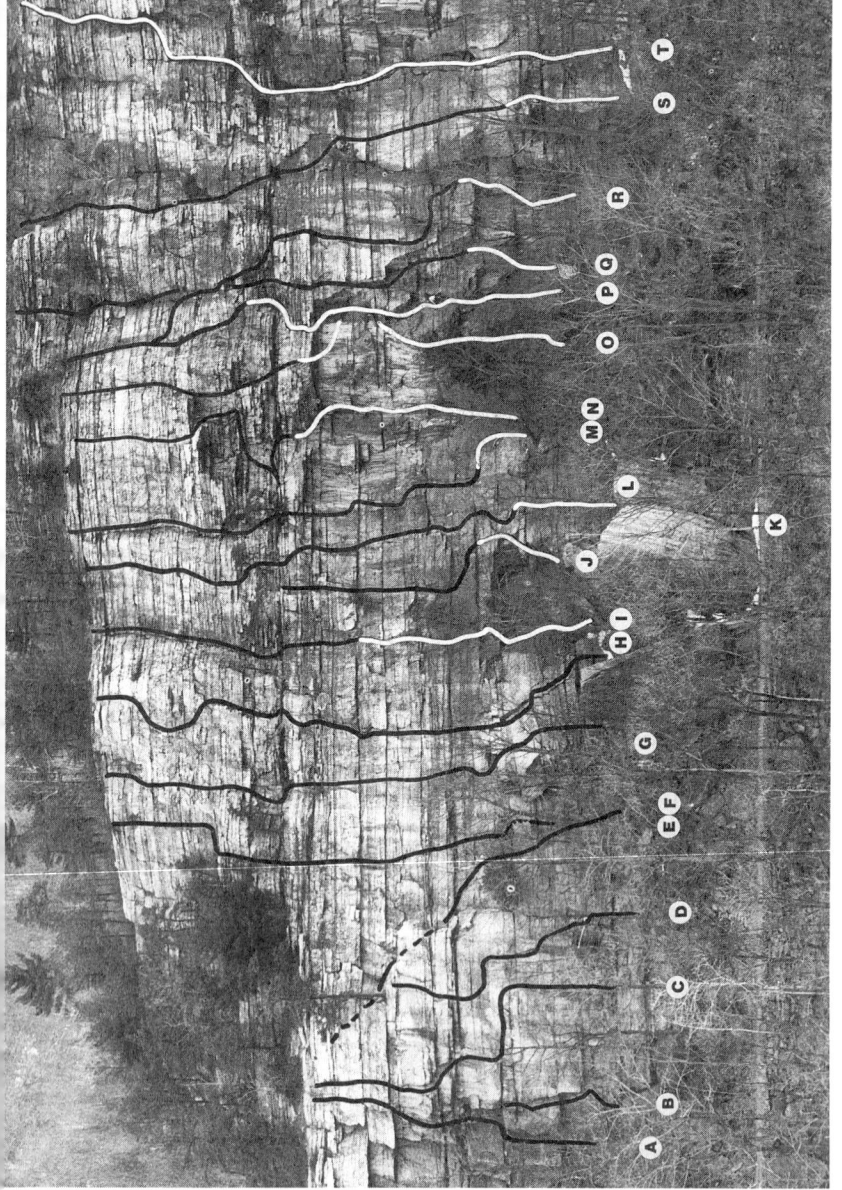

Photograph by Steven C. Faludi

- A 71. TRAPPED LIKE A RAT 5.7 G
- B 72. CILLEY DICKIN' 5.12– PG *
- C 73. STIRRUP TROUBLE 5.10 PG ***
- D 75. P38 5.10 G **
- E 76. RADCLIFFE 4th Class
- F 77. BADCLIFF 5.10– PG
- G 78. DENNIS 5.5 G *
- H 79. BELLY ROLL 5.4 PG *
- I 80. RODDEY 5.2 PG
- J 81. DAYDREAM 5.8 PG

- K THE CHOCKSTONE BOULDER
- L 82. JACKIE 5.5 G **
- M 83. CLASSIC 5.7 PG **
- N 84. PINK LAUREL 5.9 G **
- O 85. A-GAPE 5.11– PG *
- P 86. APE CALL 5.8 PG–R *
- Q 87. APE AND ESSENCE 5.9+ PG
- R 89. R.M.C. 5.5– G *
- S 90. RAUBENHEIMER SPECIAL 5.7– PG *
- T 91. BETTY 5.3– G *

74, 88 'not shown

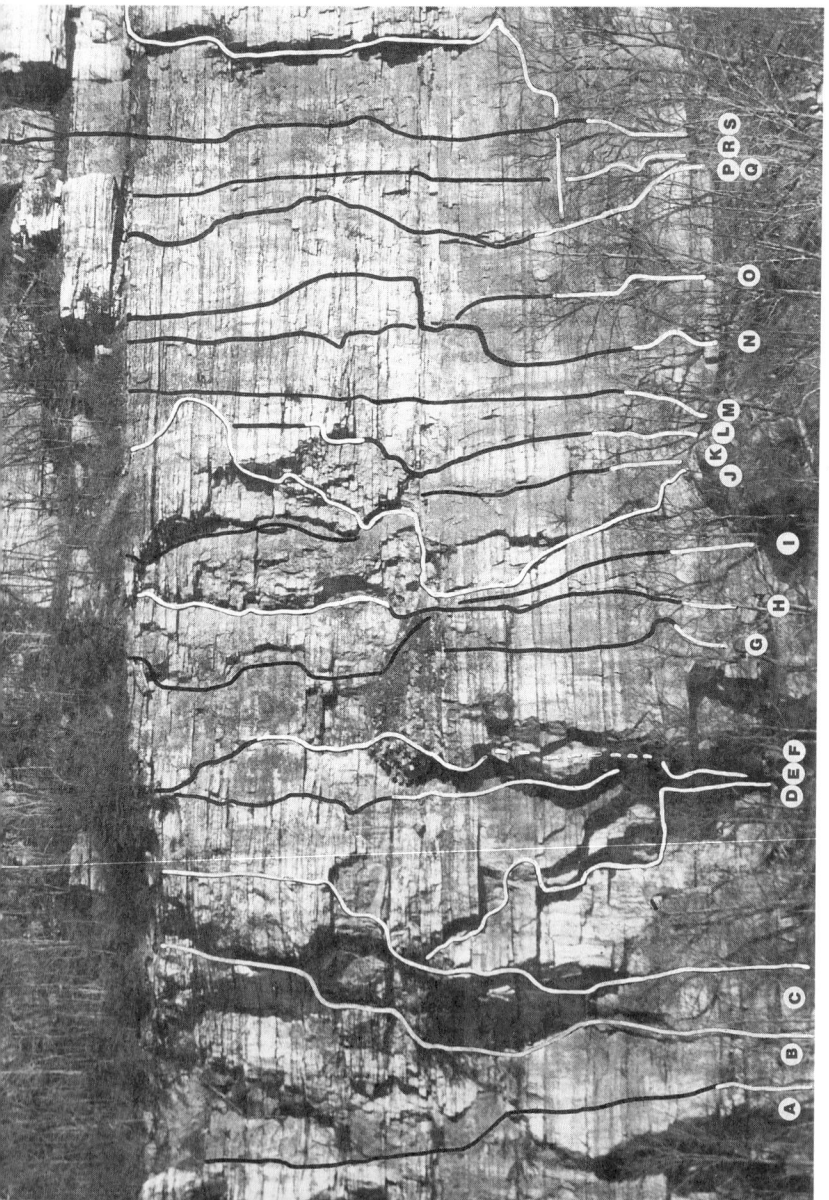

THE TRAPPS

- **A** 90. RAUBENHEIMER SPECIAL 5.7– PG *
- **B** 91. BETTY 5.3– G *
- **C** 92. THE BLACKOUT 5.8 R *
- **D** 94. MATINEE 5.10+ G ***
- **E** 96. BIG CHIMNEY 5.5 PG
- **F** 97. MISS BAILEY 5.6 PG
- **G** 98. FETUS 5.9+ PG–R
- **H** 99. BABY 5.6 G–PG ***
- **I** 100. TWISTED SISTER 5.8 G
- **J** 101. EASY OVERHANG 5.2 PG **
- **K** 102. QUEASY O 5.10– R–X
- **L** 103. SON OF EASY O 5.8 G ***
- **M** 104. HEATHER 5.9 R–X
- **N** 105. PAS DE DEUX 5.8 PG **
- **O** 106. CITY LIGHTS 5.7 G–PG **
- **P** 107. FROG'S HEAD 5.6– G ***
- **Q** 108. MARIA 5.6+ PG **
- **R** 109. SUNDOWN 5.8+ PG
- **S** 110. KAMA SUTRA 5.12– R

93, 95 not shown

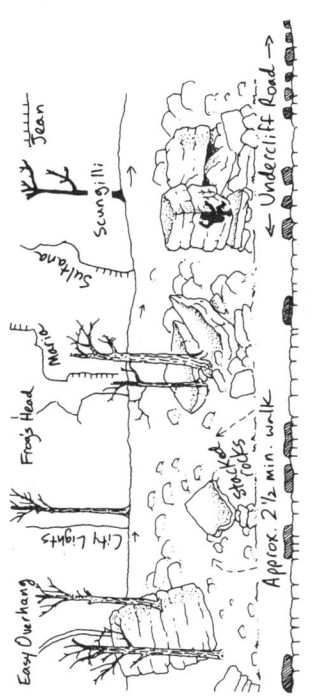

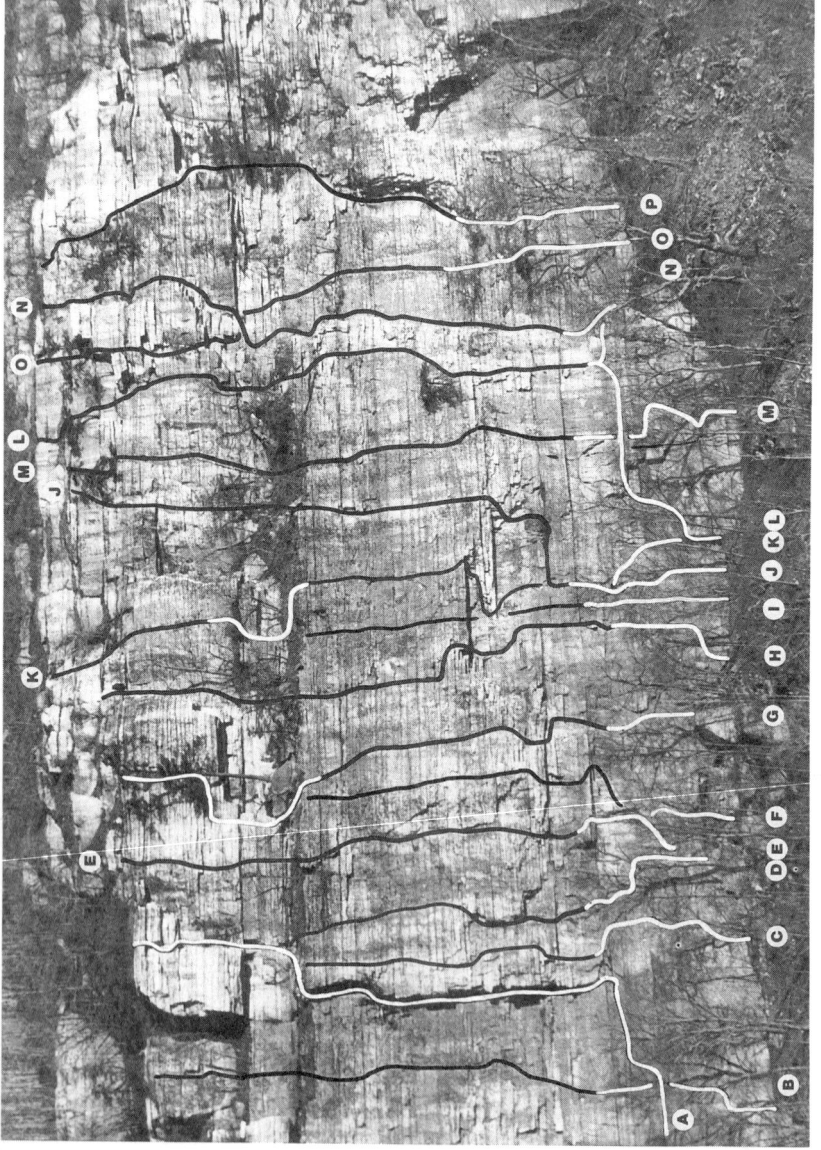

THE TRAPPS

- A 108. MARIA 5.6+ PG **
- B 110. KAMA SUTRA 5.12– R
- C 111. SULTANA 5.8 PG
- D 112. SCUNGILLI 5.7 PG
- E 113. JEAN 5.9 PG *
- F 114. PRECARIOUS PERCH 5.9 PG
- G 115. SIXISH 5.4+ G ***
- H 117. DRUNKARD'S DELIGHT 5.8– PG **
- I 118. FIVE TENDONS 5.10+ R
- J 119. MORNING AFTER 5.8– PG *
- K 120. BLOODY MARY 5.6 PG
- L 121. RUSTY TRIFLE 5.5 G *
- M 123. ROCK AND BREW 5.9 PG–R
- N 126. BLOODY BUSH 5.7 G
- O 127. UNCLE RUDY 5.8 PG
- P 128. WRIST 5.6 G *

109, 116, 122, 124-125 not shown

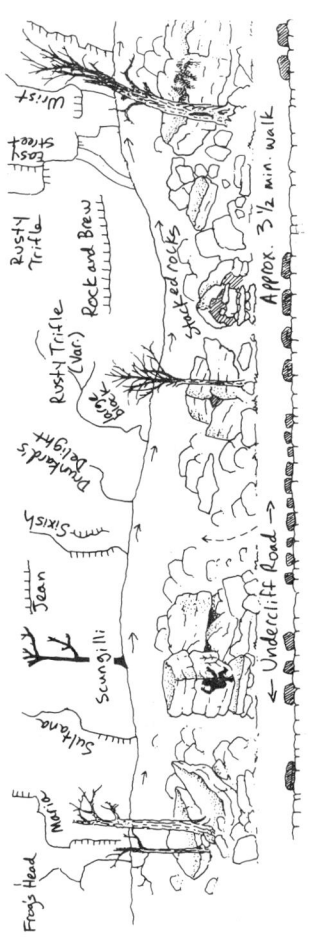

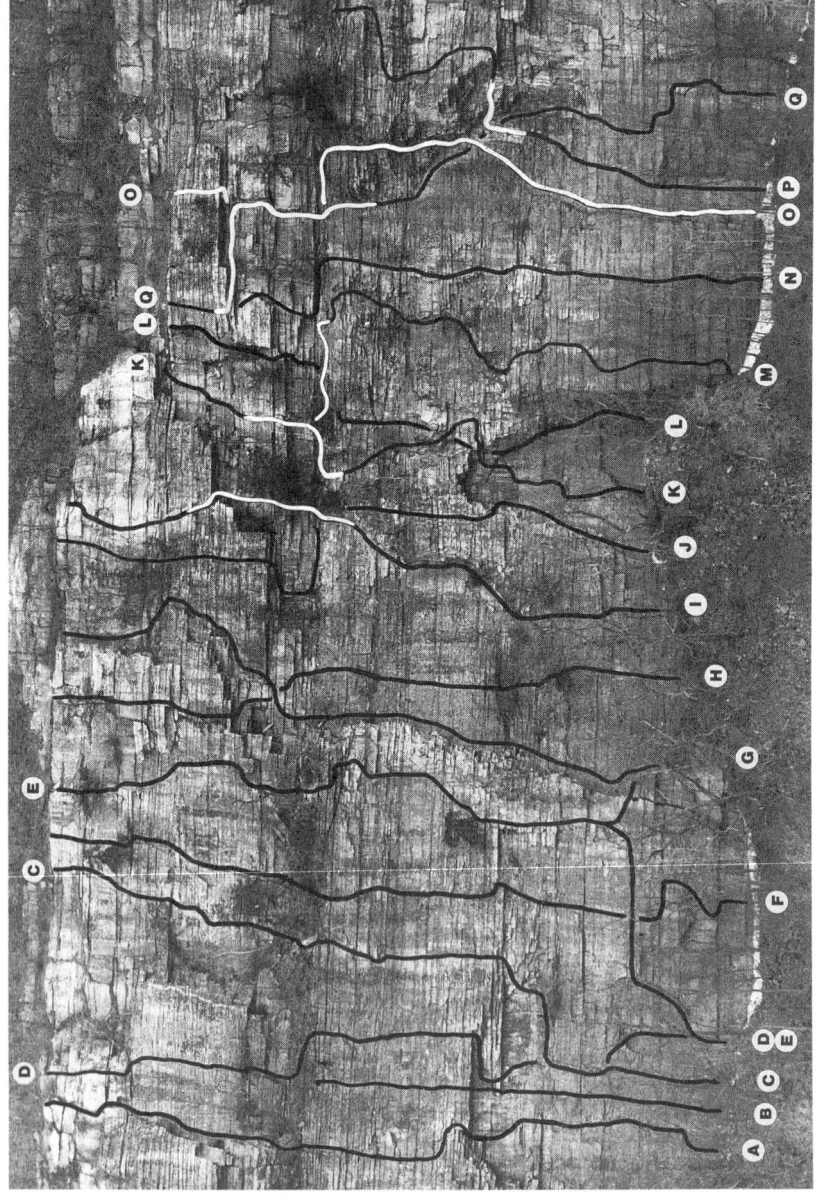

THE TRAPPS 281

Photograph by Steven C. Faludi

- **A** 117. DRUNKARD'S DELIGHT 5.8– PG **
- **B** 118. FIVE TENDONS 5.10+ R
- **C** 119. MORNING AFTER 5.8– PG *
- **D** 120. BLOODY MARY 5.6 PG
- **E** 121. RUSTY TRIFLE 5.5 G *
- **F** 123. ROCK AND BREW 5.9 PG–R
- **G** 126. BLOODY BUSH 5.7 G
- **H** 127. UNCLE RUDY 5.8 PG
- **I** 128. WRIST 5.6 G *
- **J** 129. INVITATION TO HELL 5.10+ PG
- **K** 130. ARCH 5.5– PG *
- **L** 131. BILLY SHEARS 5.9– PG
- **M** 134. RIBS 5.4 PG
- **N** 135. CALISTHENIC 5.7 PG
- **O** 136. GORILLA MY DREAMS 5.7 PG
- **P** 137. SPLASHTIC 5.9– PG–R *
- **Q** 138. GASTON 5.8 PG 122, 124-125, 132-133 not shown

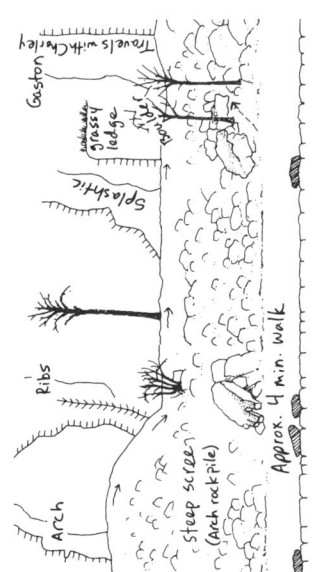

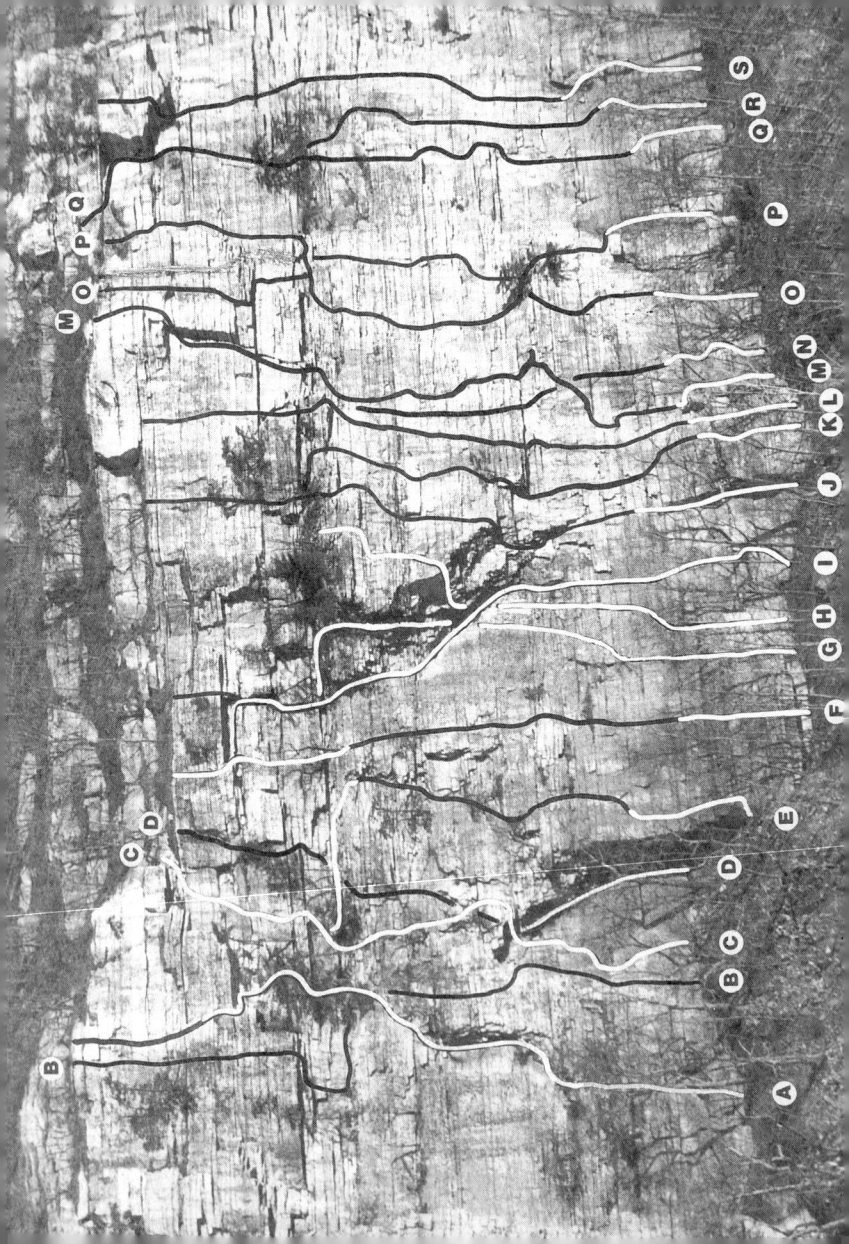

THE TRAPPS

- A 128. WRIST 5.6 G *
- B 129. INVITATION TO HELL 5.10+ PG
- C 130. ARCH 5.5– PG *
- D 131. BILLY SHEARS 5.9– PG
- E 134. RIBS 5.4 PG
- F 135. CALISTHENIC 5.7 PG
- G 136. GORILLA MY DREAMS 5.7 PG
- H 137. SPLASHTIC 5.9– PG-R *
- I 138. GASTON 5.8 PG
- J 139. TRAVELS WITH CHARLEY 5.8– R
- K 140. STRICTLY FROM NOWHERE 5.7 PG **
- L 141. EPICLEPSY 5.10 X
- M 142. SHOCKLEY'S CEILING 5.6 G ***
- N 143. MISTER TRANSISTOR 5.10– PG
- O 145. GRIM-ACE FACE 5.9 PG **
- P 148. HIGH CORNER 5.5 PG
- Q 150. GLYPTODON 5.8 PG *
- R 151. NEMESIS 5.10– PG
- S 152. MIDNIGHT COWBOY 5.9+ R *

132-133, 144, 146-147, 149 not shown

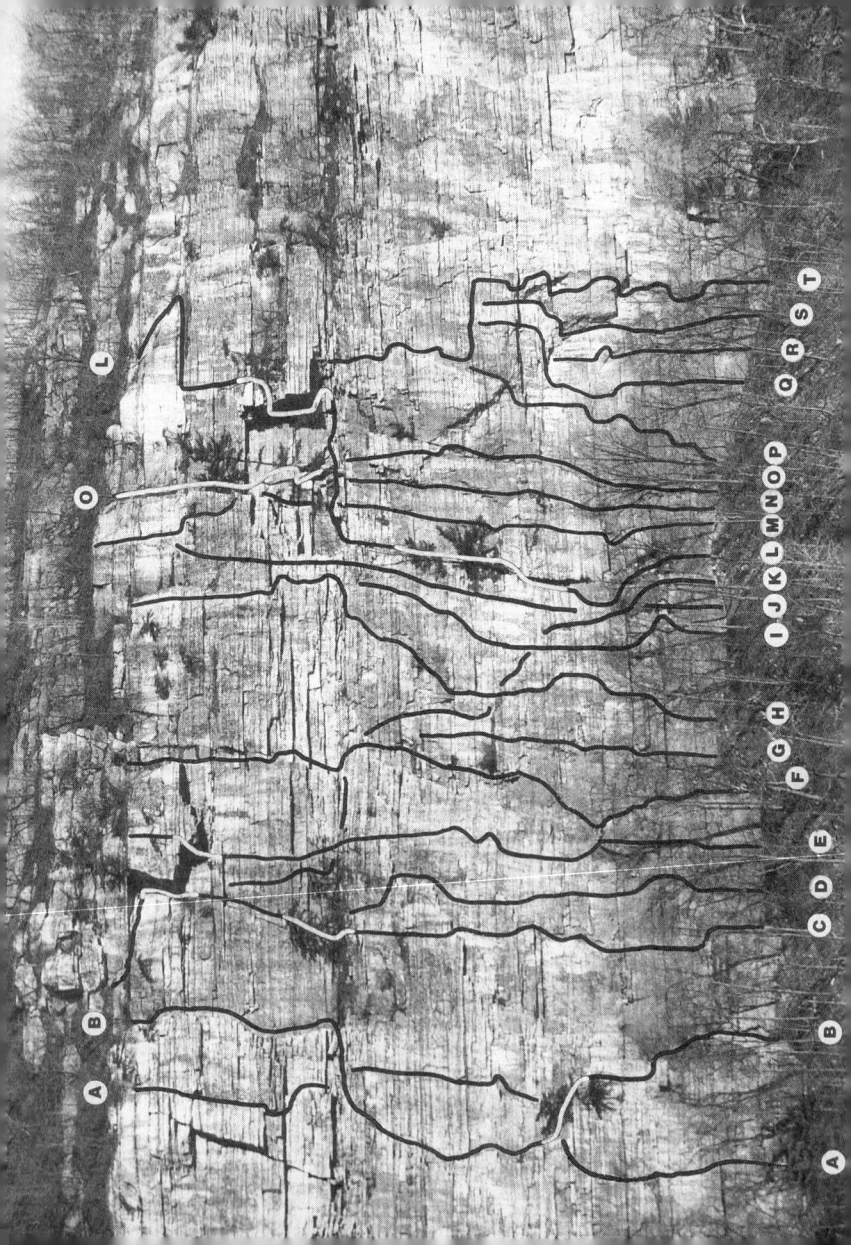

THE TRAPPS

- A   145. GRIM-ACE FACE 5.9 PG **
- B   148. HIGH CORNER 5.5 PG
- C   150. GLYPTODON 5.8 PG *
- D   151. NEMESIS 5.10– PG
- E   152. MIDNIGHT COWBOY 5.9+ R *
- F   153. GLYPNOD 5.8 PG *
- G   154. YESTERDAY'S LEMONADE 5.10– PG–R
- H   155. ANGUISH 5.8 PG
- I   156. RUBY SATURDAY 5.9– PG
- J   157. RASPBERRY SUNDAE 5.9+ PG
- K   158. SIMPLE CEILINGS 5.5 PG
- L   159. THREE PINES 5.3 G ***
- M   160. SOMETHING BORING 5.9 X
- N   161. SOMETHING OR OTHER 5.10– R
- O   162. SOMETHING INTERESTING 5.8 G ***
- P   163. HIGHER STANNARD 5.9– PG **
- Q   164. BIRDIE PARTY 5.10– PG **
- R   165. INTERSTICE 5.10+ R *
- S   166. MOTHER'S DAY PARTY 5.10 PG **
- T   167. M.F. 5.9 PG ***
  146-147, 149 not shown

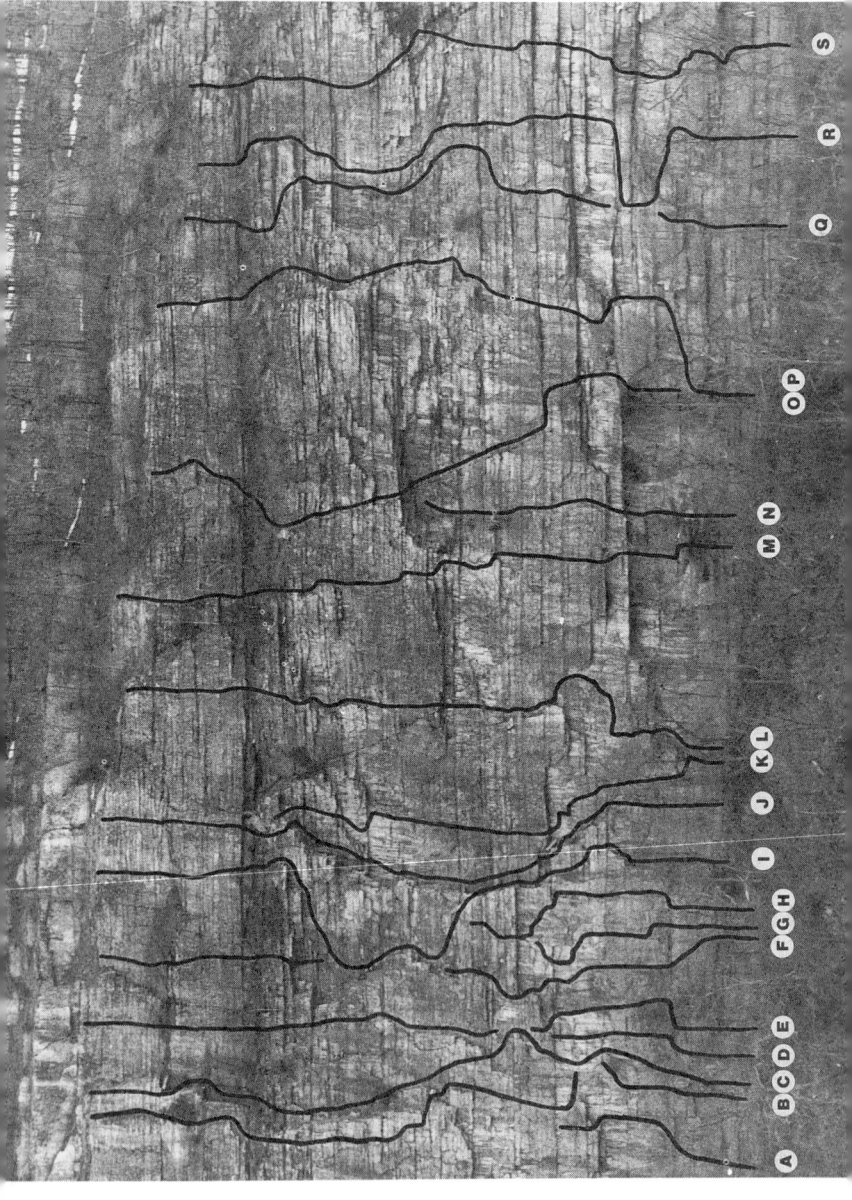

THE TRAPPS

Photograph by Steven C. Faludi

- **A** 168. WATER KING 5.10+ R
- **B** 169. MEN AT ARMS 5.9 PG *
- **C** 170. TRY AGAIN 5.10 PG **
- **D** 171. FLY AGAIN 5.11+ PG
- **E** 172. COEXISTENCE 5.10+ PG ***
- **F** 173. STAR ACTION 5.10 PG **
- **G** 175. GRAVEYARD SHIFT 5.10+ PG–R ***
- **H** 176. TOUGH SHIFT 5.10 R **
- **I** 177. OVERHANGING LAYBACK 5.7 PG
- **J** 178. NO EXISTENCE 5.9 R-X
- **K** 179. SCENE OF THE CLIMB 5.11– PG ***
- **L** 180. LAND'S END 5.9– PG
- **M** 182. ORGANIC IRON 5.12+ R *
- **N** 183. IMPENETRABLE CEILINGS 5.11 PG
- **O** 184. SCOTCH ON THE ROCKS 5.10+ PG
- **P** 185. DRY MARTINI 5.7 PG
- **Q** 187. PT. PHONE HOME 5.10+ PG
- **R** 188. CO-OP 5.9– PG
- **S** 190. WELCOME TO THE GUNKS 5.10 PG–R ***

174, 181, 186, 189 not shown

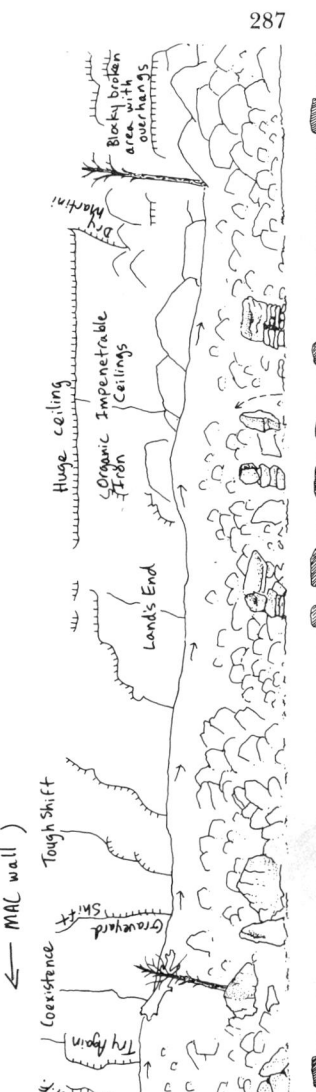

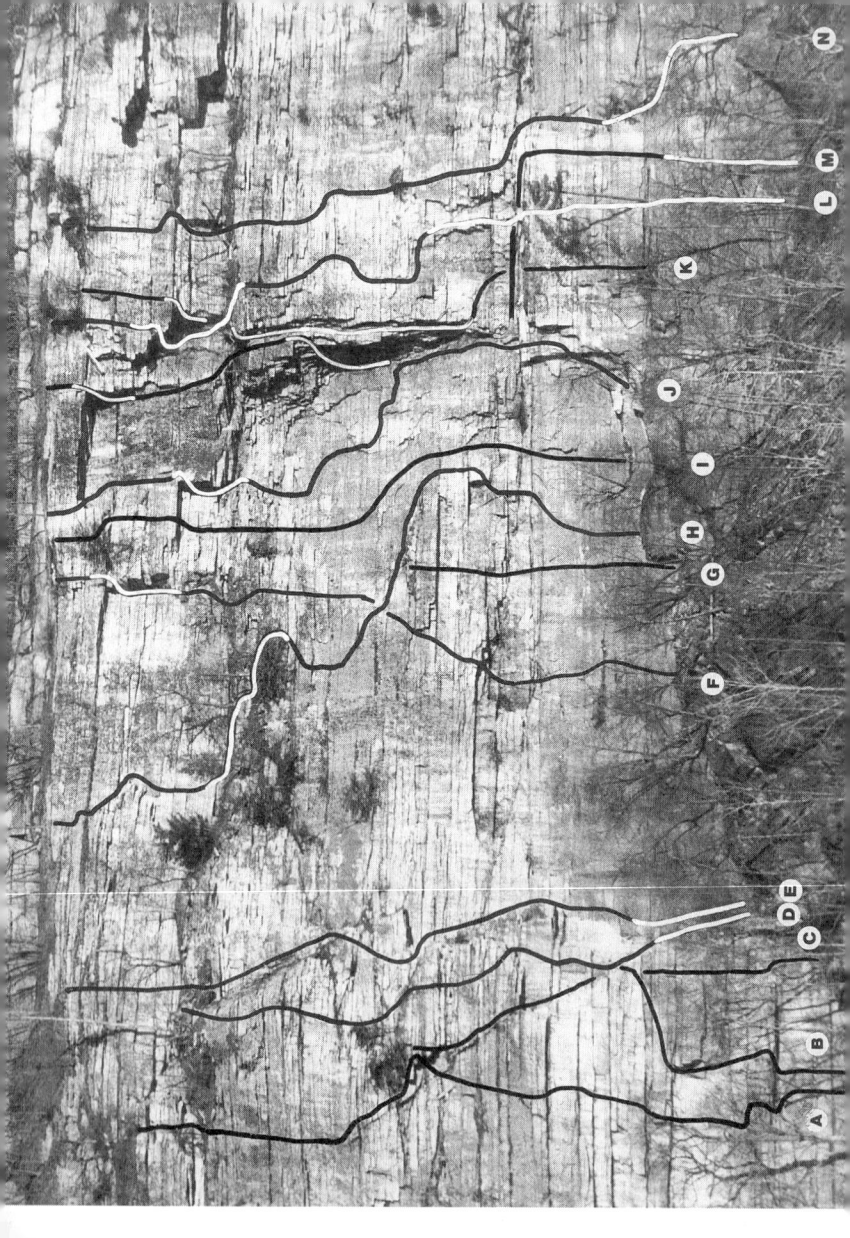

THE TRAPPS   289

A 190. WELCOME TO THE
       GUNKS
       5.10 PG-R ***

B 191. LAUGHING MAN
       5.11 PG

C 192. TREE'S A CROWD
       5.9 G

D 193. CREDIBILITY GAP
       5.6 PG

E 194. ASPHODEL 5.5 G

F 195. BEATLE BROW BULGE
       5.9+ PG

G 196. BLUEBERRY WINE
       5.10+ R

H 197. BLUEBERRY LEDGES
       5.5- G

I 198. SELDOM MUSTARD,
       NEVER RELISH
       5.10 G

J 199. BEGINNER'S DELIGHT
       5.3 PG ***

K 200. OCTOBERFEST
       5.9- R-X

L 201. SNOOKY'S RETURN
       5.8 PG **

M 202. FRIENDS AND LOVERS
       5.9 PG

N 203. MINTY 5.3 G **

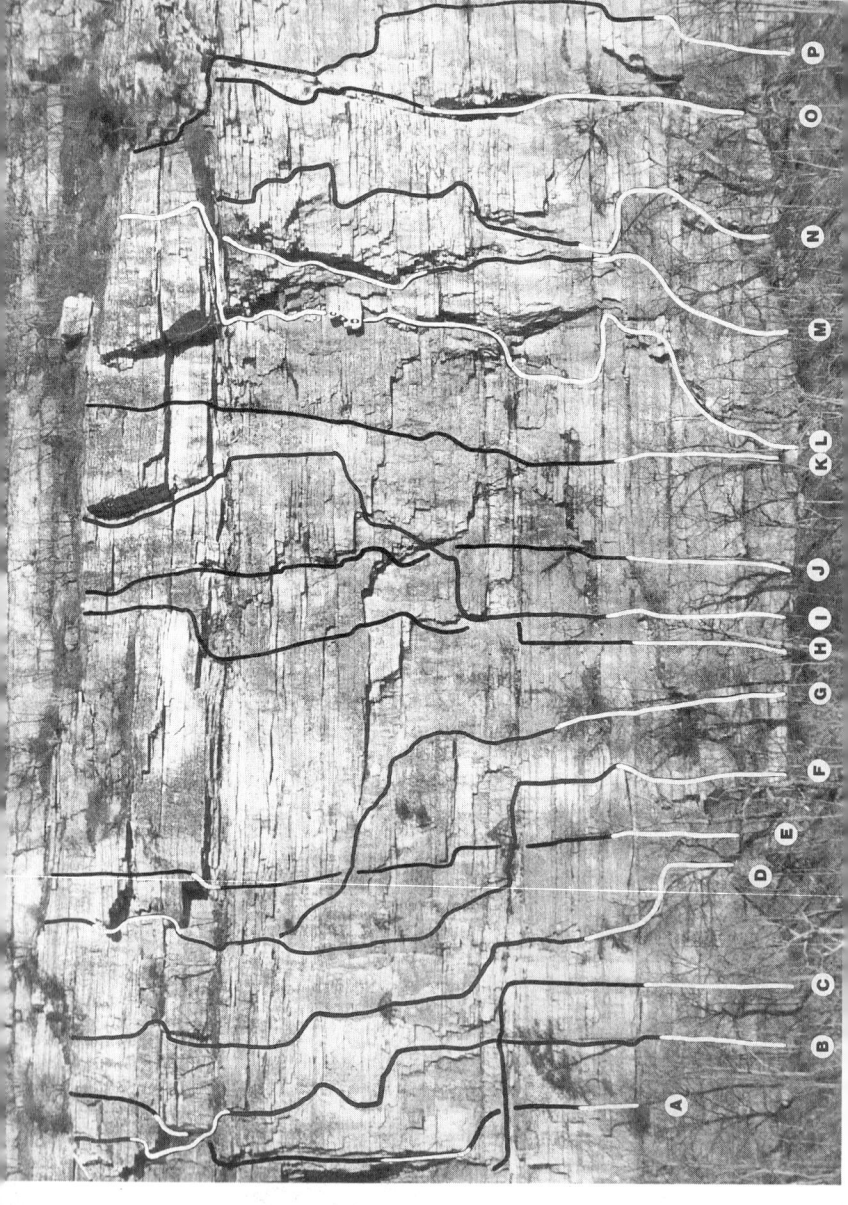

THE TRAPPS

- A 200. OCTOBERFEST 5.9– R-X
- B 201. SNOOKY'S RETURN 5.8 PG **
- C 202. FRIENDS AND LOVERS 5.9 PG
- D 203. MINTY 5.3 G **
- E 204. BAG'S END 5.8+ PG
- F 205. TIPSY TREES 5.3 G
- G 206. THE WOMB STEP 5.7 PG
- H 207. CHIMANGO 5.9+ PG
- I 208. HAWK 5.4+ PG *
- J 209. PEREGRIN 5.8 PG
- K 210. REACH OF FAITH 5.10– PG
- L 211. SOUTHERN PILLAR 5.2 G *
- M 212. COLUMBIA 5.9– G
- N 213. MADAME GRUNNE-BAUM'S WULST 5.6 G ***
- O 215. LE TETON 5.9 G **
- P 216. NORTHERN PILLAR 5.2 G **

214 not shown

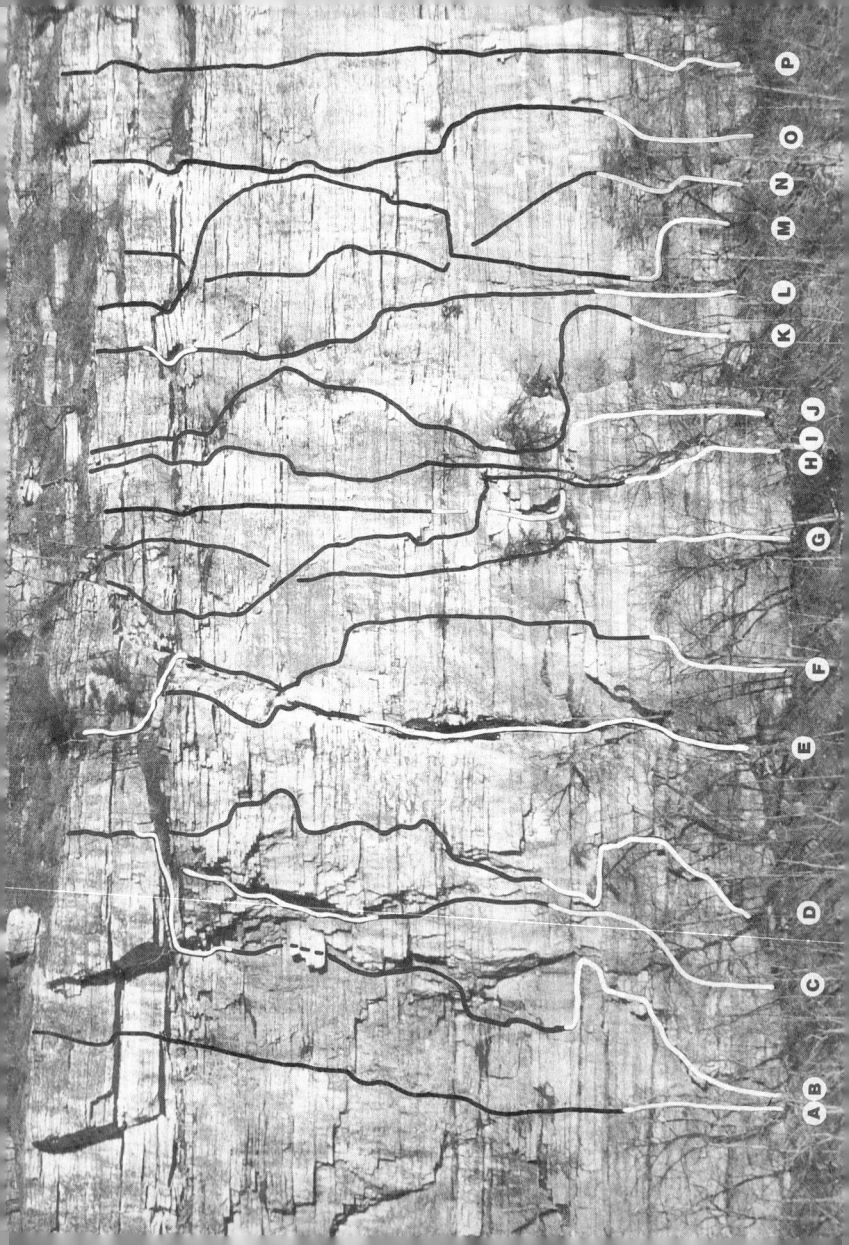

THE TRAPPS

- A 210. REACH OF FAITH 5.10– PG
- B 211. SOUTHERN PILLAR 5.2 G *
- C 212. COLUMBIA 5.9– G
- D 213. MADAME GRUNNEBAUM'S WULST 5.6 G ***
- E 215. LE TETON 5.9 G **
- F 216. NORTHERN PILLAR 5.2 G **
- G 217. HYJEK'S HORROR 5.8– PG *
- H 218. TWIN OAKS 5.3 PG
- I 219. TRIPLE BULGES 5.5 PG
- J 220. DELUSIONS OF GRANDEUR 5.9+ PG
- K 221. WILLIE'S WEEP 5.2 G
- L 222. DON'T SHOOT 5.6 G
- M 223. LAT-ON THE SEASON 5.7 PG
- N 224. GLEET STREET 5.8 R
- O 225. FUNNY FACE 5.5– PG
- P 226. SON OF BITCHY VIRGIN 5.6 PG

214 not shown

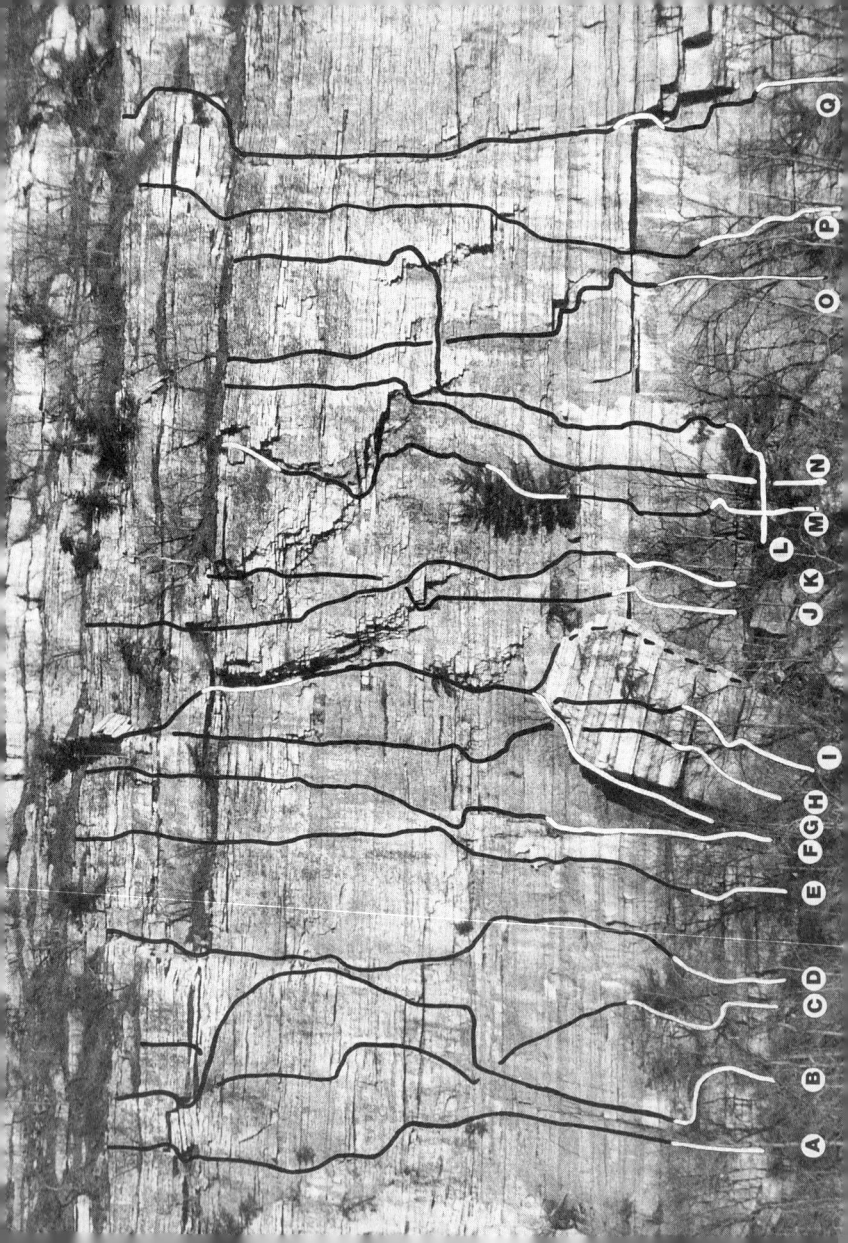

THE TRAPPS

- A 222. DON'T SHOOT 5.6 G
- B 223. LAT-ON THE SEASON 5.7 PG
- C 224. GLEET STREET 5.8 R
- D 225. FUNNY FACE 5.5– PG
- E 226. SON OF BITCHY VIRGIN 5.6 PG
- F 228. BITCHY VIRGIN 5.6 R *
- G 229. UNNAMED 5.2 G
- H 230. DAT MANTEL 5.10 PG
- I 231. DIS-MANTEL 5.10 G
- J 233. HIGH TIMES 5.9+ PG-R
- K 234. STOP THE PRESSES, MR. WILLIAMS 5.8+ PG
- L 235. GORY THUMB 5.8+ G–PG *
- M 236. RAUNCHY 5.8 PG *
- N 237. WILD HORSES 5.11+ R *
- O 239. HELP! 5.11+ R
- P 240. PLEH! 5.11+ R
- Q 241. V-3 5.7 G **

227, 232, 238 not shown

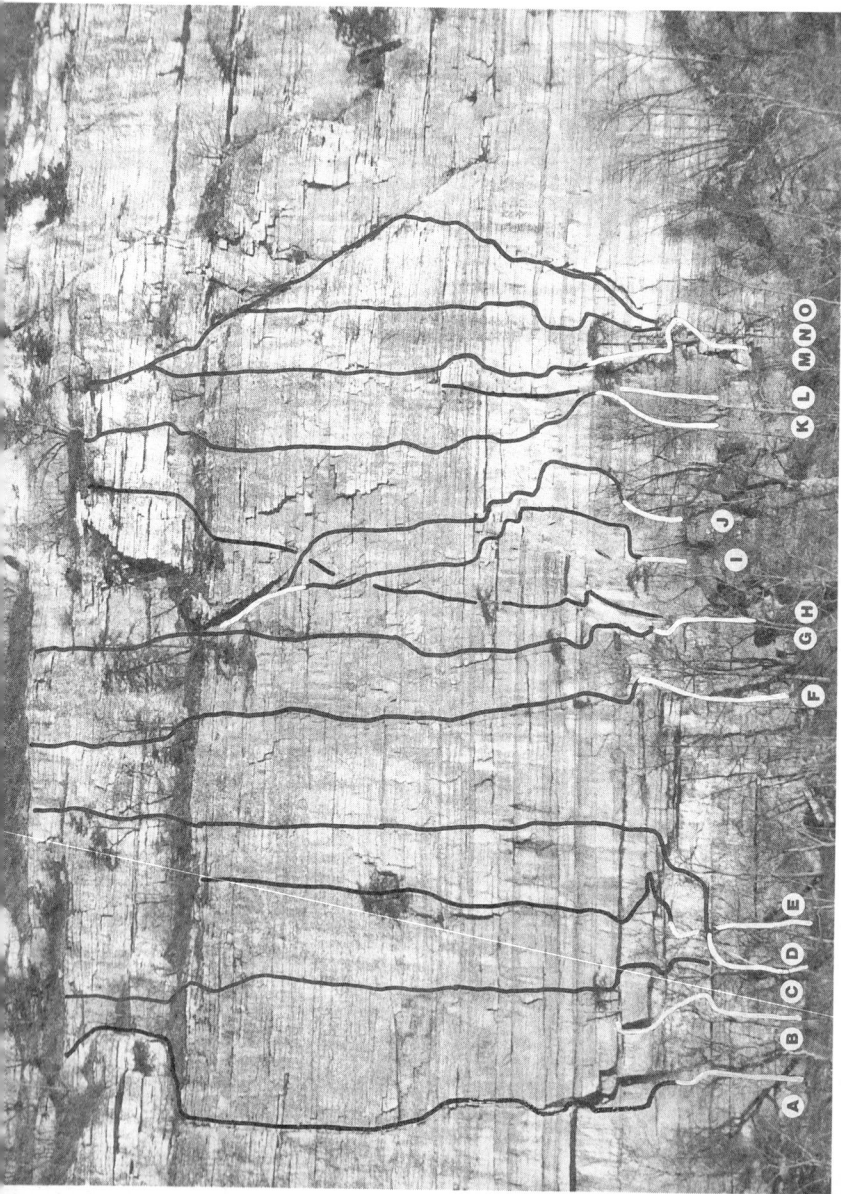

THE TRAPPS

- A 241. V-3 5.7 G **
- B 242. CITY STREETS 5.10 PG
- C 243. COUNTRY ROADS 5.10 PG *
- D 244. COMMANDO RAVE 5.9 PG *
- E 245. METROPOLIS 5.11+ PG-R *
- F 246. BEYOND THE FRINGE 5.9 R
- G 247. BALROG 5.10 G-PG *
- H 248. BULLFROG 5.12– PG-R
- I 250. DRY HEAVES 5.8 PG
- J 251. ALLEY OOP 5.7 PG *
- K 252. CHEAP THRILLS 5.10 PG *
- L 253. DEEP CHILLS 5.11+ R-X
- M 254. CAKEWALK 5.7 PG *
- N 256. TURDLAND 5.10+ PG *
- O 257. TRIANGLE 5.9– PG

249, 255 not shown

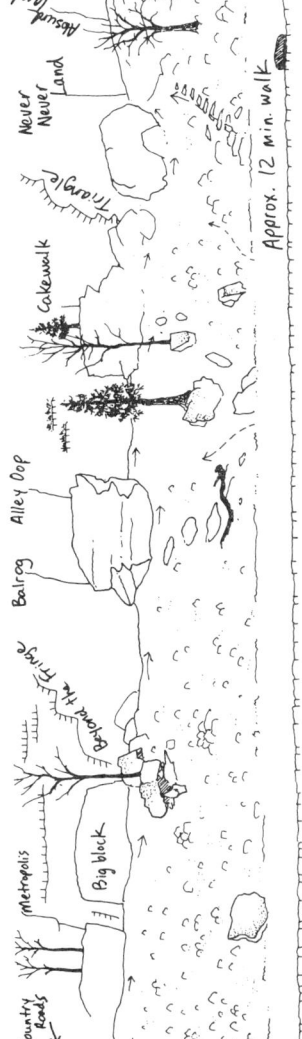

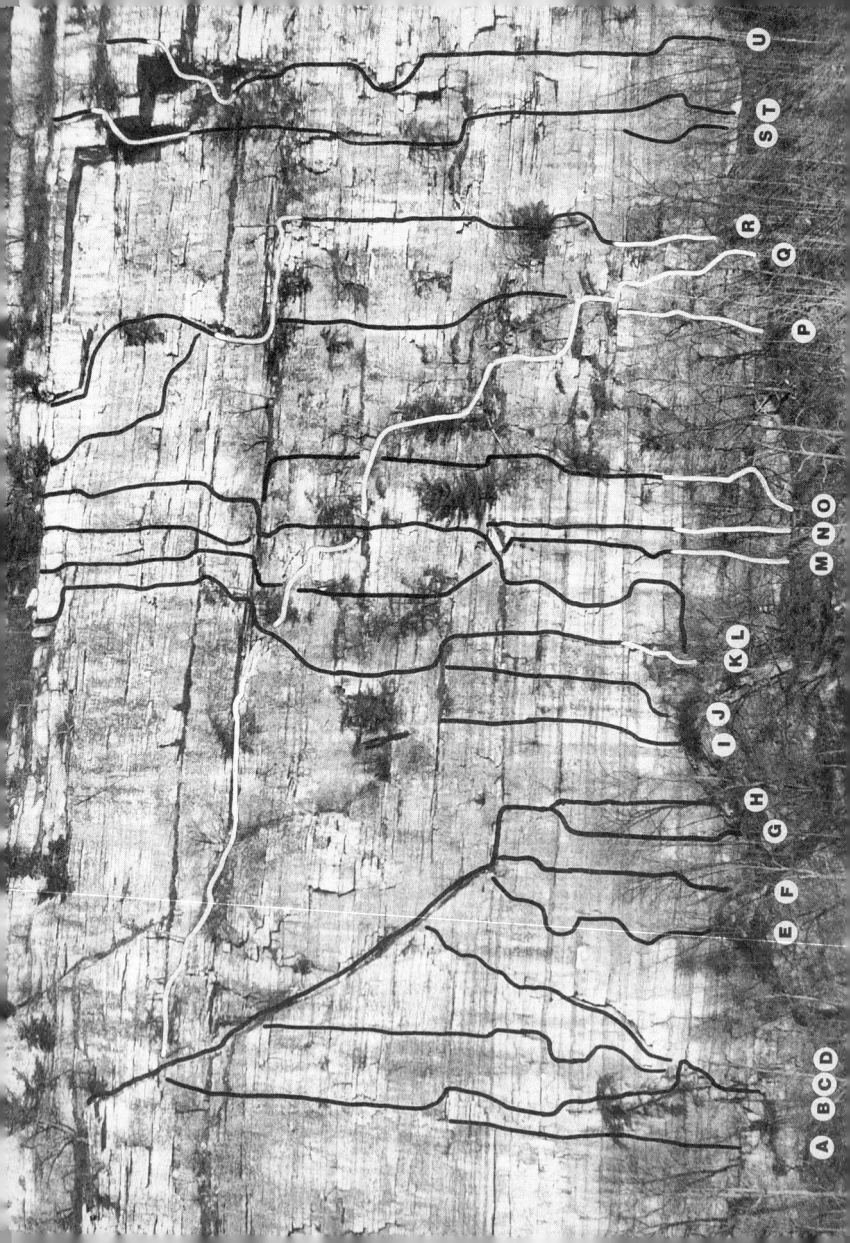

THE TRAPPS

- **A** 253. DEEP CHILLS 5.11+ R-X
- **B** 254. CAKEWALK 5.7 PG *
- **C** 256. TURDLAND 5.10+ PG *
- **D** 257. TRIANGLE 5.9– PG
- **E** 258. NEVERMORE 5.10 PG–R
- **F** 259. NEVER SAY NEVER 5.10 R-X
- **G** 260. NEVER NEVER LAND 5.10– PG ***
- **H** 261. J'ACCUSE 5.10 R
- **I** 263. ABSURDLAND 5.9 PG *
- **J** 264. BLUNDERBUS 5.9 R
- **K** 265. WISECRACK 5.6 G
- **L** 266. WONDERLAND 5.8 PG
- **M** 267. FAITHFUL JOURNEY 5.8+ G
- **N** 268. MIDDLE EARTH 5.7– G *
- **O** 269. BOMBS AWAY DREAM BABY 5.8 G
- **P** 271. RED'S RUIN 5.2 G
- **Q** 272. SMEGMA GARDEN and PIGEON 4th Class
- **R** 273. SNOWPATCH 5.5 PG
- **S** 274. SENTÉ 5.9– PG *
- **T** 276. THIN SLABS 5.7 PG–R *
- **U** 277. ON ANY MONDAY 5.11– PG *

255, 262, 270, 275 not shown

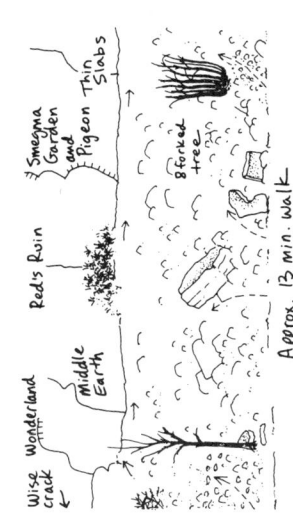

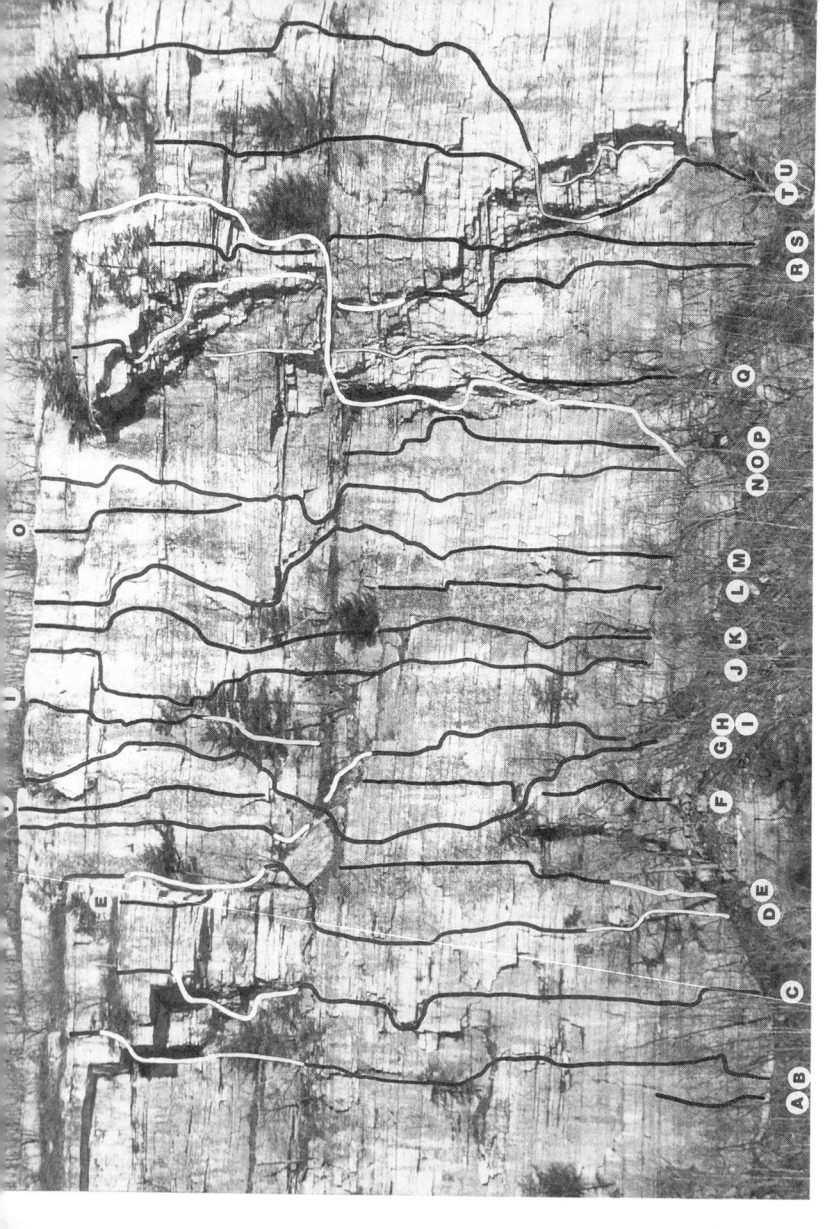

THE TRAPPS

- A 274. SENTÉ 5.9– PG *
- B 276. THIN SLABS 5.7 PG–R *
- C 277. ON ANY MONDAY 5.11– PG *
- D 278. SNAKE 5.6 PG
- E 279. TALUS OF POWDER 5.8 PG
- F 280. STEEP HIKIN' 5.8+ PG
- G 281. RED PILLAR 5.5 G
- H 282. DEEP LICHEN 5.10 X
- I 283. HAWKEYE 5.9+ PG
- J 284. THREE DOVES 5.8+ PG **
- K 285. ANNIE OH! 5.8 PG
- L 286. ROAD LESS TRAVELED 5.9– PG
- M 287. LIMELIGHT 5.7 PG **
- N 288. ARROW 5.8 PG ***
- O 289. QUIVER 5.9 PG
- P 290. EASY VERSCHNEI-DUNG 5.2 G *
- Q 291. COLD TURKEYS 5.9– G
- R 292. NURSE'S AID 5.10 R **
- S 293. SUPPER'S READY 5.12– PG **
- T 294. HANS' PUSS 5.7 PG *
- U 295. THE FEAST OF FOOLS 5.10 PG **

275 not shown

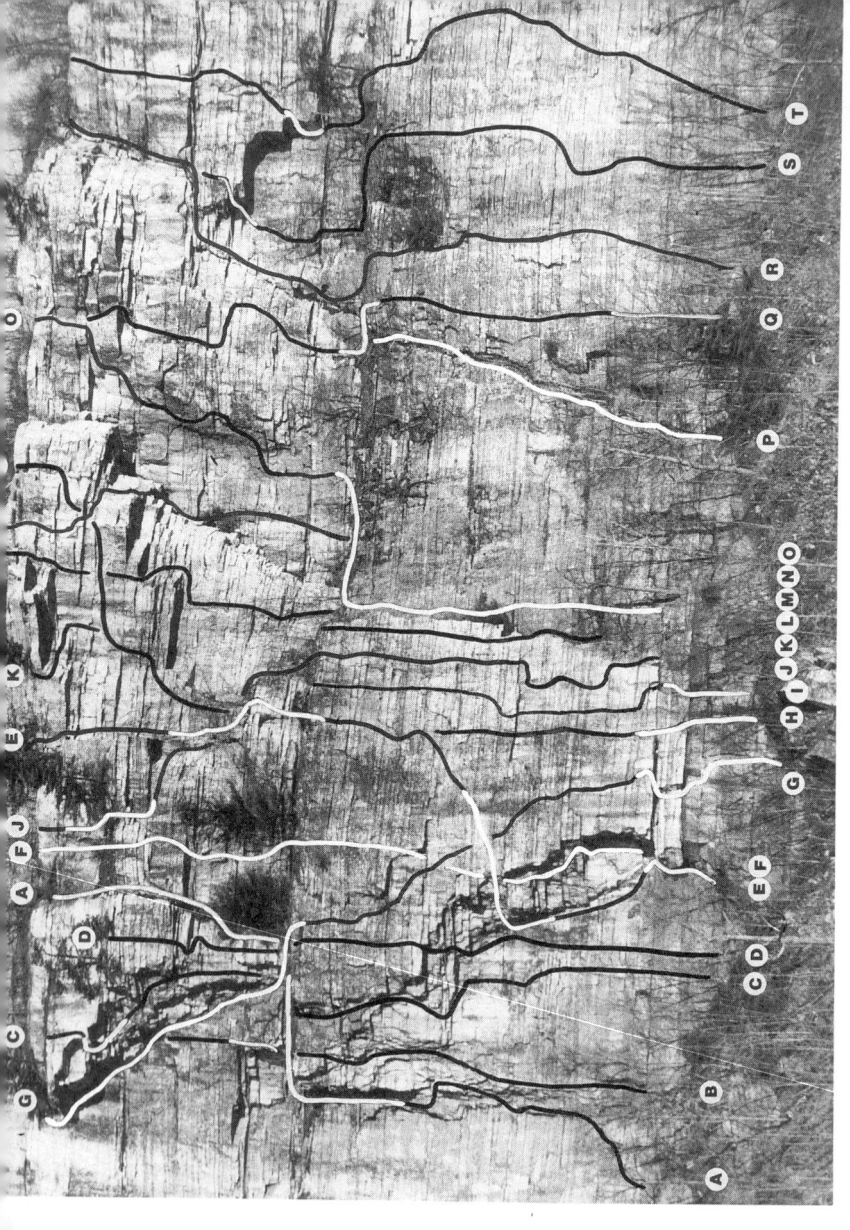

THE TRAPPS

- **A** 290. EASY VERSCHNEI-DUNG 5.2 G *
- **B** 291. COLD TURKEYS 5.9– G
- **C** 292. NURSE'S AID 5.10 R **
- **D** 293. SUPPER'S READY 5.12– PG **
- **E** 294. HANS' PUSS 5.7 PG *
- **F** 295. THE FEAST OF FOOLS 5.10 PG **
- **G** 297. PROCTOSCOPE 5.9+ PG
- **H** 298. SNAGGLEPUSS 5.8 PG
- **I** 299. PROCTOR SILEX 5.9+ PG *
- **J** 300. SILHOUETTE 5.7+ PG–R *
- **K** 301. MAN'S QUEST FOR FLIGHT 5.8 PG
- **L** 302. TRAVERSE OF THE CLODS 5.8 PG
- **M** 303. SKELETAL REMAINS 5.11+ X
- **N** 304. TWIGHLIGHT ZONE 5.7 PG A3
- **O** 306. ANDREW 5.4 PG **
- **P** 307. GOLDNER'S GRUNGE 4th Class
- **Q** 308. ANDROID 5.10– PG
- **R** 309. THREE VULTURES 5.9 PG *
- **S** 310. FACE TO FACE 5.9 PG
- **T** 311. NO GLOW 5.9 PG *

296, 305 not shown

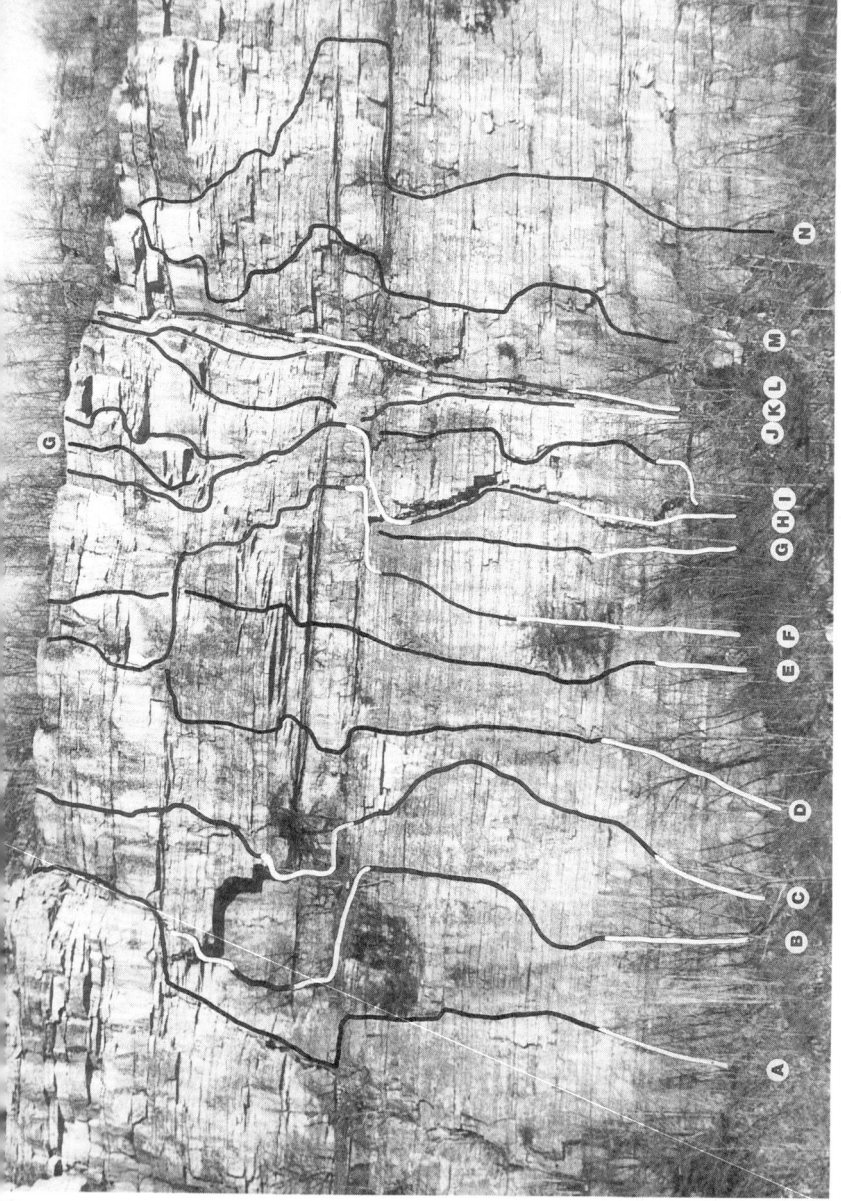

THE TRAPPS

305

- A   309. THREE VULTURES 5.9 PG *
- B   310. FACE TO FACE 5.9 PG
- C   311. NO GLOW 5.9 PG *
- D   312. SHELL SHOCK 5.10+ PG
- E   313. WOP STOP 5.11– PG
- F   314. KEEP ON STRUTTIN' 5.9 PG–R *
- G   315. STEP LIVELY 5.9+ PG
- H   316. MOONLIGHT 5.6 PG *
- I   317. POINT BLANK 5.12 R
- J   318. ERECT DIRECTION 5.10 PG ***
- K   319. CRACK'N-UP 5.11+ PG–R **
- L   320. UPDRAFT 5.5 G *
- M   321. CASCADING CRYSTAL KALEIDOSCOPE 5.8 PG ***
- N   322. DIANA 5.8– PG

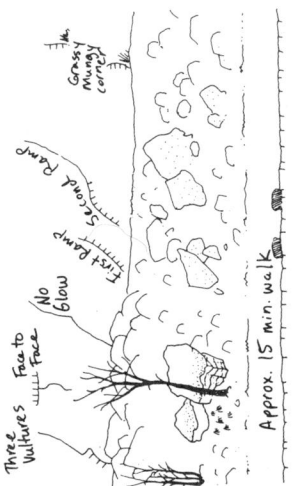

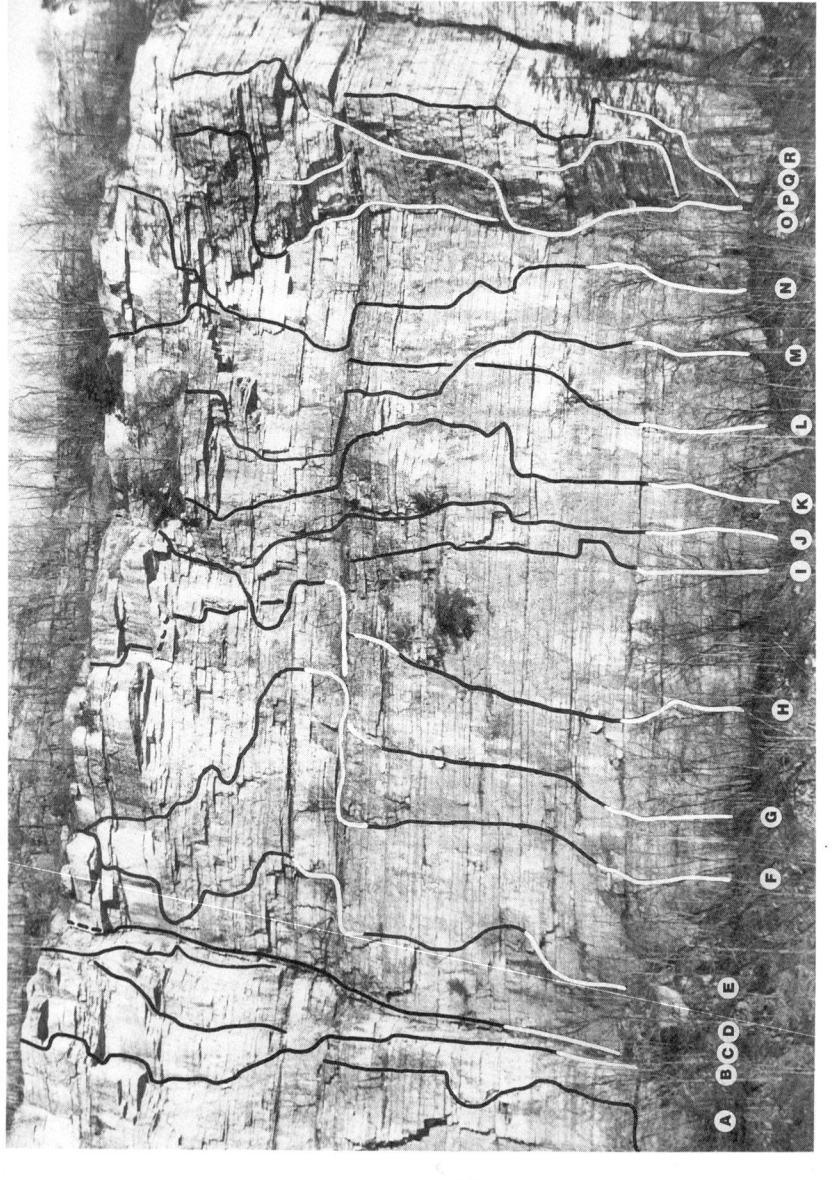

THE TRAPPS

- A 317. POINT BLANK 5.12 R
- B 318. ERECT DIRECTION 5.10 PG ***
- C 319. CRACK'N-UP 5.11+ PG–R **
- D 320. UPDRAFT 5.5 G *
- E 321. CASCADING CRYSTAL KALEIDOSCOPE 5.8 PG ***
- F 322. DIANA 5.8– PG
- G 323. KEN'S BLIND HOLE 5.6 PG
- H 324. UNHOLY WICK 5.8 G
- I 325. LOST AND FOUND 5.7 PG
- J 326. THE LAST WILL BE FIRST 5.6 PG
- K 327. STROLLING ON JUPITER 5.10+ PG–R
- L 328. EXIT STAGE LEFT 5.9 PG
- M 329. JIM'S GEM 5.8 PG
- N 330. MODERN TIMES 5.8+ PG **
- O 331. PSYCHEDELIC 5.8+ PG
- P 332. HIGH EXPOSURE 5.6+ G–PG ***
- Q 333. BEYOND GOOD AND EVIL 5.11– PG
- R 334. DIRECTISSIMA 5.9 G ***

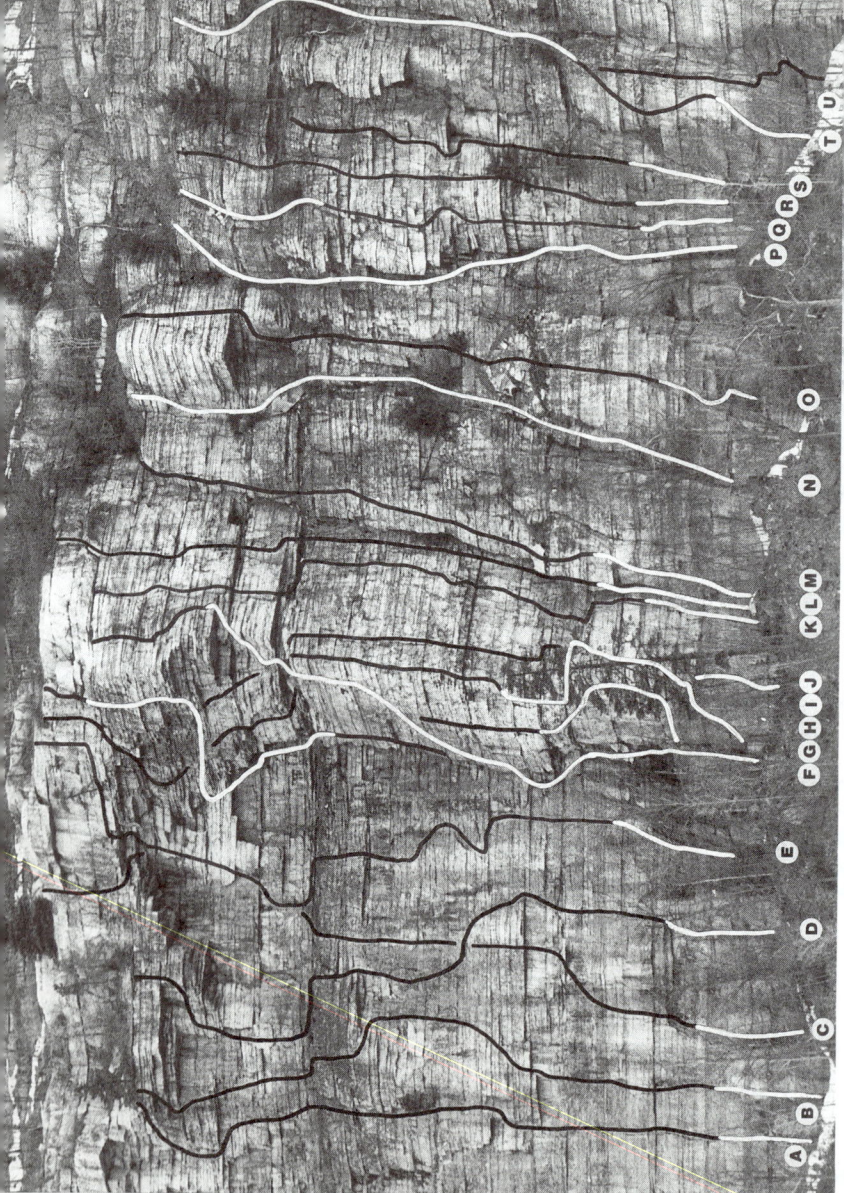

Photograph by Steven C. Faludi

THE TRAPPS

A 326. THE LAST WILL BE FIRST 5.6 PG
B 327. JUPITER 5.10+ PG–R
C 328. EXIT STAGE LEFT 5.9 PG
D 329. JIM'S GEM 5.8 PG
E 330. MODERN TIMES 5.8+ PG **
F 331. PSYCHEDELIC 5.8+ PG
G 332. HIGH EXPOSURE 5.6+ G–PG ***
H 333. BEYOND GOOD AND EVIL 5.11– PG
I 334. DIRECTISSIMA 5.9 G ***
J 335. ENDURO MAN 5.11 R ***
K 336. DIRECTISSISSIMA 5.10 PG ***
L 337. LAKATAKISSIMA 5.10 R–X
M 338. FIRST TRAPPS CHIMNEY 5.3 G
N 339. SECOND TRAPPS CHIMNEY 5.4 G
O 340. BUCKETS ABOVE 5.9+ G
P 341. THIRD TRAPPS CHIMNEY 5.3 G
Q 342. OBSTACLE DELUSION 5.10– PG
R 343. INSUHLATION 5.9 PG
S 344. ALPINE DIVERSIONS 5.8 G
T 346. 50-50 5.5 G
U 347. 60-40 5.7 PG

345 not shown

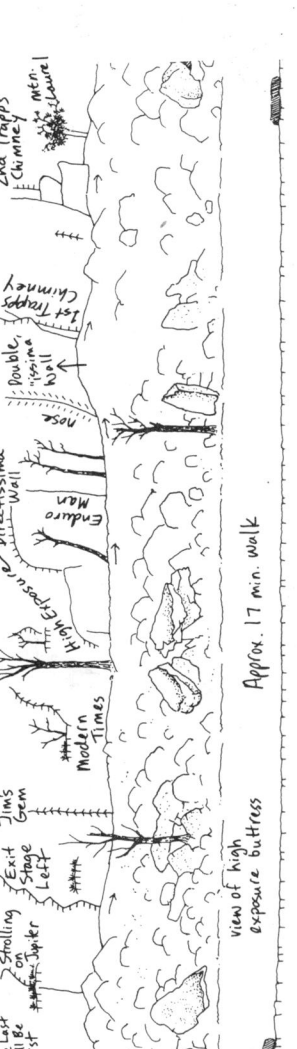

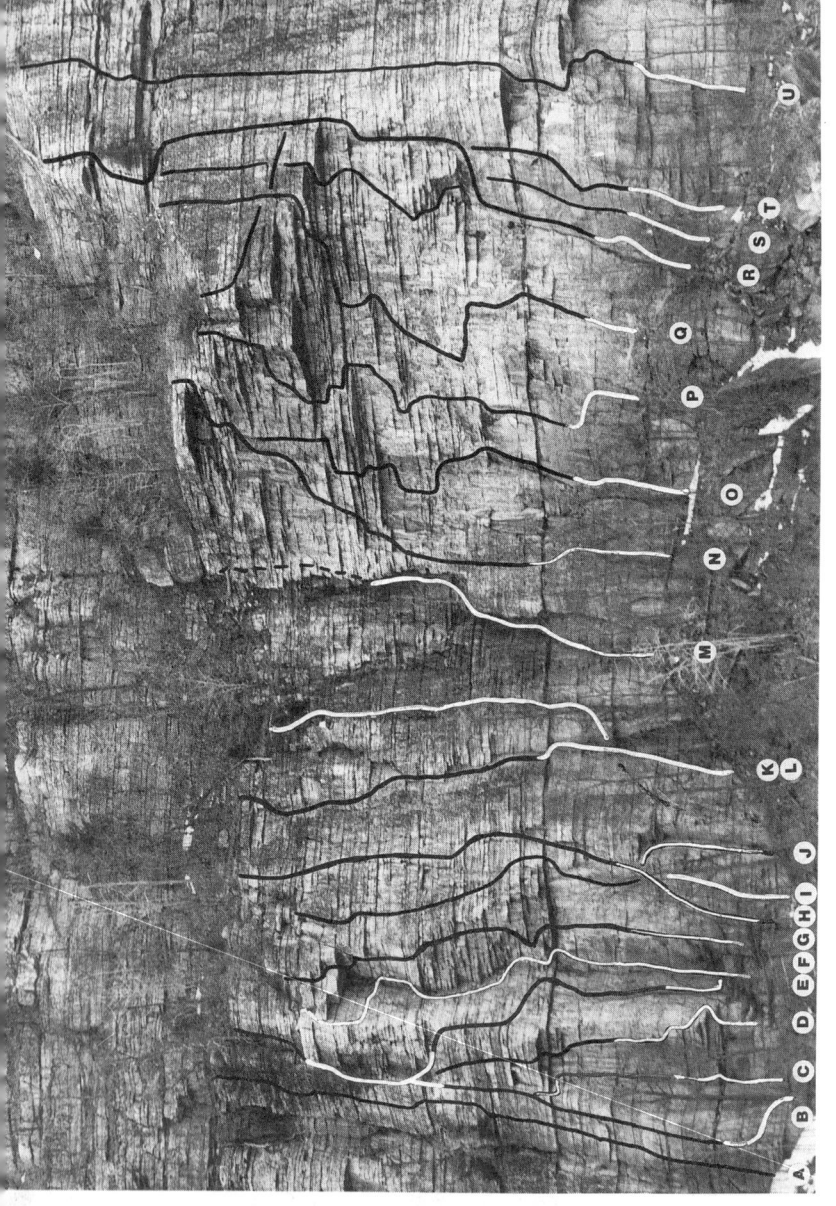

THE TRAPPS

Photograph by Steven C. Faludi

- **A** 348. LICHEN 40 WINKS 5.7 PG
- **B** 349. SLEEPWALK 5.7 PG
- **C** 350. ANTS' LINE 5.9 G **
- **D** 351. CONDEMNED MAN 5.12– R
- **E** 352. THE THRONE 5.12– PG *
- **F** 353. BONNIE'S ROOF 5.9 G–PG ***
- **G** 354. KNOCKOUT DROPS 5.11 R
- **H** 355. URSULA 5.5 PG
- **I** 356. NOSE DROPS 5.9+ PG
- **J** 357. GROOVY 5.9– G
- **K** 359. IN THE GROOVE 5.6
- **L** 360. IN THE SILLY 5.3 G
- **M** 363. SILLY CHIMNEY 5.1 G
- **N** 364. NO MAN'S LAND 5.11 PG **
- **O** 365. TIERS OF FEAR 5.12 PG **
- **P** 366. THE YELLOW WALL 5.11 PG–R ***
- **Q** 367. SCARY AREA 5.12 G *
- **R** 369. AIRY ARIA 5.8 G **
- **S** 370. CARBS AND CAFFEINE 5.11– R *
- **T** 371. LOTS OF MALARKEY 5.7 PG
- **U** 372. WASP STOP 5.11+ G

358, 361-362, 368 not shown

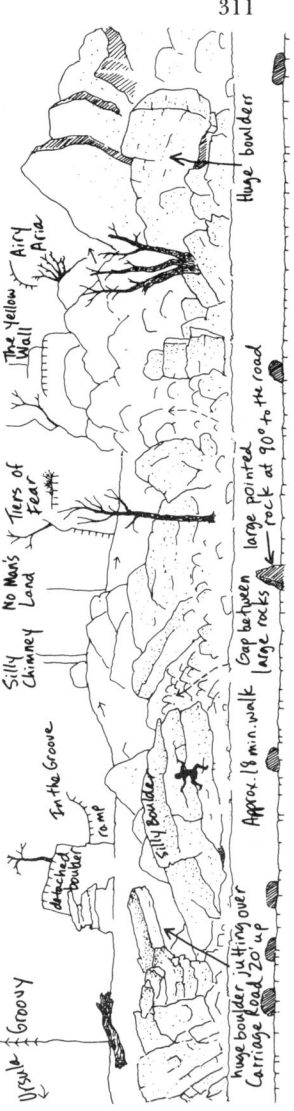

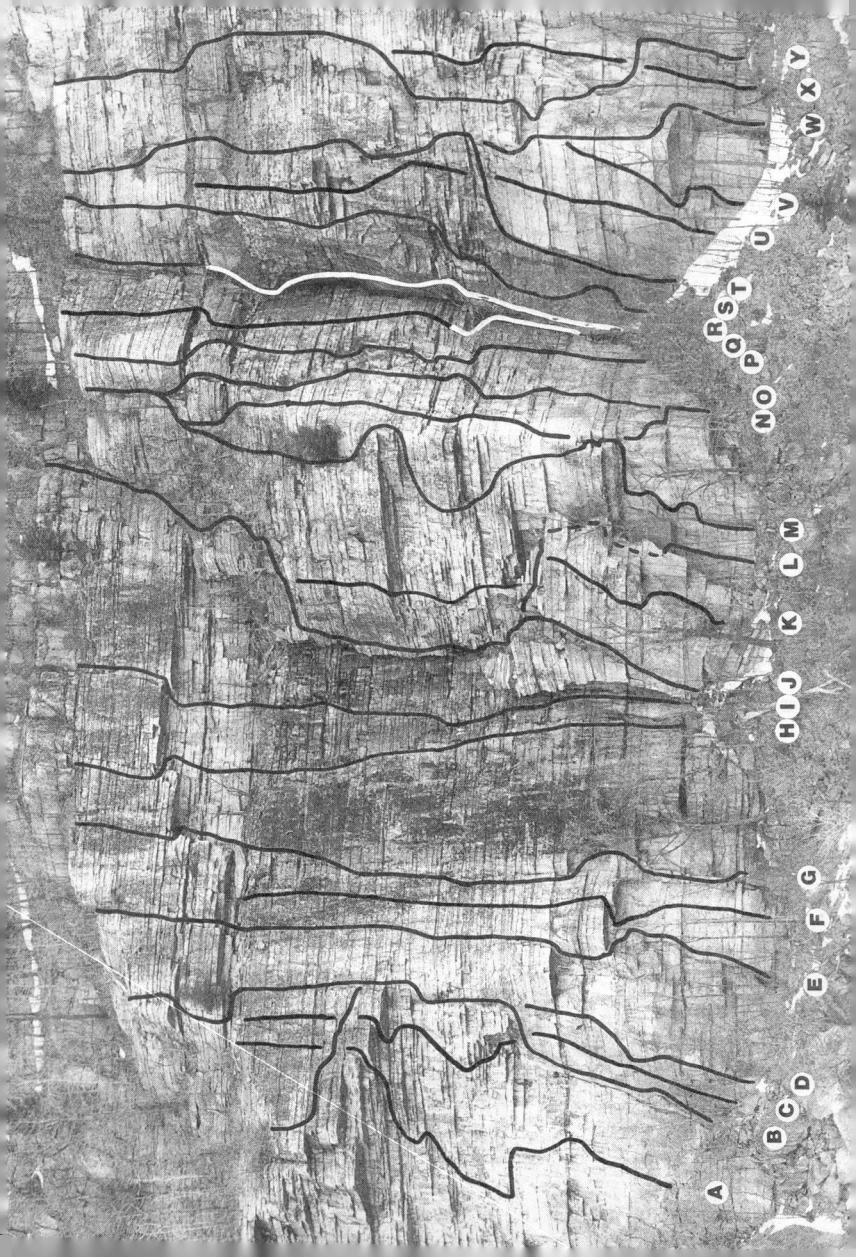

A	367. SCARY AREA 5.12 G *	K	378. VADER 5.10 R
B	369. AIRY ARIA 5.8 G **	L	379. VENTRE DE BOEUF 5.9 PG
C	370. CARBS AND CAFFEINE 5.11– R *	M	380. UPHILL ALL THE WAY 5.12– PG *
D	371. LOTS OF MALARKEY 5.7 PG	N	381. WHERE FOOLS RUSH IN 5.11– R
E	372. WASP STOP 5.11+ G	O	382. DOUBLE CRACK 5.8 G **
F	373. THE STING 5.11+ PG **	P	383. LITO AND THE SWAN 5.9 R
G	374. LISA 5.9 G	Q	384. IVAN AND THE SAUM 5.9 PG
H	375. FULL FACE 5.8 PG	R	386. BROKEN HAMMER 5.3 PG
I	376. LONELY RUNNER 5.10 G	S	387. THE ZIGZAG FACE 5.7– R
J	377. 48 5.2 G	T	388. 49 5.2 G
		U	389. FORCES OF NATURE 5.11 PG
		V	390. QUIÉN SABE 5.10– PG-R
		W	391. THE NOSE 5.7 PG-R
		X	392. LADY'S LAMENT 5.10– G
		Y	393. FILLIPINA 5.9– G
			368, 385 not shown

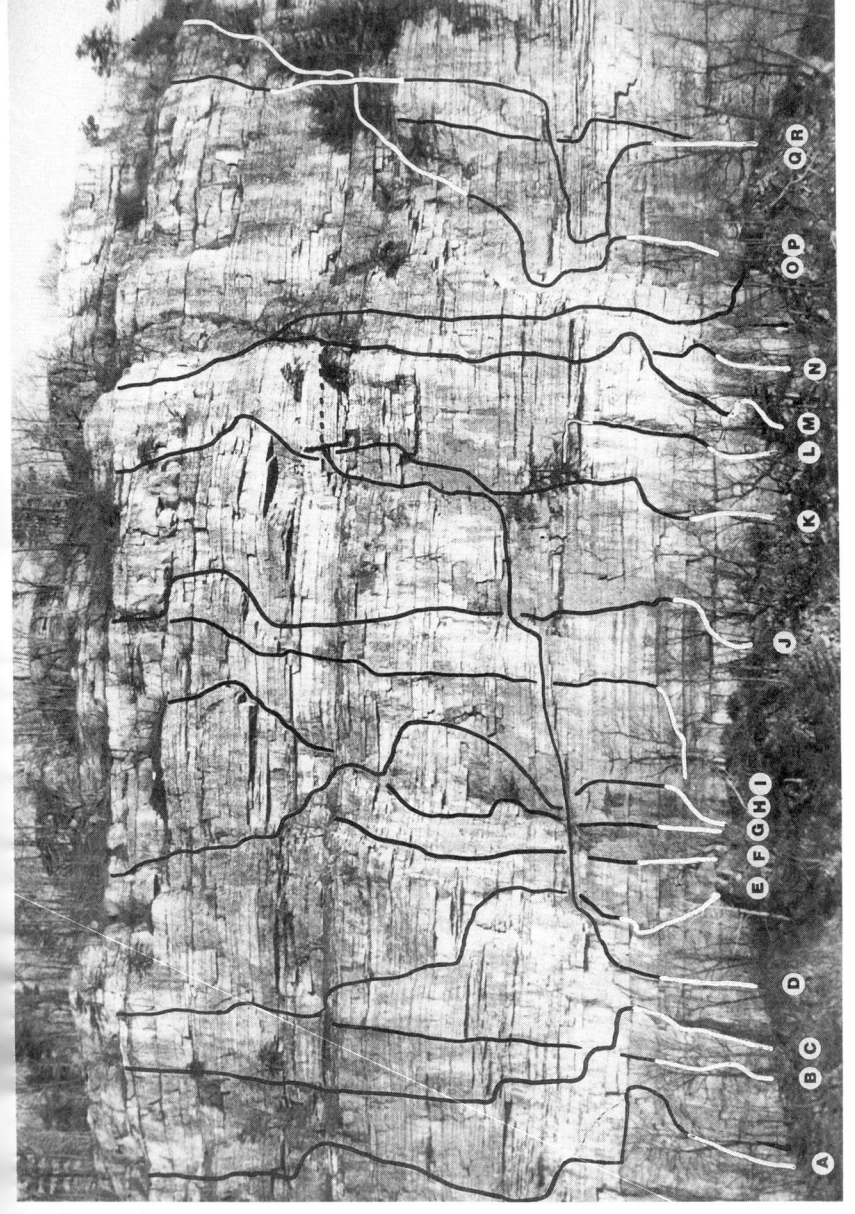

THE TRAPPS

- A 395. BOLD-VILLE 5.8 G *
- B 398. THE FALL 5.11– R *
- C 400. THE SPRING 5.10 PG–R **
- D 401. OBLIQUE TWIQUE 5.8 G
- E 402. SHIT CREEK 5.7 PG
- F 403. UNSLUNG HEROES 5.10– PG–R
- G 404. LOS TRES CABRONES 5.9 PG
- H 405. BLISTERED TOE 5.8– PG
- I 406. TORTURE GARDEN 5.8 PG
- J 407. LAST FRONTIER 5.10 G
- K 408. THE YELLOW CRACK 5.12 R-X
- L 409. THE BRAGG-HATCH ROUTE 5.10+ PG
- M 410. KLIGFIELD'S FOLLIES 5.11+ PG ***
- N 411. CLUNEY'S JOLLIES 5.12 R
- O 412. SIMPLE SUFF 5.10– G **
- P 414. THE BLUE STINK 5.3 PG
- Q 415. HOOKY 5.6– PG
- R 416. YESTERDAY 5.10– PG 394, 396-397, 399, 413 not shown

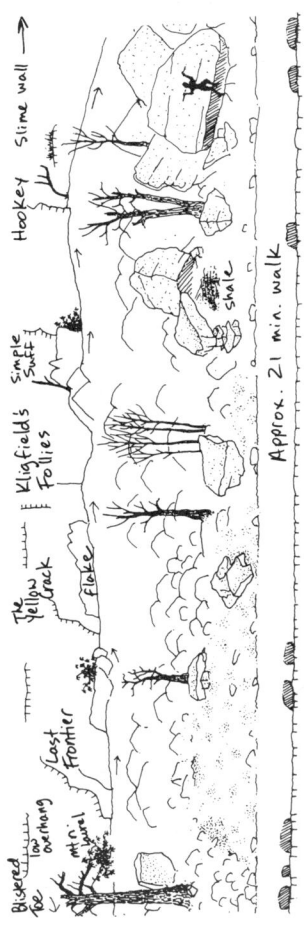

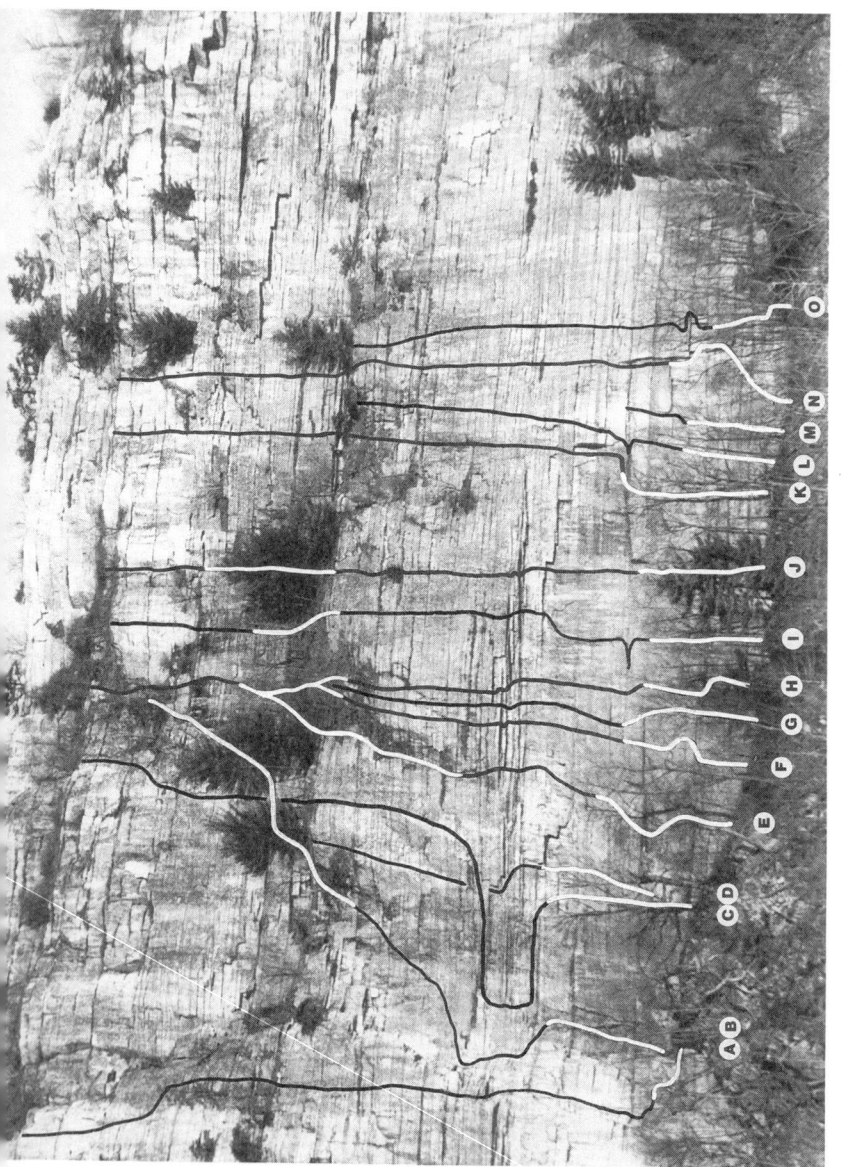

THE TRAPPS

- **A** 412. SIMPLE SUFF
  5.10– G **
- **B** 414. THE BLUE STINK
  5.3 PG
- **C** 415. HOOKY 5.6– PG
- **D** 416. YESTERDAY 5.10– PG
- **E** 417. TOMORROW AND
  TOMORROW AND
  TOMORROW 5.11 R
- **F** 418. FALLED ON ACCOUNT
  OF STRAIN
  5.10– PG–R *
- **G** 419. WET DREAM 5.12– R
- **H** 420. APRIL SHOWERS
  5.11 PG *
- **I** 421. GOLDEN SHOWERS
  5.11 G *
- **J** 422. CALLED ON ACCOUNT
  OF RAIN 5.11+ R
- **K** 423. COMEDY IN THREE
  ACTS 5.11 PG *
- **L** 424. DROP ZONE 5.12– R
- **M** 425. PRESSURE DROP
  5.11+ R
- **N** 426. FRUSTRATION
  SYNDROME
  5.10 G **
- **O** 427. THE STAND
  5.11– PG *

413 not shown

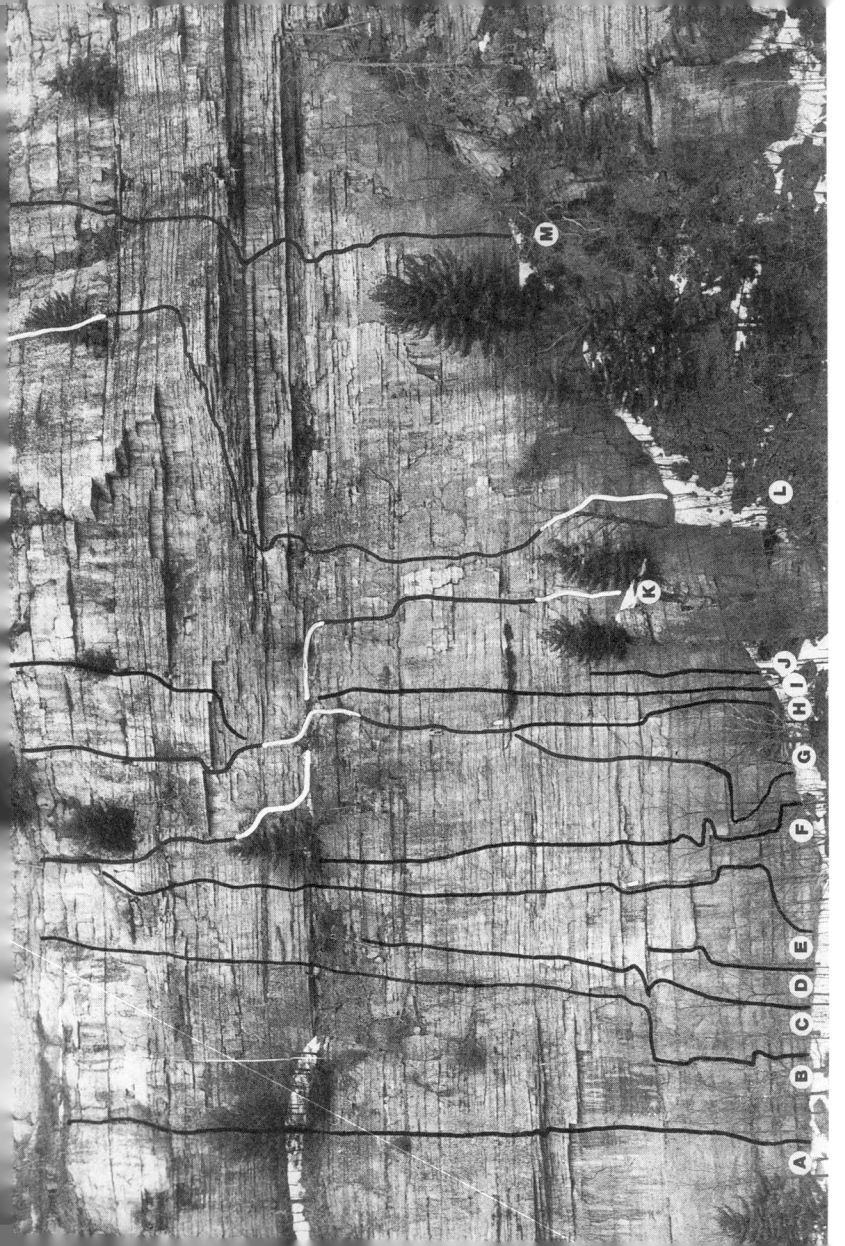

THE TRAPPS

Photograph by Steven C. Faludi

A 422. CALLED ON ACCOUNT OF RAIN 5.11+ R
B 423. COMEDY IN THREE ACTS 5.11 PG *
C 424. DROP ZONE 5.12– R
D 425. PRESSURE DROP 5.11+ R
E 426. FRUSTRATION SYNDROME 5.10 G **
F 427. THE STAND 5.11– PG *
G 428. COPROPHAGIA 5.10– PG
H 429. W.A.S.P. 5.9 PG **
I 430. J.A.P. 5.10 PG
J 431. EXPEDITION TO NOWHERE 5.10– R
K 432. STICKY GATE 5.3 PG
L 433. MUD, SWEAT, AND TEARS 5.10– PG
M 434. WITHERING HEIGHTS 5.11 PG-R

THE TRAPPS

- **A** 435. MOONDANCE
  5.6 G–PG
- **B** 436. SUNDANCE 5.6 PG *
- **C** 437. GHOSTDANCE
  5.7 PG–R
- **D** 438. RAINDANCE 5.5 G
- **E** 439. CONTRADANCE
  5.6– PG
- **F** 440. ROGER'S ESCAPE
  HATCH 3rd Class

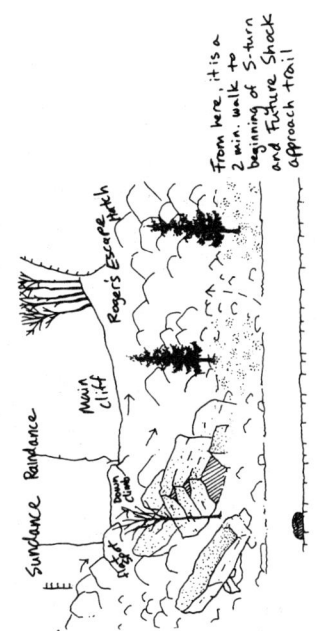

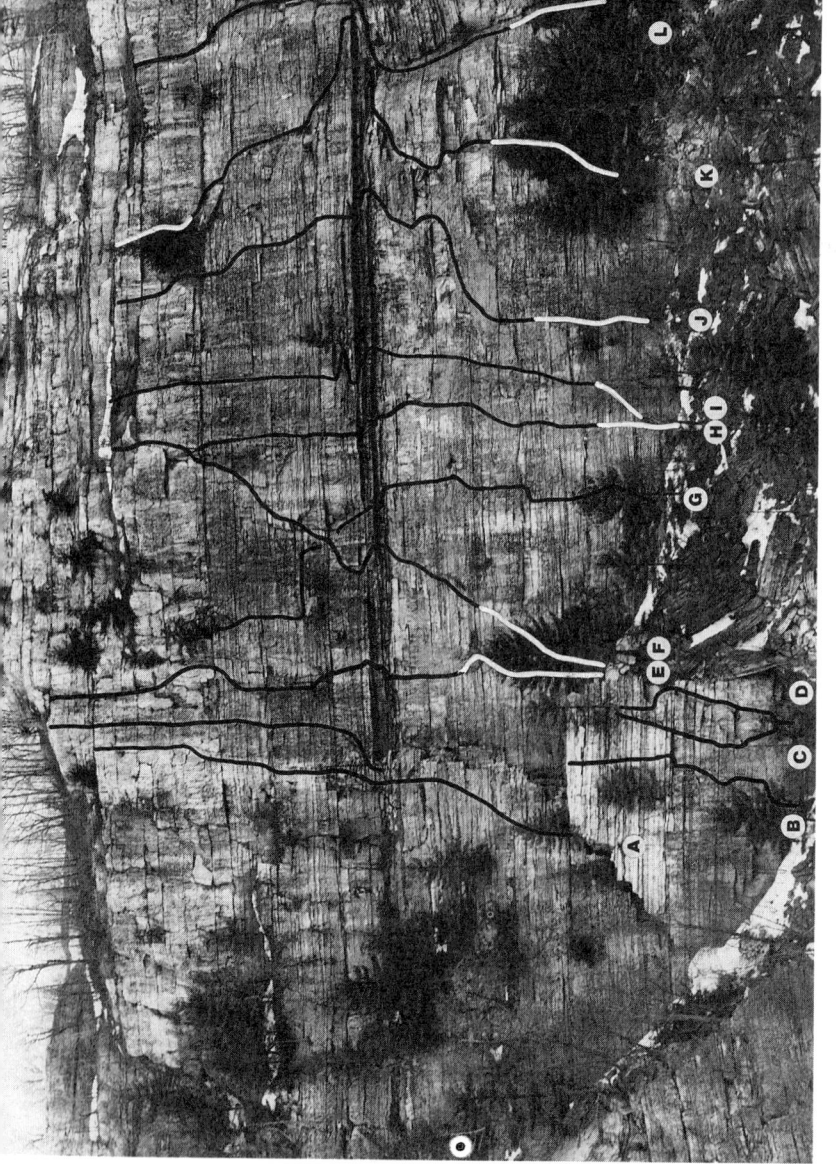

Photograph by Steven C. Faludi

- **A** 441. CASA EMILIO 5.2 PG *
- **B** 442. CREAKY JOINTS AND TRIGGER POINTS 5.10 PG
- **C** 443. THE DEVIL MADE ME DO IT 5.9 R
- **D** 444. ALMOST PURE AND SIMPLE 5.8 G
- **E** 446. CASABLANCA 5.8 PG *
- **F** 447. EMILIO 5.7+ PG
- **G** 448. CASANOVA 5.8 PG-R
- **H** 449. INDEPENDENT HANGOVER 5.10+ PG-R
- **I** 450. YO MAMA 5.10 PG
- **J** 451. WORP FACTOR 1 5.11+ R-X
- **K** 452. INTERSTELLAR OVERDRIVE 5.8 PG
- **L** 453. EMILIETTA 5.3 G

445 not shown

THE TRAPPS

Photograph by Steven C. Faludi

- **A** 454. COUNTERSTRIKE 5.9 PG
- **B** 455. SUDDEN DEATH 5.8+ X
- **C** 456. TRIGGER POINT 5.6 G
- **D** 457. CRACK OF DESPONDENCY 5.4 G
- **E** 458. PFUI TEUFEL 5.3 G
- **F** 459. FOUR-FOOT FACE 5.3 G
- **G** 460. THOM'S THUMB, LEFT HAND 5.4 PG
- **H** 461. FUTURE SHOCK 5.12– R
- **I** 464. ART'S ROUTE 5.9 G
- **J** 468. RANGER'S REVENGE 5.5 PG
- **K** 469. TRUE BRIT 5.7 G
- **L** 470. THE CIRCUMCISOR 5.12 R
- **M** 471. BONE HARD 5.12 PG
- **N** 474. CIRCUMCISION 5.7 PG
- **O** 477. DICK'S PRICK 5.6 PG
- **P** 482. THE LONE RANGER 5.3 G

462–463, 465–467, 472–473, 475–476, 478–481 not shown

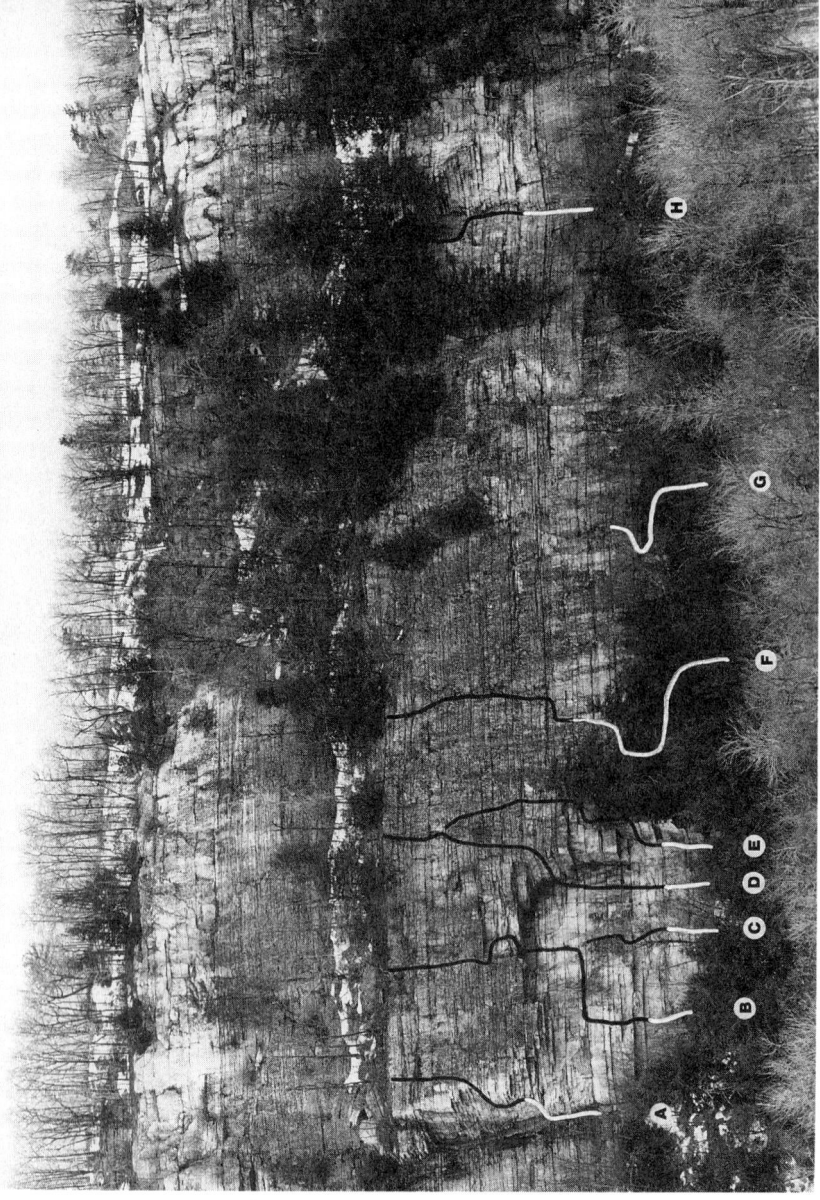

THE TRAPPS

327

Photograph by Steven C. Faludi

- **A** 483. AFTER THE PRICK 5.4 PG
- **B** 485. WEGETABLES I'VE NEVER SEEN BEFORE 5.10+ PG *
- **C** 486. TENNISH, ANYONE? 5.10 PG
- **D** 488. FOOTLOOSE 5.8 PG
- **E** 490. FANCY FREE 5.8+ PG
- **F** 492. CRUSTACEAN SYNDROME 5.8 PG
- **G** 494. SWAMP GAS 5.10+ PG
- **H** 495. A LONG WALK FOR MAN, A SHORT CLIMB FOR MANKIND 5.4 G

484, 487, 489, 491, 493 not shown

Indexes

Climbs by Grade

THE NAME OF THE ROUTE IS preceded by its number. Routes are listed in their Grade without regard to plus (+) or minus (−) variations.

Boulders
— Chockstone Boulder
— Mental block

Third Class
440. Roger's Escape Hatch

Fourth Class
307. Goldner's Grunge
 76. Radcliffe
272. Smega Garden and Pidgeon

5.0
 67. Crimson Corner
 39. Dirty Chimney

5.1
 57. Flake, The
363. Silly Chimney

5.2
441. Casa Emilio
  8. Easy Keyhole
101. Easy Overhang
290. Easy Verschneidung
377. "48"
388. "49"
 70. Harvard
216. Northern Pillar
271. Red's Ruin
 80. Roddey

211. Southern Pillar
 15. Sudoriferous
229. Unnamed
221. Willie's Weep

5.3
199. Beginner's Delight
 91. Betty
414. Blue Stink, The
386. Broken Hammer
 45. Das Wiggles
453. Emilietta
338. First Trapps Chimney
459. Four-Foot Face
360. In the Silly
482. Lone Ranger, The
203. Minty
458. Pfui Teufel
 12. "69"
432. Sticky Gate
341. Third Trapps Chimney
159. Three Pines
205. Tipsy Trees
218. Twin Oaks
 68. Yale

5.4
483. After the Prick
306. Andrew
 79. Belly Roll
 23. Bunny
457. Crack of Despondency
208. Hawk
495. Long Walk for Man, A Short Climb for Mankind, A
345. Missing, but not Lost
 13. No Picnic
134. Ribs
339. Second Trapps Chimney
 11. Short Job
115. Sixish
 49. Squiggles
 66. Star Route, The
460. Thom's Thumb, Left Hand

5.5
130. Arch
194. Asphodel
 96. Big Chimney
  9. Black Fly
197. Blueberry Ledges
 60. Boston
 78. Dennis
 27. Double Chin
346. "50-50"
225. Funny Face
148. High Corner
 35. Horseman
 82. Jackie
438. Raindance
468. Ranger's Revenge
281. Red Pillar
133. Ribless
 89. RMC
121. Rusty Trifle
158. Simple Ceilings
273. Snowpatch
219. Triple Bulges
320. Updraft
355. Ursula

5.6
 99. Baby
228. Bitchy Virgin

CLIMBS BY GRADE

- 120. Bloody Mary
- 6. Brat, The
- 439. Contradance
- 193. Credibility Gap
- 54. Crowberry Ridge
- 477. Dick's Prick
- 222. Don't Shoot
- 29. Eyebrow
- 69. Eyesore
- 22. Fancy Idiot
- 107. Frog's Head
- 332. High Exposure
- 415. Hooky
- 227. Immaculate Conception
- 359. In the Groove
- 323. Ken's Blind Hole
- 326. Last Will Be First, The
- 213. Madame Grunnebaum's Wulst
- 108. Maria
- 97. Miss Bailey
- 435. Moondance
- 316. Moonlight
- 36. Pony Express
- 43. Rhododendron
- 142. Shockley's Ceiling
- 278. Snake
- 226. Son of Bitchy Virgin
- 436. Sundance
- 456. Trigger Point
- 265. Wisecrack
- 128. Wrist

5.7

- 251. Alley Oop
- 126. Bloody Bush
- 34. Bridle Path
- 254. Cakewalk
- 135. Calisthenic
- 65. C. C. Route
- 474. Circumcision
- 106. City Lights
- 83. Classic
- 42. Clover
- 185. Dry Martini
- 447. Emilio
- 437. Ghostdance
- 136. Gorilla My Dreams
- 7. Handy Andy
- 294. Hans' Puss
- 5. Katzenjammer
- 58. Ken's Crack
- 4. Keyhole
- 223. Lat-on the Season
- 41. Laurel
- 348. Lichen 40 Winks
- 287. Limelight
- 325. Lost and Found
- 371. Lots of Malarkey
- 268. Middle Earth
- 391. Nose, The
- 177. Overhanging Layback
- 473. Penal Colony
- 90. Raubenheimer Special
- 112. Scungilli
- 402. Shit Creek
- 1. Short and Simple
- 300. Silhouette
- 347. "60-40"
- 349. Sleepwalk
- 140. Strictly from Nowhere
- 186. Tequila Mockingbird
- 276. Thin Slabs
- 71. Trapped Like a Rat
- 469. True Brit
- 304. Twilight Zone

241. V-3
206. Womb Step, The
387. Zigzag Face, The

5.8
369. Airy Aria
444. Almost Pure and Simple
344. Alpine Diversions
155. Anguish
285. Annie Oh!
 86. Ape Call
288. Arrow
204. Bag's End
 92. Blackout, The
249. Blind Alley
405. Blistered Toe
395. Bold-ville
269. Bombs Away Dream Baby
446. Casablanca
448. Casanova
321. Cascading Crystal Kaleidoscope
492. Crustacean Syndrome
 81. Daydream
322. Diana
382. Double Crack
117. Drunkard's Delight
250. Dry Heaves
267. Faithful Journey
490. Fancy Free
 62. Fitschen's Folly
488. Footloose
 21. Friday the 13th
375. Full Face
138. Gaston
224. Gleet Street
153. Glypnod
150. Glyptodon
149. Glyptomaniac
235. Gory Thumb
 17. Herdie Gerdie
217. Hyjek's Horror
452. Interstellar Overdrive
 88. Jane
329. Jim's Gem
232. Kernmantle
214. Madame Grunnebaum's Sorrow
301. Man's Quest for Flight
330. Modern Times
119. Morning After
401. Oblique Twique
105. Pas de Deux
478. Penis Colada
209. Peregrine
331. Psychedelic
 32. Ralph's Climb
236. Raunchy
 14. Shit or Go Blind
298. Snagglepuss
201. Snooky's Return
162. Something Interesting
103. Son of Easy O
280. Steep Hikin'
234. Stop the Presses, Mr. Williams
455. Sudden Death
111. Sultana
109. Sundown
279. Talus of Powder
284. Three Doves
406. Torture Garden
139. Travels with Charley
302. Traverse of the Clods
100. Twisted Sister
127. Uncle Rudy

CLIMBS BY GRADE

324. Unholy Wick
 47. Walter Mitty
266. Wonderland

5.9
263. Absurdland
350. Ants' Line
 87. Ape and Essence
 37. Apoplexy
122. Arc of a Diver
464. Art's Route
238. Badfinger
195. Beatle Brow Bulge
246. Beyond the Fringe
131. Billy Shears
  2. Birthday Biscuit Boy
264. Blunderbus
353. Bonnie's Roof
340. Buckets Above
207. Chimango
291. Cold Turkeys
212. Columbia
244. Commando Rave
188. Co-op
454. Counterstrike
220. Delusions of Grandeur
443. Devil Made Me Do It, The
334. Directissima
 18. Dirty Gerdie
 50. Dislocation
 30. Double Clutch
328. Exit Stage Left
310. Face to Face
 98. Fetus
393. Fillipina
202. Friends and Lovers
  3. Great Wall of China
145. Grim-ace Face
357. Groovy
283. Hawkeye
104. Heather
147. Hi Coroner!
385. High Jinx
233. High Times
163. Higher Stannard
343. Insuhlation
384. Ivan and the Saum
113. Jean
 40. Junior
314. Keep on Struttin'
180. Land's End
215. Le Teton
374. Lisa
383. Lito and the Swan
404. Los Tres Cabrones
169. Men at Arms
167. M.F.
178. No Existence
311. No Glow
356. Nose Drops
200. Octoberfest
 84. Pink Laurel
114. Precarious Perch
299. Proctor Silex
297. Proctoscope
289. Quiver
157. Raspberry Sundae
 19. Red Cabbage
286. Road Less Traveled
123. Rock and Brew
156. Ruby Saturday
274. Senté
362. Silly Groove
160. Something Boring
137. Splashtic

315. Step Lively
309. Three Vultures
296. Too Old to Know Better
192. Tree's a Crowd
257. Triangle
125. Trusty Rifle
379. Ventre de Boeuf
429. W.A.S.P.
237. Wild Horses
265A. Wiseland

5.10
63. Alphabet Arête
308. Android
10. Astro Traveler
77. Badcliff
247. Balrog
44. Birch
164. Birdie Party
196. Blueberry Wine
489. Boron Destroyer, The
394. Boulder-Ville
409. Bragg-Hatch Route, The
61. Charie
252. Cheap Thrills
242. City Streets
172. Coexistence
428. Coprophagia
38. Coronary
243. Country Roads
442. Creaky Joints and Trigger Points
230. Dat Mantel
64. D.D. Route
282. Deep Lichen
336. Directississima
231. Dis-Mantel
141. Epiclepsy

318. Erect Direction
431. Expedition to Nowhere
418. Falled on Account of Strain
295. Feast of Fools, The
118. Five Tendons
476. Foreign Lesion
426. Frustration Syndrome
175. Graveyard Shift
487. Hawaii Five-Ten
491. Headless Horseman
16. Heel Hook and Hack-It
449. Independent Hangover
165. Interstice
129. Invitation to Hell
261. J'Accuse
53. Jacob's Ladder
430. J.A.P.
270. Journey's End
392. Lady's Lament
337. Lakatakissima
407. Last Frontier
376. Long Distance of the Lonely Runner
48. Low Exposure
124. Make Haste or Tomato Paste
94. Matinee
462. Meat By-products
152. Midnight Cowboy
143. Mister Transistor
166. Mother's Day Party
433. Mud, Sweat and Tears
151. Nemesis
260. Never Never Land
259. Never Say Never
258. Nevermore
146. No Belle Prize

CLIMBS BY GRADE

 26. Nosedive
255. Nurdland
292. Nurse's Aid
342. Obstacle Delusion
116. One Blunder and It's Six Feet Under
 59. Phoebe
187. P. T. Phone Home
 75. P38
102. Queasy O
390. Quién Sabe
210. Reach of Faith
 20. Red Cabbage Right
 24. Retribution
184. Scotch on the Rocks
198. Seldom Mustard, Never Relish
312. Shell Shock
412. Simple Suff
361. Slipping into Incipiency
161. Something or Other
 28. Something Scary
358. Space Invaders
400. Spring, The
 51. Squiggles Direct
173. Star Action
 73. Stirrup Trouble
327. Strolling on Jupiter
 56. Susie A
494. Swamp Gas
481. 10,000 Restless Virgins
486. Tennish, Anyone?
467. Thom's Thumb, Right Hand
176. Tough Shift
170. Try Again
256. Turdland
403. Unslung Heroes
378. Vader
479. V.D.
168. Water King
485. Vegetables I've Never Seen Before
262. Welcome to My Nightmare
190. Welcome to the Gunks
397. Winter, The
396. Winterlude
275. Yenta
416. Yesterday
154. Yesterday's Lemonade
450. Yo Mama

5.11

 85. A-Gape
420. April Showers
333. Beyond Good and Evil
422. Called on Account of Rain
370. Carbs and Caffeine
423. Comedy in Three Acts
319. Crack'n-up
 95. Creature Features
253. Deep Chills
174. Don't Shift
 33. Doug's Roof
335. Enduro Man's Longest Hangout
398. Fall, The
189. Fall to Grace
171. Fly Again
389. Forces of Nature
421. Golden Showers
239. Help!
 55. Hudson's Boulder Problem

183. Impenetrable Ceilings
410. Kligfield's Follies
354. Knockout Drops
191. Laughing Man
245. Metropolis
364. No Man's Land
277. On Any Monday
240. Pleh!
144. P.R.
425. Pressure Drop
475. Prophylactic
179. Scene of the Climb
 46. Shitty Mitty
303. Skeletal Remains
427. Stand, The
373. Sting, The
399. Summer, The
417. Tomorrow and Tomorrow and Tomorrow
132. Vicious Rumors
372. Wasp Stop
381. Where Fools Rush In
434. Withering Heights
313. Wop Stop
451. Worp Factor 1
366. Yellow Wall, The

5.12

305. Best Things in Life Aren't Free, The
471. Bone Hard
248. Bullfrog
 72. Cilley Dickin'
470. Circumcisor, The
411. Cluney's Jollies
351. Condemned Man
472. Death's Head Mask
 52. Devine Wind
424. Drop Zone
461. Future Shock
 31. Gill's Boulder Problem
480. Girls Just Want to Have Fun
181. Jane Fonda Workout for Pregnant Women, The
110. Kama Sutra
 93. Late Show
 74. Mohel, The
 25. No Solution
463. Numbers Racket, The
182. Organic Iron
317. Point-Blank
465. Renaissance
367. Scary Area
368. Scary Area Direct
484. Shut Up and Eat Your Greens
493. Slime World
445. Strings Attached
293. Supper's Ready
413. Techo-Stuff
352. Throne, The
365. Tiers of Fear
380. Uphill all the Way
419. Wet Dream
408. Yellow Crack, The

5.13

466. Modern Love

Index

Absurdland, 158
After the Prick, 250
A-Gape, 88
Airy Aria, 210
Alley Oop, 153
Almost Pure and Simple, 239
Alphabet Arête, 80
Alpine Diversions, 198
Andrew, 177
Android, 178
Anguish, 115
Annie Oh!, 167
Ants' Line, 200
Ape and Essence, 89
Ape Call, 88
Apoplexy, 73
April Showers, 230
Arc of a Diver, 102
Arch, 105

Arrow, 168
Art's Route, 246
Asphodel, 130
Astro Traveler, 64

Baby, 93
Badcliff, 84
Badfinger, 149
Bag's End, 134
Balrog, 152
Beatle Brow Bulge, 130
Beginner's Delight, 132
Belly Roll, 85
Best Things in Life Aren't Free, The, 177
Betty, 90
Beyond Good and Evil, 193
Beyond the Fringe, 152
Big Chimney, 92

Billy Shears, 106
Birch, 75
Birdie Party, 119
Birthday Biscuit Boy, 61
Bitchy Virgin, 145
Black Fly, 64
Blackout, The, 90
Blind Alley, 153
Blistered Toe, 223
Bloody Bush, 103
Bloody Mary, 101
Blue Stink, The, 227
Blueberry Ledges, 131
Blueberry Wine, 131
Blunderbus, 158
Bold-ville, 220
Bombs Away Dream Baby, 160
Bone Hard, 247
Bonnie's Roof, 202
Boston, 80
Boron Destroyer, The, 253
Boulder-ville, 219
Bragg-Hatch Route, The, 225
Brat, The, 62
Bridle Path, 72
Broken Hammer, 217
Buckets Above, 197
Bullfrog, 152
Bunny, 67

Cakewalk, 155
Calisthenic, 107
Called on Account of Rain, 231
Carbs and Caffeine, 210
Casa Emilio, 238
Casablanca, 239
Casanova, 240
Cascading Crystal Kaleidoscope, 184
C. C. Route, 81
Charie, 80
Cheap Thrills, 154
Chimango, 135
Chockstone Boulder, 84
Cilley Dickin', 82
Circumcision, 248
Circumcisor, The, 247
City Lights, 96
City Streets, 150
Classic, 87
Clover, 75
Cluney's Jollies, 226
Coexistence, 122
Cold Turkeys, 170
Columbia, 137
Comedy in Three Acts, 231
Commando Rave, 151
Condemned Man, 202
Contradance, 237
Co-op, 128
Coprophagia, 233
Coronary, 74
Counterstrike, 243
Country Roads, 151
Crack of Despondency, 244
Crack'n-Up, 183
Creaky Joints and Trigger Points, 238
Creature Features, 92
Credibility Gap, 130
Crimson Corner, 81
Crowberry Ridge, 78
Crustacean Syndrome, 254

Das Wiggles, 75
Dat Mantel, 146

Daydream, 86
D.D. Route, 80
Death's Head Mask, 248
Deep Chills, 154
Deep Lichen, 166
Delusions of Grandeur, 142
Dennis, 84
Devil Made Me Do It, The, 239
Devine Wind, 77
Diana, 186
Dick's Prick, 249
Directissima, 193
Directississima, 196
Dirty Chimney, 74
Dirty Gerdie, 66
Dislocation, 77
Dis-Mantel, 146
Don't Shift, 123
Don't Shoot, 142
Double Chin, 70
Double Clutch, 71
Double Crack, 215
Doug's Roof, 72
Drop Zone, 232
Drunkard's Delight, 100
Dry Heaves, 153
Dry Martini, 126

Easy Keyhole, 63
Easy Overhang, 94
Easy Verschneidung, 170
Emilietta, 242
Emilio, 240
Enduro Man's Longest Hangout, 195
Epiclepsy, 109
Erect Direction, 183
Exit Stage Left, 189

Expedition to Nowhere, 234
Eyebrow, 70
Eyesore, 82

Face to Face, 179
Faithful Journey, 159
Fall, The, 221
Fall to Grace, 128
Falled on Account of Strain, 229
Fancy Free, 254
Fancy Idiot, 67
Feast of Fools, The, 173
Fetus, 93
"50-50", 199
Fillipina, 219
First Trapps Chimney, 196
Fitschen's Folly, 80
Five Tendons, 100
Flake, The, 57
Fly Again, 121
Footloose, 253
Forces of Nature, 218
Foreign Lesion, 249
"48", 213
"49", 218
Four-Foot Face, 244
Friday the 13th, 67
Friends and Lovers, 133
Frog's Head, 96
Frustration Syndrome, 232
Full Face, 212
Funny Face, 144
Future Shock, 245

Gaston, 108
Ghostdance, 237
Gill's Boulder Problem, 71

Girls Just Want to Have Fun, 249
Gleet Street, 143
Glypnod, 114
Glyptodon, 113
Glyptomaniac, 113
Golden Showers, 230
Goldner's Grunge, 178
Gorilla My Dreams, 107
Gory Thumb, 147
Graveyard Shift, 123
Great Wall of China, 61
Grim-Ace Face, 111
Groovy, 205

Handy Andy, 63
Hans' Puss, 171
Harvard, 82
Hawaii Five-Ten, 253
Hawk, 136
Hawkeye, 167
Headless Horseman, 254
Heather, 95
Heel Hook and Hack-It, 66
Help!, 149
Herdie Gerdie, 66
Hi Coroner!, 112
High Corner, 112
High Exposure, 190
High Jinx, 217
High Times, 146
Higher Stannard, 118
Hooky, 228
Horseman, 73
Hudson's Boulder Problem, 78
Hyjek's Horror, 141

Immaculate Conception, 145
Impenetrable Ceilings, 126
In the Groove, 205
In the Silly, 206
Independent Hangover, 241
Insuhlation, 198
Interstellar Overdrive, 242
Interstice, 119
Invitation to Hell, 105
Ivan and the Saum, 215

J'Accuse, 157
Jackie, 87
Jacob's Ladder, 77
Jane, 89
Jane Fonda Workout for Pregnant Women, The, 125
J.A.P., 234
Jean, 99
Jim's Gem, 189
Journey's End, 160
Junior, 74

Kama Sutra, 97
Katzenjammer, 62
Keep on Struttin', 181
Ken's Blind Hole, 186
Ken's Crack, 79
Kernmantle, 146
Keyhole, 62
Kligfield's Follies, 226
Knockout Drops, 204

Lady's Lament, 219
Lakatakissima, 196
Land's End, 125
Last Frontier, 224
Last Will Be First, The, 188
Late Show, 91
Lat-on the Season, 143

INDEX

Laughing Man, 129
Laurel, 74
Le Teton, 140
Lichen 40 Winks, 199
Limelight, 168
Lisa, 212
Lito and the Swan, 215
Lone Ranger, The, 250
Long Distance of the Lonely Runner, 213
Long Walk for Man, A Short Climb for Mankind, A, 255
Los Tres Cabrones, 223
Lost and Found, 187
Lots of Malarkey, 210
Low Exposure, 76

Madame Grunnebaum's Sorrow, 138
Madame Grunnebaum's Wulst, 138
Make Haste or Tomato Paste, 103
Man's Quest for Flight, 175
Maria, 97
Matinee, 91
Meat By-products, 245
Mental Block, 68
Men at Arms, 120
Metropolis, 151
M.F., 120
Middle Earth, 160
Midnight Cowboy, 114
Minty, 134
Miss Bailey, 92
Missing, But Not Lost, 199
Mister Transistor, 111
Modern Love, 246

Modern Times, 190
Mohel, The, 83
Moondance, 236
Moonlight, 182
Morning After, 101
Mother's Day Party, 119
Mud, Sweat, and Tears, 235

Nemesis, 113
Never Never Land, 157
Never Say Never, 157
Nevermore, 156
No Belle Prize, 112
No Existence, 124
No Glow, 180
No Man's Land, 207
No Picnic, 65
No Solution, 68
Northern Pillar, 140
Nose, The, 219
Nose Drops, 205
Nosedive, 68
Number's Racket, The, 245
Nurdland, 155
Nurse's Aid, 171

Oblique Twique, 222
Obstacle Delusion, 197
Octoberfest, 132
On Any Monday, 165
One Blunder and It's Six Feet Under, 100
Organic Iron, 125
Overhanging Layback, 123

Pas de Deux, 95
Penal Colony, 248
Penis Colada, 249

Peregrine, 136
Pfui Teufel, 244
Phoebe, 79
Pink Laurel, 87
Pleh!, 149
Point Blank, 182
Pony Express, 73
P.R., 111
Precarious Perch, 99
Pressure Drop, 232
Proctor Silex, 174
Proctoscope, 174
Prophylactic, 248
Psychedelic, 190
P.T. Phone Home, 127
P38, 83

Queasy O, 94
Quién Sabe, 218
Quiver, 170

Radcliffe, 83
Raindance, 237
Ralph's Climb, 71
Ranger's Revenge, 247
Raspberry Sundae, 116
Raubenheimer Special, 90
Raunchy, 148
Reach of Faith, 136
Red Cabbage, 66
Red Cabbage Right, 67
Red Pillar, 166
Red's Ruin, 161
Renaissance, 246
Retribution, 68
Rhododendron, 75
Ribless, 106
Ribs, 106

RMC, 89
Road Less Traveled, 168
Rock and Brew, 102
Roddey, 86
Roger's Escape Hatch, 237
Ruby Saturday, 115
Rusty Trifle, 102

Scary Area, 209
Scary Area Direct, 209
Scene of the Climb, 124
Scotch on the Rocks, 126
Scungilli, 98
Second Trapps Chimney, 197
Seldom Mustard, Never Relish, 131
Senté, 162
Shell Shock, 180
Shit Creek, 222
Shit or Go Blind, 65
Shitty Mitty, 75
Shockley's Ceiling, 110
Short and Simple, 61
Short Job, 64
Shut Up and Eat Your Greens, 250
Silhouette, 175
Silly Chimney, 206
Silly Groove, 206
Simple Ceilings, 116
Simple Suff, 226
Sixish, 99
"69", 64
"60-40", 199
Skeletal Remains, 176
Sleepwalk, 200
Slime World, 255
Slipping into Incipiency, 206

INDEX

Smegma Garden and Pigeon, 161
Snagglepuss, 174
Snake, 165
Snooky's Return, 133
Snowpatch, 161
Something Boring, 117
Something Interesting, 118
Something or Other, 117
Something Scary, 70
Son of Bitchy Virgin, 144
Son of Easy O, 95
Southern Pillar, 137
Space Invaders, 205
Splashtic, 108
Spring, The, 221
Squiggles, 76
Squiggles Direct, 77
Stand, The, 232
Star Action, 122
Star Route, The, 81
Steep Hikin', 166
Step Lively, 182
Sticky Gate, 234
Sting, The, 211
Stirrup Trouble, 83
Stop the Presses, Mr. Williams, 147
Strictly from Nowhere, 109
Strings Attached, 239
Strolling on Jupiter, 188
Sudden Death, 243
Sudoriferous, 65
Sultana, 98
Summer, The, 221
Sundance, 236
Sundown, 97
Supper's Ready, 171
Susie A, 79
Swamp Gas, 255

Talus of Powder, 165
Techo-Stuff, 227
10,000 Restless Virgins, 250
Tennish, Anyone?, 253
Tequila Mockingbird, 127
Thin Slabs, 162
Third Trapps Chimney, 197
Thom's Thumb, Left Hand, 244
Thom's Thumb, Right Hand, 246
Three Doves, 167
Three Pines, 116
Three Vultures, 179
Throne, The, 202
Tiers of Fear, 207
Tipsy Trees, 134
Tomorrow and Tomorrow and Tomorrow, 228
Too Old to Know Better, 173
Torture Garden, 224
Tough Shift, 123
Trapped Like a Rat, 82
Travels with Charley, 108
Traverse of the Clods, 175
Tree's a Crowd, 129
Triangle, 156
Trigger Point, 243
Triple Bulges, 141
True Brit, 247
Trusty Rifle, 103
Try Again, 121
Turdland, 155
Twilight Zone, 176

Twin Oaks, 141
Twisted Sister, 93

Uncle Rudy, 104
Unholy Wick, 187
Unnamed, 145
Unslung Heroes, 223
Updraft, 184
Uphill All the Way, 214
Ursula, 204

Vader, 213
V.D., 249
Ventre de Boeuf, 214
Vicious Rumors, 106
V-3, 150

Walter Mitty, 76
W.A.S.P., 233
Wasp Stop, 211
Water King, 120
Vegetables I've Never Seen Before, 251
Welcome to My Nightmare, 157

Welcome to the Gunks, 129
Wet Dream, 229
Where Fools Rush In, 214
Wild Horses, 148
Willie's Weep, 142
Winter, The, 220
Winterlude, 220
Wisecrack, 158
Wiseland, 158
Withering Heights, 235
Womb Step, The, 135
Wonderland, 159
Wop Stop, 181
Worp Factor 1, 241
Wrist, 104

Yale, 81
Yellow Crack, The, 225
Yellow Wall, The, 207
Yenta, 162
Yesterday, 228
Yesterday's Lemonade, 115
Yo Mama, 241

Zigzag Face, The, 217